EFFECTIVE ENFORCEMENT OF PLANNING CONTROL

EFFECTIVE ENFORCEMENT OF PLANNING CONTROL

JOHN ALDER LLB, BCL

*with Scottish section by E. Young MA, LLB, solicitor
and Northern Ireland section by W. D. Trimble LLB, barrister*

BSP PROFESSIONAL BOOKS
OXFORD LONDON EDINBURGH
BOSTON MELBOURNE

Copyright © John Alder 1989
© E. Young 1989 – Scottish
section
© W. D. Trimble 1989 –
Northern Ireland section
All rights reserved. No part of this
publication may be reproduced, stored
in a retrieval system, or transmitted,
in any form or by any means, electronic,
mechanical, photocopying, recording
or otherwise without the prior
permission of the copyright owner.

First published 1989

British Library
Cataloguing in Publication Data

Alder, John
   Effective enforcement of planning control.
   1. England.   Enforcement notices.   Law
   I. Title
   344.2064'5

ISBN 0-632-02154-3

BSP Professional Books
A division of Blackwell Scientific
   Publications Ltd
Editorial Offices:
Osney Mead, Oxford OX2 0EL
   (Orders: Tel: 0865 240201)
8 John Street, London WC1N 2ES
23 Ainslie Place, Edinburgh EH3 6AJ
3 Cambridge Center, Suite 208, Cambridge
   MA 02142, USA
107 Barry Street, Carlton, Victoria 3053,
   Australia

Typeset by Action Typesetting Limited,
Gloucester

Printed and bound in Great Britain by
Mackays of Chatham PLC, Chatham, Kent

The specimen enforcement notice from Circular 38/81, which appears in Appendix III, is reproduced by kind permission of the Controller of Her Majesty's Stationery Office.

Contents

Preface   ix

1 The development control system in outline   1
    Introduction
    An outline of the enforcement process
    The legal background
    The decision makers
    The courts and enforcement

2 Development and planning permission   11
    Development
    Planning permission
    Conclusion

3 The decision to take enforcement action   34
    The discretionary power
    Obtaining information
    Breach of planning control
    Bars to enforcement action

4 Drafting an enforcement notice   52
    Introduction
    The contents of an enforcement notice
    The nature of the breach
    Time limits
    The steps required to remedy the breach

5 Service of an enforcement notice   66
    Persons to be served
    Method of service
    The effect of a failure to serve a notice
    Defective service
    Service and the right of appeal

Contents

6	**Challenging an enforcement notice**	72
	General principles	
	Appeals to the Secretary of State	
	Challenging the Secretary of State's decision	
	Challenging an enforcement notice in the courts	
7	**Implementing an enforcement notice**	93
	The effect of an enforcement notice	
	When does an enforcement notice take effect?	
	Criminal proceedings	
	The offences	
	Power of entry	
	Conclusion	
8	**Supplementary methods of enforcement**	111
	Stop notices	
	Injunctions	
	'Section 52 agreements'	
9	**Crown land, Scotland and Northern Ireland**	122
	Introduction	
	Crown land – special enforcement notices	
	Scotland	
	Northern Ireland	
10	**Enforcement in special cases – (I) Conservation**	145
	Listed buildings	
	Trees	
11	**Enforcement in special cases – (II) Amenity and safety**	161
	Derelict land	
	Hazardous substances	
	Advertisements	
12	**Reforms?**	174
	Select bibliography	179
	Appendix I The allocation of enforcement functions	180

Contents vii

Appendix II **Town and Country Planning Act 1971 (as amended) – extracts** **183**

Appendix III **Specimen enforcement notices** **189**
                    (1) – Operational development
                    (2) – Material change of use
                    (3) – Breach of condition

Table of cases **198**

Table of statutes **204**

Index **209**

Preface

The law relating to the enforcement of planning control is complicated, technical and full of pitfalls for the unwary. Local planning authorities often find it difficult to take swift and effective action and developers are able to exploit the law's delays. There are also opportunities for conflict between local and central government.

My aim in writing this book has been to provide a straightforward but critical account of the general principles underlying the law in the hope that it will be useful to people on both sides of the battle lines, to local authorities and planning inspectors faced with the technicalities of the legislation and the endlessly proliferating case law, and to developers and their advisers. Students of law and land management may also find the book useful as providing a more detailed overview than is possible in the confines of a general students' text book. Finally, I have tried to provide a starting point for the legal practitioner and for this purpose I have included references to some leading and illustrative cases and have tried to emphasise the main arguments in controversial areas. Non-legal readers need not be distracted by the case references.

After two general introductory chapters, the enforcement process is discussed in Chapters 3 to 7 stage by stage from the decision to take enforcement action to the final criminal sanctions. Chapter 8 deals with some additional methods of enforcement and Chapter 9 with variations in the law applying to Crown Land and in Scotland and Northern Ireland. Chapters 10 and 11 concentrate on the enforcement regimes applicable in certain special cases where more stringent controls have been imposed in the interests of conservation, amenity and safety. Finally, Chapter 12 looks at some suggestions for reform of the enforcement system.

Enforcement of planning control cannot be understood in isolation from the planning system as a whole. I have therefore discussed the law relating to development, planning permission, listed buildings, etc. sufficiently to make sense of the relevant enforcement regime. I have not, however, included such matters as the procedure for applying for planning permission or planning appeal procedure. These topics are catered for in other volumes in this series.

At the time of writing, the enforcement system is undergoing one of its periodic reviews and it is hoped that as on previous occasions some useful practical reforms will result. Despite all its weaknesses, the enforcement system is a lot more satisfactory than it was 10 years ago.

I should like to thank Eric Young of Strathclyde University, and David Trimble of The Queen's University, Belfast, for contributing the sections on Scotland and Northern Ireland respectively, Grahame Rowe of East Devon District Council for reading and commenting on several chapters and Michael Pattison of Exeter University for helping with the proofs. I owe a particular debt of gratitude to Anne Waters for producing the manuscript in what, for me, is record time.

As always, I am indebted to the help supplied, sometimes unknowingly, by generations of students and for the forbearance of my family in putting up with my reclusive habits.

I have attempted to describe the law as it was on 20 April 1989, but the law rarely stands still and I have included some further developments at the proof stage.

John Alder
Exeter, July 4th 1989

Chapter 1

The development control system in outline

Introduction

Land use planning control in the United Kingdom takes an unusual form compared to that in many other countries. The Town and Country Planning Act 1971 embodies a system of discretionary decision making powers exercisable by local and central government in respect of individual pieces of land. These powers are triggered by a landowner (or indeed any person) committing an act of 'development' without planning permission or breaching a condition of a planning permission. The local planning authority can issue an 'enforcement notice' requiring the developer to take steps specified in the notice to remedy what he has done wrong. It is a criminal offence to disobey an enforcement notice and the authority can enter the land and carry out remedial work. Development without planning permission, although unlawful, is not an offence in itself. Nor is unlawful development actionable in the courts by a private individual.

There are two kinds of development. These must be kept distinct:

(i) 'Operational' development consists of carrying out 'building engineering mining or other operations' in, on, over or under land. (Town and Country Planning Act, 1971, section 22(1).) This involves altering the land itself or physical structures on it.
(ii) Change of use development consists of making a 'material' change in the purpose for which buildings or other land is used (*ibid.*) for example, using a private dwelling as an hotel or office. No physical operations need necessarily be involved.

Change of use development raises difficult enforcement problems and is the subject of the majority of enforcement notices. For example, it is sometimes difficult to prove that a change of use has occurred. Activities such as retail sales may be intermittent, leave little physical evidence on the land and are easily removed. It may be impossible to discover when a change of use took place and unlawful activities are often physically intermingled with lawful ones. The world of change of use is dominated by motor vehicle related cases, caravans, scrap dealing, catering and ephemeral small businesses. Multiple occupation of dwelling houses is also a common problem.

The enforcement system comes under particular pressure where land values are increasing, because of the temptation for developers to jump the gun. In 1986 there were 1789 enforcement appeals concerning change of use, compared with 950 relating to other kinds of development and 520 concerning breaches of condition (DoE 1988). Not surprisingly, the bulk of enforcement activity is to be found in the more affluent suburban or other areas of high land values.

Although it is the 'sharp end' of the planning system, enforcement is the Cinderella of the planning world. The powers of investigation available to a local planning authority are weak and most enforcement notices are the result of random complaints from the public or from other local authority departments. Not all local authorities have specialised enforcement staffs and in many cases enforcement officers are not professional planners. Very few local authorities employ enforcement specialists with comprehensive control over all aspects of the enforcement process. By contrast, developers are often represented by highly qualified professionals.

The enforcement process is very slow and complex. Enforcement notices have to contain specified information which may not be readily obtainable. Copies must be served on the right people, and there are strict time limits. On average, there is a time gap of three to six months between a complaint being received and a resolution to issue an enforcement notice, and one of three to four months between the resolution and the actual notice.

There is a right of appeal to the Secretary of State for the Environment in which the planning aspects of the case can be reconsidered and planning permission granted. There is a further right of appeal to the High Court. These appeals may take many months and sometimes years, during which the enforcement notice is suspended. Finally, the authority must launch a prosecution in a context which to many people is regarded as 'red tape' rather than truly criminal and where the penalties are small. The case could be adjourned to allow the accused to apply for planning permission and to appeal against any refusal, and at the end of the day it may be worth the developer's while to pay the fine and continue to break the law. The criminal process may itself take several months (see below).

The enforcing authority is therefore faced with a formidable and lengthy obstacle course. It is not surprising that more than 60% of enforcement notices are appealed against, of which some 35% are successful, and that less than 10% of complaints end in successful prosecutions. The Department of the Environment has recently published a report which makes several recommendations for making the appeal process more efficient and speedy (see *Planning Control: Enforcement Notice Appeals, Efficiency, Scrutiny and Action Plan*, HMSO 1988). Most of these recommendations involve changes of practice within the DoE for the purpose of speeding up the procedure and monitoring the flow of information. A 'target' timetable of 22 to 28 weeks is proposed.

An outline of the enforcement process

An enforcement notice can be issued when it 'appears to the authority that there has been a breach of planning control after the end of 1963' and if they consider it 'expedient' to do so (section 87(1)). In the case of (i) operational development and (ii) a change of use to use as a single dwelling, the time limit is four years. It is worth noting at the outset that in order to issue an enforcement notice there does not actually *have* to be a breach of planning control. If the authority's belief is wrong, for example, if what is complained of is not development, the remedy lies in an appeal to the Secretary of State. If the landowner fails to take advantage of the right of appeal, the local planning authority can lawfully implement the enforcement notice.

There is a breathing space of at least 28 days after service of an enforcement notice before it can take effect. After that, a reasonable time for compliance must be permitted. During the 28 days anyone with an interest in the land can appeal to the Secretary of State. There is a further right of appeal to the High Court on a point of law. During all these appeal stages the notice remains suspended. On appeal, the Secretary of State can re-examine the whole matter. He can quash or alter the notice and can grant planning permission for the development specified in the notice or modify any existing permission.

The appeal process may involve a public local inquiry although in about 50% of cases the appeal is heard by means of written representations. This requires the consent of both parties. Most appeals are decided by inspectors attached to the DoE under powers delegated by the Secretary of State. There is a body of inspectors specialising in enforcement appeal work. They operate within the constraints of central government policy but are as far as possible impartial and independent of the mainstream planning work of the DoE. The appeal process may take from about 35 working days in simple written representation cases to over three years where legal challenge is involved. It can be complex and technical. Even where the developer has previously been refused planning permission and has lost earlier appeals, he can attempt to persuade the inspector to grant him planning permission.

The whole process is designed to ensure that developers have a fair hearing and many people argue that it goes too far in that direction. Coupled with the automatic suspension of the enforcement notice, the appeal process can be effectively used to postpone the day of reckoning. Delay centring upon appeals is the biggest single criticism of the enforcement system. A fee is payable for the deemed application for planning permission which is automatically included in every enforcement appeal but this is relatively small. About a third of appellants do not pay and there is no effective means of recovering the money.

If the Secretary of State's appeal decision is unsuccessfully challenged in the courts, the matter is referred back to him to be decided again in the light of the courts' ruling. In addition, the enforcement notice itself could be challenged on the ground that it is so seriously defective as to be a nullity and as such merely waste paper (see below). This can be argued at a late stage as a defence to a prosecution. If the notice is a nullity, a new notice must be issued and the proceedings commence all over again.

There are special remedies designed to provide speedier and more draconian methods of control than ordinary enforcement notices. A local planning authority can serve a 'stop notice' which makes disobedience to the enforcement notice a criminal offence immediately, whether or not an appeal is pending. However, if the enforcement notice is later quashed on legal grounds, compensation must be paid. The authority may also obtain an injunction from the court to restrain extreme abuses of the law, but this will only be

The development control system in outline

granted in exceptional cases where the ordinary enforcement machinery is clearly not adequate.

Special enforcement provisions apply to the Crown and to land in which the Crown has an interest.

There are additional enforcement powers in special cases concerned with local amenities. These include:

- buildings listed as of special architectural or historic interest
- special consents for the placing of hazardous substances on land
- trees protected by Tree Preservation Orders
- waste land
- advertisements

These will be discussed towards the end of the book.

The legal background

The background against which planning law must be discussed is that of *public law* which concerns principles of good administration — fair procedures, relevance, rationality — applied by the courts to the exercise of government powers: see *O'Reilly* v. *Mackman* (1983). The law relating to enforcement is to be found mainly in the Town and Country Planning Act 1971, Part V (as later amended) and all statutory references will be to this Act unless stated otherwise. Some of the law is to be found in regulations made by the Secretary of State for the Environment under powers conferred by the Act. Of these the most important as regards enforcement notices are the Town and Country Planning (Enforcement Notices and Appeals) Regulations 1981 (SI 1981 No 1742) which deal with the content of an enforcement notice and the provision of information relating to appeals, and the Town and Country Planning (Enforcement) (Inquiries Procedure) Rules 1981 (SI 1981 No 1743).

There are other regulations of general importance. These are:

(i) the Town and Country Planning (Use Classes) Order 1987 (SI 1987 No 764). This designates 16 classes of use of land and provides that a change of use *within* any single class is not development (see below). The purpose of the order is to provide a degree of freedom for changes between uses that are compatible with each other.

(ii) The Town and Country Planning (General Development) Order 1988 (SI 1988 No 1813). This fulfils several functions. Firstly, it grants automatic planning permission for prescribed classes of development (see below). Secondly, the GDO lays down procedural requirements for applications for planning permission and for appeals against refusal of planning permission including duties to consult other public bodies. These do not apply to enforcement decisions. Thirdly, the GDO provides for a public register of planning applications, planning permissions and other related orders and for a similar register of enforcement and stop notices. Finally, the GDO regulates the procedure for 'established use certificates'. This concerns the time limit for issuing an enforcement notice (see below).

There are also circulars issued by the DoE and the Welsh Office outlining government policies and explaining procedures, e.g. Circulars 22/80 and 14/85 (general), 38/81 (appeals), 20/85 (enforcement and appeals), 4/87 (stop notices) and 2/87 (costs). These documents, together with all the relevant legislation, are published in the *Encyclopaedia of Planning Law and Practice.* They do not have the force of law except where they contain 'directions' made by the Secretary of State about particular matters. However, circulars often attempt to explain the law and contain useful guidance about particular policies, e.g. 1/88 (minerals), 16/87 (agricultural land), 2/86 (small businesses) and 15/84 (land for housing). They must be taken into account by local planning authorities and appeal inspectors but must *not* be treated as absolutely binding.

A series of planning policy guidance notes issued by the DoE outlines the major planning policies both generally and in relation to particular subjects.

The decision makers

The planning authority to which applications for planning permission must be made and which issues enforcement notices is usually a district council, metropolitan district council or London Borough council. Some kinds of development, notably mineral working and

The development control system in outline 7

associated matters, are matters for county councils, and there are special arrangements for national parks. We shall detail this indigestible material in an appendix. An Urban Development Corporation may be designated by the Secretary of State as the planning authority for its area, thus replacing an elected local council with a body of central government appointees (Local Government Planning and Land Act 1980, section 149).

A local planning authority, other than an urban development corporation, may delegate the power to take enforcement action to any committee, sub-committee or officer, or to a joint committee of two or more authorities, or to any other local authority (Local Government Act 1972, section 101).

This is a very wide power of delegation but has important limitations. Power cannot be delegated to an individual councillor so that the device of 'chairman's action' is not lawful (see *R.* v. *Secretary of State for the Environment ex parte Hillingdon Borough Council* (1986). There cannot be a committee of one. However, power can be delegated to an *officer* in consultation with a councillor (*Fraser* v. *Secretary of State* (1988), and the decision of a councillor could be ratified by a committee (see *West Glamorgan County Council* v. *Rafferty* (1987).

If power has been validly delegated to an officer, a member of his staff can act in his name. In *Cheshire County Council* v. *Secretary of State* (1988), power to issue enforcement notices was formally delegated to the County Secretary and Solicitor. In practice, the matter was handled jointly by the Chief Assistant Solicitor and the planning officer. The County Secretary was not necessarily aware of the issue of particular enforcement notices. The Secretary of State took the view that all notices issued under these arrangements were invalid. The court held that the arrangement was perfectly lawful. The court's reasoning depended on the language of section 101 which permits councils 'to *arrange* for the discharge of their functions' by officers. The practice of leaving the matter to the more junior officers amounted to such an arrangement. Thus delegation need not take the form of a formal resolution but can be the subject of informal arrangements. This commonsense principle has much to be said for it although uncertainty may result for a member of the public as to whether he is dealing with the right person.

Local planning authorities often enter into negotiations with landowners before commencing enforcement action. An assurance, promise or advice given by an official to whom the power has not been delegated cannot normally bind the authority (*Western Fish Products* v. *Penwith District Council* (1981). Nevertheless, if there has actually been a regular practice under which the official normally makes decisions of the kind in issue, the authority could be bound.

Officials who give misleading advice may also be liable in damages for negligence. In *Davy* v. *Spelthorne District Council* (1983), an official improperly told the developer that if he refrained from appealing against an enforcement notice, the authority would not take action against him. This did not prevent the authority from taking action but it did make the authority liable for damages. An officer is deemed to know all facts available to his committee.

Local authorities must publish a list of powers where delegation arrangements have been made. In practice, delegation of the decision to issue an enforcement notice to an official is relatively unusual. Decisions are normally taken by the planning or development committee. Such functions as carrying out investigations and giving advice can, of course, always be exercised by officials, but unless there is a full delegation of power the committee cannot simply 'rubber stamp' an official recommendation. The committee itself must genuinely consider the matter on the basis of summaries of evidence presented by officers.

The Secretary of State has power to 'call in' any application for planning permission to be decided at central government level and also to issue an enforcement notice (sections 34 and 276(5A)). These powers are sparingly exercised and the usual role of the Secretary of State is to decide appeals. His appeal powers are very wide. He can consider the whole matter afresh and is not limited to ensuring that the local authority has acted properly. The balance of power in development control, legally at any rate, lies with the central government, the local authority being primarily an initiator and a filter for relatively uncontroversial cases.

The courts and enforcement

The judges have often expressed horror at the technical complexities of enforcement notice law and the delays that may result. For example, in *Britt* v. *Buckinghamshire County Council* (1963), Lord Justice Harman said:

'Hard indeed are the paths of local authorities in striving to administer the town and country planning legislation of recent years... It is a subject which stinks in the noses of the public and not without reason. Local authorities... have had practically to employ conveyancing counsel to settle these notices which they serve in the interests of planning the countryside or the towns which they control. Instead of their trying to make this thing simpler, lawyers succeeded day by day in making it more difficult and less comprehensible until it has reached a stage where it is very much like the state of the land which the plaintiff landowner has brought about by his operations − an eyesore, a wilderness and a scandal.'

Since then, courts and Parliament have attempted to overcome the technical complexities of the enforcement process but with only limited success: see e.g. *Eldon Garages* v. *Kingston upon Hull Borough Council* (1974); *Miller-Mead* v. *Minister of Housing and Local Government* (1963). These and other examples will be discussed in their contexts.

The problems are caused partly by the complexities of the law relating to development and planning permission. This affects the drafting of an enforcement notice. The authority has to identify what sort of development is involved and to draft the notice accordingly. Difficulties also arise in cases where some sort of permission is in force but has been violated. Has there been a breach of condition, a breach of a limitation or a full-blooded 'development without planning permission' (see below)?

The draftsman must attempt to pinpoint the breach with sufficient certainty, but without excessive detail which could create a risk of error. Problems also arise in relation to the service of an enforcement notice and to specifying the steps required to obey it.

Matters are often made worse by the complex facts involved. These may require the authority to unravel a mixture of lawful and unlawful uses existing on a site, some of them going back many years and without adequate powers of investigation and entry to the land. The courts are sympathetic to these practical difficulties and will often apply the law liberally in favour of local planning authorities in order that the system does not collapse. For example, in *Ferris* v. *Secretary of State* (1988), Mr Graham Eyre QC emphasised that a planning authority was entitled to issue an enforcement notice without a full investigation of the facts and it was up to the developer to show grounds for challenging the notice (see below). Nor did the authority have to specify in the notice what was the 'base use' of the land before the alleged development took place. As Mr Graham Eyre QC said, 'The burden of monitoring each planning unit in its administrative area...would collapse the administration of the whole scheme of legislation.'

These problems are highlighted by the very generous rights of appeal available to the citizen. As we have seen, not only can the technical requirements of the notice and the basic question whether there has been a breach of planning control be raised but the Secretary of State or Inspector can also reconsider the planning merits of the case. He can decide to grant planning permission or to alter any condition attached to a planning permission, even where the developer had previously lost an appeal to the Secretary of State against a refusal of permission on the same facts.

An official deciding a planning appeal is bound by findings of *fact* made at a previous appeal, except where the circumstances have changed, but is not bound by findings of law or judgments on matters of planning policy and discretion (*Thrasyvoulou* v. *Secretary of State* (1988)). In general, the appeal process is unpredictable and haphazard.

There is a right of appeal to the High Court against the Secretary of State's decision, but only on a point of law. The High Court's only powers are either to dismiss the appeal or to refer the notice back to the Secretary of State. If the notice is referred back, the Secretary of State cannot merely correct the legal error but has a clean sheet and must reconsider the whole matter, at least where new circumstances have arisen since the notice was previously before him (*Kingswood District Council* v. *Secretary of State* (1988)).

In recent years, statutory reforms and a flexible approach by the courts have improved the position, and yet in a recent case Graham Eyre QC was moved to say that 'this court had been treated to a rehearsal of somewhat arid technicalities most of which had a ring of nostalgia in its true sense, and largely unwelcome familiarity' (*West Oxfordshire District Council* v. *Secretary of State* (1988)). Lawyers dealing with an enforcement notice are therefore well advised to take a broad commonsense approach to technical problems.

Chapter 2

Development and planning permission

Enforcement law can only be understood against the background of the basic concepts of development and planning permission. If no development has taken place or if a planning permission is in force, an activity can only be prohibited by means of a discontinuance order under section 51, or in the case of mineral workings under section 51A. A discontinuance order must be confirmed by the Secretary of State and compensation must be paid since rights conferred by planning law are being taken away.

Development

It is initially for the local planning authority to decide whether development has taken place. The Act provides a general definition of development (section 22) but the courts will not interfere with the local authority's application of that definition in an individual case unless it has taken an entirely improper approach or acted without evidence.

For enforcement purposes it is vital to distinguish between the two kinds of development. Not only are the time limits for issuing an enforcement notice different (see below) but the offences and the local authority's powers operate differently.

(1) 'Operational' development consists of 'building, engineering, mining or other operations in or over or under land' (section 22(1)).
(2) Change of use development consists of making a material change in the use of buildings or other land (ibid).

OPERATIONAL DEVELOPMENT (section 22(1))

BUILDING OPERATIONS

An 'operation' is essentially a physical alteration to the land itself or to a building on it. However, the courts have held that the *demolition* of a building is not necessarily development (*Coleshill Investments* v. *Minister of Housing* (1969)). Why this should be so is obscure. Demolishing *part* of a building is development because the Act expressly includes altering a building as a building operation (section 290(1), the definition section) and the large-scale removal of earth is an engineering operation. Alterations to a building which are purely internal or which do not affect its external appearance are not development (section 22(2)).

The meaning of building is very wide and bears little resemblance to ordinary usage. 'Building' includes any 'structure or erection' but not plant or machinery comprised in a building. A part of a building is itself a building (section 290(1)). For example, a fence, a flagpole, a radio mast and a model village have all been treated as buildings. Anything artificial which is physically attached to the land is a building. Indeed, it has been held that a large crane fixed to a concrete platform which rests on the land on its own weight is a building so that placing it on site is a building operation (*Barvis* v. *Secretary of State* (1971)). This is because the crane was functionally similar to a building: it was large, could be moved only with difficulty and was intended to be on site for a long time. By contrast, swingboats on a beach that were readily transportable without being dismantled were not buildings (*James* v. *Brecon County Council* (1963)). A caravan is apparently not a building for planning purposes unless, perhaps, its wheels are removed. Therefore placing a caravan on a site if it is development at all would be a 'change of use' and not operational development (*Wealden District Council* v. *Secretary of State* (1988)). Illuminating a building is not development because the building itself is not altered. Painting a building, on the other hand, is development.

ENGINEERING OPERATIONS

These are not defined in detail by the Act which is content only to remark that 'the formation and laying out of means of access to the highway' are included (section 290(1)). Apart from that, it would seem that the gist of an engineering operation is the removal or manipulation of materials from the ground on a substantial scale — digging a swimming pool, for example. Some forms of demolition may therefore count as engineering operations (see *Coleshill Investments Ltd v. Minister of Housing* above).

MINING OPERATIONS

This term is given an elaborate meaning. Basically, mining operations involve the removal of minerals from the land. 'Minerals' includes all minerals and substances worked for removal by underground or surface working except that it does not include peat cut for purposes other than sale (section 290(1)). Mining operations also include:

(a) the removal of material of any description
 (i) from a mineral working deposit;
 (ii) from a deposit of pulverised fuel ash or other furnace ash or clinker; or
 (iii) from a deposit of iron, steel or other metallic slags; and
(b) the extraction of minerals from a disused railway embankment.

The special problems with mining operations are firstly, that they are continuing activities similar in many ways to uses, and secondly, that they permanently damage the environment. These problems led to the enactment of special measures relating to planning permission for mining development (see Town and Country Planning (Minerals) Act 1981). They include powers to impose 'aftercare conditions' and special compensation arrangements. As far as enforcement is concerned, mining development can be enforced only by the County Council in its capacity as mineral planning authority (Local Government Act 1972, Schedule 16, para 24.4).

OTHER OPERATIONS

In accordance with the courts' traditional approach to the reading of statutes, the phrase 'other operations' does not include *all* other operations but is limited by the notions of building, engineering and mining operations. Thus an 'other' operation is an operation that is similar in some respect to a building, engineering or mining operation but which does not quite fit the normal meaning of these categories. Given the width of the three concepts, it is difficult to guess what might count as an 'other' operation. The courts have not ruled on the matter (see generally *Coleshill Investments* v. *Minister of Housing* above). Examples of 'other operations' might include the laying out of gardens or parks or drilling holes in the ground (cf. *Bedford County Council* v. *Central Electricity Generating Board* (1985) — small boreholes for the investigation of whether ground was suitable for dumping nuclear waste, probably not development).

MATERIAL CHANGE OF USE

This aspect of development has attracted considerable case law and is by far the most difficult in relation to enforcement. A material change of use does not necessarily involve any physical alteration to the land itself but concerns the purpose to which the land is put. The courts have stressed that the proper approach is to look for 'a change in the character of the land' and not 'the particular purpose of the particular occupier'. *East Barnet Urban District Council* v. *BTC* (1961) is a case that has been approved many times and illustrates this. A yard was previously used for storing coal for transhipment by rail. It was then used for storing crated cars, again for rail transhipment. It was held that no development took place. The successive owners' purposes were, of course, different but the character of the use — storage and the associated movements remained similar.

East Barnet also illustrates that the change must be material from the point of view of planning policy. The kind of goods stored on the land was different but this raised no new planning implications in terms of impact on the environment. By contrast, in *Williams* v. *Minister of Housing* (1967) a site was used as a smallholding and the produce was sold to passers-by. Later, imported fruit was sold from the site in addition to homegrown produce. It was held that the local planning authority was entitled to regard this as development even though the imported element was only about 15% of sales. There is a crucial distinction in planning terms between sales which are incidental to agricultural activities and retail sales generally. The sale of imported produce was the thin end of an unwanted wedge.

The decision of the House of Lords in *Westminster City Council* v. *British Waterways Board* (1985) provides a further illustration of the general principle. There was a dispute between the council as tenant and the board as landlord. The council was using the land as a depot for storing road cleaning equipment. It resisted the board's claim to terminate the lease on the ground that the lawful use was that of a 'local authority depot' and that if the Board resumed control of the land, planning permission would be required for any other use. This would probably be refused. Their Lordships held that the council had taken the wrong approach to the question of development. The identity of the occupier – in this case a local authority – was normally irrelevant, as was the destination of the vehicles after they left the site, in this case to clean the local roads. The use was that of storing vehicles and miscellaneous equipment. Under that head, the Board could use the land beneficially without the need for planning permission. Following *East Barnet* (see above), their Lordships emphasised that the character of the land in relation to its surroundings was the crucial factor.

However, the identity of the occupiers in the sense of the way of life associated with particular kinds of person may sometimes be relevant. It has been held, for example, that a change of use of residential premises to a short-term hostel for the homeless can be development (*Panyani* v. *Secretary of State* (1985)), as can a change from a local government headquarters to commercial offices (*London Residuary Body* v. *Secretary of State* (1988)). The matter depends upon whether there is a distinction between the two uses to be compared in terms of planning policy. It is relevant, but not conclusive, to be able to attach a different 'label' to the new use than that appropriate to the previous use, e.g. 'private dwelling' to 'lodging house'.

In extreme cases, a large-scale increase in the level of a use can be development even where the description of the use or its label remains the same. In *Brooks and Burton* v. *Secretary of State* (1978), concrete blocks were originally manufactured on the site at a rate of less than 300 000 per year. After modernisation, production began to run at the rate of 1 200 000 a year. This increase was held in principle to be capable of being development although it was protected by a statutory exemption (the Use Classes Order (see below). This doctrine of 'intensification' has been much criticised (see e.g. *Royal Borough of Kensington and Chelsea* v. *Secretary of State* (1981)). It raises particular problems for enforcement because the level of activity before the intensification took place cannot be interfered with. In cases of gradual, or 'creeping', intensification this may be impossible to determine. However, as we shall see, the courts have taken a sympathetic approach to the problem.

MULTIPLE USES

There are complications where a site has more than one use, particularly where the various activities on a site are physically intermingled as in the case of many small businesses. Enforcers must disentangle lawful from unlawful uses and determine when each began and the precise relationship between them. Three kinds of multiple use must be distinguished.

(i) Seasonal uses

This is where two or more uses fluctuate on a regular basis over a period of time, e.g. a field is used for parking cars in winter and for camping in the summer. In *Webber* v. *Minister of Housing* (1968), the Court of Appeal held that the seasonal changes between the two uses did not require planning permission. The introduction of each use for the first time would, of course, require permission.

(ii) Composite or concurrent uses

Here the land is used for separate purposes which are independent of each other but geographically mixed up. Each use must be treated separately, and changes of use analysed in accordance with ordinary principles. There is one special rule: this is the doctrine of 'encroachment'. Where one of the uses substantially expands at the expense of the other so that the *balance* between the two has changed, the authority is entitled to treat this as development (e.g. *Brooks* v. *Gloucestershire County Council* (1967) – dwelling house used as shop and cafe). The expanded uses need not absorb the whole site (*Philglow* v. *Secretary of State* (1985)).

(iii) Ancillary uses

An ancillary use is a use which could exist in its own right but in fact is carried out in connection with another major or dominant use, for example, a restaurant exclusively serving a factory or block of flats. An ancillary use is not treated as a use in its own right but takes on the same planning characteristics as its parent use. For example, in *G. Percy Trentham Ltd* v. *Gloucestershire County Council* (1966), a building on a farm was used for storing building materials for use on the farm. This was ancillary to the major agricultural use of the site. Later, the farm activities were discontinued and the building was used for storing building materials for the purpose of the owners' building trade. It was held that development had taken place even though, if the building were to be taken in isolation, the activities within it would remain the same. The cessation of the umbrella agricultural use meant that the storage use automatically ceased to be ancillary.

An ancillary use might expand to become independent of its parent. For example, if land is used to repair vehicles in connection with the owner's road haulage business but in addition vehicles are repaired for the general public, development may take place once the 'public' element becomes substantial. As usual, the question is one of fact and degree.

It is arguable that an ancillary use must be a use that is *normally* ancillary and not one which is ancillary because of some idiosyncracy of the landowner, e.g. using a caravan to reside in and also to keep pigs (see *Wealden District Council* v. *Secretary of State* (1988)).

In principle, a use should not be ancillary to a use on another site which is geographically separate. In *Jones* v. *Secretary of State* (1974) and *Lewis* v. *Secretary of State* (1971), workshops were used in connection with haulage businesses that later closed down. In both cases the workshops continued catering for the public. In *Lewis* this was not development because the haulage business had been based elsewhere and the workshops had been the only relevant use of the site. In *Jones* the haulage business had been on the same site. The workshops were therefore ancillary and development had now occurred.

Despite the seeming anomaly, it would surely be undesirable to look at other sites to determine whether a particular use was ancillary. Nevertheless, in *Swinbank* v. *Secretary of State* (1987), it was held that a use can indeed be ancillary to a use elsewhere. Farm tractors were stored on a site remote from the farm. This was held to be 'agricultural' use because the storage was ancillary to the farm. Planning permission was therefore not required, agricultural uses being given statutory exemption (see below). *Lewis* and *Jones* do not seem to have been cited to the judge in *Swinbank* so that the decision is doubtful.

THE PLANNING UNIT

Before deciding whether a material change of use has taken place the local planning authority must know precisely what area of land to look at. The *Williams* case (see above) illustrates this. Retail sales were carried out from a building on the smallholding, originally of home grown produce but later including imported fruit. Had the building alone been looked at, the use would have been at all times that of retail sales. But because the whole site was looked at, the predominant use could be seen as a smallholding. Thus the introduction of imported oranges for sale was an alien event. In *Burdle* v. *Secretary of State* (1972), Mr Justice Bridge laid down the test for identifying the planning unit. He said that:

> '...it may be a useful working rule to assume that the *unit of occupation* is the appropriate planning unit unless and until some smaller unit can be recognised as the site of activities which amount in substance to a separate use both physically and functionally.'

The unit of occupation is the whole area occupied by a person, or group of people as a single physical unit. In almost all cases this will be the planning unit. Ownership as such is immaterial. In *Johnstone* v. *Secretary of State* (1974), a group of 44 lock-up garages had previously been used by their common owner in connection with a taxi business. The garages were later let to individuals who used them for various purposes. It was held that each garage had become a separate planning unit. Therefore use rights attached to one garage could not affect the rest. (Compare *Rawlins* v. *Secretary of State* (1989).)

Occasionally, the unit of occupation will not be the planning unit. This is where smaller areas of physically separate activities can be identified within a unit of occupation, e.g. a field half of which is used for agriculture and the rest as a caravan site (*James* v. *Secretary of*

State for Wales (1986)). In this kind of case, which is a matter of fact and degree, there will be two or more separate units. A unit of this kind is a 'unit of function'. In *Burdle* (see above) Mr Justice Bridge identified three broad categories of planning unit:

(1) 'Whenever it is possible to recognise a single main purpose of the occupier's land to which secondary activities are incidental, the whole unit of occupation should be considered.'
(2) 'But secondly it may be equally apt to consider the entire unit of occupation even though the occupier carries out a variety of activities and it is not possible to say that one is incidental or ancillary to the other. This is well settled in the case of a composite use where the composite activities fluctuate in their intensity from time to time, but the different activities are not confined within separate and physically distinct areas of land.'
(3) '... it may frequently occur that within a single unit of occupation two or more physically separate and distinct areas are occupied for substantially different and unrelated purposes. In such a case each area used for a different main purpose (together with its incidental and ancillary activities) ought to be considered as a separate unit.'

In *Wood* v. *Secretary of State* (1973), it was emphasised that rarely, if ever, should a dwelling house be subdivided into separate functional units. Conversely, geographically separate pieces of land would not normally be treated as a single planning unit even if occupied by the same person and used in conjunction with each other. (see *Fuller* v. *Secretary of State* (1988); *Duffy* v. *Secretary of State* (1981)).

If a single unit of land is subdivided into two or more units, this is not automatically development. The actual uses before or after the subdivision must be compared in the normal way. (See *Winton* v. *Secretary of State* (1983)).

As well as being essential to determining whether development has taken place, the planning unit has a bearing on enforcement powers. A single unit cannot be arbitrarily divided up so as to issue more than one enforcement notice with the effect of restricting the landowner's normal freedom to dispose his activities as he likes around his unit. In *de Mulder* v. *Secretary of State* (1974), 'Mad Barn Farm' was used partly as a factory for skinning animals and partly for car repairs described as 'general dealing'. The factory use first expanded but after running into construction problems declined, while the general dealing side of the business expanded. This was a material change of use of the whole site (see below). The local planning authority served three enforcement notices, one relating to the factory building, one relating to an adjoining compound and a third to a driveway, in each case prohibiting 'general dealing' in those areas. It was held that the notices should be quashed. The landowner had a right to continue the level of general dealing that applied before the big expansion. This applied to the whole planning unit. He was therefore free to distribute the general dealing use as he wished within the unit provided that the overall level of activity did not increase.

LOSS OF USE RIGHTS

It will be recalled that planning permission is granted for a *change* of use and not for the use as such. Therefore a change from, say, factory to office back to factory requires two planning permissions unless there is a specific exemption in the Act, even if the factory uses are identical. In *Cynon Valley District Council* v. *Secretary of State* (1986), planning permission was given for a fish and chip shop in 1958. From 1978 to 1983 the premises were used temporarily as an antique shop. The owner now wished to revert to the fish and chip shop. It was held that the fact that the antique shop was only temporary was irrelevant. Once a change of use had been made, a fresh planning permission was required to revert to the previous use. In the particular circumstances, however, an automatic planning permission covered the change thanks to the General Development Order (see below).

The same may apply if a use ceases and the land remains unused. If the owner wishes to recommence the previous use, planning permission is required. It is irrelevant whether or not the previous use had planning permission (see below). However, the developer may be able to show that the previous use has not been abandoned but is merely temporarily in abeyance. If he can do this the courts will treat the use as having existed all the time. Therefore planning permission is not required. For example, a use may temporarily cease while the landowner is abroad or in hospital. It would be unfair and unreasonable to insist on a fresh planning permission in these circumstances. The developer must satisfy the authority (a) that he had an intention to resume the use and (b) that there is no other use replacing the one that is claimed (*Hartley* v. *Minister of Housing* (1970)). The state of repair of the premises is an important factor to be taken into account (see *Trustees of Castell-y-Mynach Estates* v. *Secretary of State* (1985)). This abandonment doctrine is irrelevant in a case such as *Cynon Valley* (above) where one use is replaced by another.

It also follows that if planning permission is given for a change of use from use X to use A *or* use B, then if A is in fact implemented the permission for use B is destroyed. The General Development Order 1988 Schedule 2 part 3 reflects this by giving automatic planning permission for such alternative uses provided that the use conforms with the original permission and is implemented within 10 years.

COMPLEX ACTIVITIES

We have emphasised the importance of separating change of use development from operational development and indeed of distinguishing between different kinds of operation. This factor must be borne in mind when drafting enforcement notices (see below). Planning permission for a use does *not* include permission for any operations such as erecting buildings, however necessary those buildings are to the use. However, planning permission for the erection of a building does include permission for the use for which the building is designed unless the permission states otherwise (section 33(2)).

A particular project will often include several different kinds of development. For example, in *West Bowers Farm Products* v. *Secretary of State* (1985), the landowner dug out a reservoir (engineering operation) and sold off the spoil. This was held to be a change of use requiring a separate planning permission. In *Northavon District Council* v. *Secretary of State* (1980), the landowner drained his farmland by removing topsoil. He replaced it with builder's rubble. If this were an 'operation' it would have automatic planning permission under the General Development Order (see below). If it were a change of use − the tipping of refuse − it would need planning permission. The court held that the test is the primary purpose of the landowner: was this to provide a 'last resting place for rubble' or to raise the level of the land using rubble as a convenient way of doing so? As is so often the case, this approach requires the enforcement official to have a thorough knowledge of all the relevant facts since the notion of 'primary purpose' must be examined in the context of the history of the site and the developer's activities generally. (See *Northavon District Council* v. *Secretary of State* (1980).)

SPECIAL CASES

The Act singles out some special cases. Some of these it excludes from being development, others it designates as particular kinds of development.

The following are not development.

'(a) the carrying out of works for the maintenance, improvement or other alteration of any building, being works which affect only the interior of the building or which do not materially affect the external appearance of the building and (in either case) are not works for making good war damage or works begun after 5 December 1968 for the alteration of a building by providing additional space therein below ground;

(b) the carrying out by a local highway authority of any works required for the maintenance or improvement of a road, being works carried out on land within the boundaries of the road;

(c) the carrying out by a local authority or statutory undertakers of any works for the purpose of inspecting, repairing or renewing any sewers, mains, pipes, cables or other apparatus including the breaking open of any street or other land for that purpose;

(d) the use of any building or other land within the curtilage of a dwelling house for any purpose incidental to the enjoyment of the dwelling house as such;

(e) the use of any land for the purposes of agriculture or forestry (including afforestation) and the use for any of those purposes of any building occupied together with land so used;

(f) in the case of buildings or other land which are used for a purpose of any class specified in an order made by the Secretary of State under this section, the use of the buildings or other land or, subject to the provisions of the order, of any part thereof for any other purpose of the same class.'

(e) and (f) deserve further discussion.

Development and planning permission

Agricultural use

This is defined by section 290(1) as 'including horticulture, fruit growing, seed growing, dairy farming, the breeding and keeping of livestock (including any creature kept for the production of food, wool, skins or fur, or for the purpose of its use in the farming of land), the use of land as grazing land, meadow land, osier land, market gardens and nursery grounds, and the use of land for woodlands where that use is ancillary to the farming of land for other agricultural purposes, and "agricultural" shall be construed accordingly'.

The definition must be applied in the light of the planning unit doctrine discussed earlier. For example, the grazing of horses for use in sporting activities elsewhere is agricultural (*Sykes* v. *Secretary of State* (1981)), but not where horse training or showjumping is carried on within the site (*Belmont Farms* v. *Secretary of State* (1962)). In *Gill* v. *Secretary of State* (1985), it was held that the large-scale slaughter of foxes bred on the site was not an agricultural use although breeding foxes for slaughter elsewhere is (*North Warwickshire District Council* v. *Secretary of State* (1983)).

The sale of produce from the land, and the manufacture of equipment for the agricultural use, are ancillary uses. The sale of imported goods, as is the case with many so-called 'farm shops', is development.

The agricultural exemption relates only to uses and not to building and other operations. However, many operations connected with agriculture have automatic planning permission under the General Development Order (Schedule 2, Part 6). A problem here arises where a building is used for the industrial processing of agricultural products – factory farming. In *Jones* v. *Stockport Borough Council* (1984), the Court of Appeal thought that such processes were sufficiently related to agricultural use to benefit from the GDO.

The Use Classes Order 1987

The Use Classes Order states that a change from a use within any class specified in the Order to another use within the same class is not development. The Order does not in any sense grant planning permission. The first use must already be in existence and must itself either have planning permission or have begun before the end of 1963 (the time limit for taking enforcement action). If the land is subdivided, the use of each part must be compared with the previous use of the whole unit. For example, suppose a department store is subdivided into separate units of shops, restaurants, offices, etc. The shop units will not need planning permission because most shops fall within a single use class (see below). The office and restaurant units fall within a different use class and need planning permission.

Changes *between* classes or outside the classes are not necessarily development. Ordinary principles must be applied.

The various use classes can be summarised as follows:-

A1	Shops including 'cold food' takeaways such as sandwich bars.
A2	Financial and professional services such as estate agents and solicitors. Medical services are not included and the use must be appropriate to a shopping area and be available to visiting members of the public.
A3	Restaurants, pubs and hot food takeaways.
B1	Other offices, research and development and light industrial processes which do not harm local amenities. This class caters for modern 'high-tech' businesses where the office and production sides are intermingled. The standard is that of a *hypothetical* residential area against which the particular use must be assessed (*Lamb* v. *Secretary of State* (1983); *Essex County Council* v. *Secretary of State* (1974)).
B2	General Industrial Uses.
B3 to B7	Classes of specific industrial uses classified in descending order of unpleasantness, e.g. B7 includes 'boiling or cleaning tripe and glue manufacturing'.
B8	Storage or use as a distribution centre.
C1	Hotels and hostels.
C2	Residential institutions providing care. Hospitals, nursing homes, boarding schools, colleges or training centres.
C3	Certain dwelling houses (see above).
D1	Various non-residential public institutions, e.g. day nurseries, schools, libraries, museums, public halls, churches.

Development and planning permission 25

D2   Cinemas, concert halls, bingo halls, casinos, dance halls, sports centres not involving motorised vehicles or firearms.

Some uses which might otherwise fall within the Order are excluded from any class (Art 3(6)). These include theatres, amusement arcades and funfairs, launderettes, petrol stations, car sales shops, taxi and car hire businesses, scrapyards and motor vehicle breakers. The Order is, of course, completely irrelevant to all other uses and of no help in deciding questions about the general meaning of development. It is merely a governmental regulation dealing with a specific list of uses. It must be interpreted literally, so that any use within its language is protected, but not so as to have any wider significance.

ACTS WHICH ARE DEVELOPMENT

By virtue of section 22(3) which is said to be 'for the avoidance of doubt', certain uses and operations are stated to be development. These are as follows:

(a) The *use* of any building previously used as a single dwelling house as two or more separate dwelling houses. No physical subdivision is needed. The test is whether the planning authority can reasonably decide that separate living units have been created (*Wakelin* v. *Secretary of State* (1978)).

(b) The deposit of refuse or waste is a material change of use even on an existing refuse dump if the area or height above ground is increased. Use of a new tip is, of course, a material change of use unless it can be regarded as incidental to another kind of development e.g. *Northavon District Council* v. *Secretary of State* (1980) (see above).

(c) Section 22(3A) extends the definition of mining operation (see above) and section 22(4) makes the use of the outside of a building for the display of advertisements a material change of use if that part of the building is not normally used for that purpose.

(d) Finally, two special cases apply to Greater London:
    (i) The provision of (up to 90 days') temporary sleeping accommodation on residential premises for payment or by

reason of the employment of the occupant is a material change of use (Greater London (General Powers) Act 1973, section 25).

(ii) Timesharing schemes constitute a material change of use (Greater London Council (General Powers) Act 1984, section 5).

Planning permission

THE EFFECT OF A PLANNING PERMISSION

Planning permission is normally granted as a result of an application made in an individual case. A planning permission benefits any owner, occupier or user of the land unless it is made purely personal (section 33). A developer can hold as many unimplemented permissions as he wishes. However, a planning permission normally lapses unless implementation is commenced within five years (sections 42, 43). Similarly, a permission may lapse if the development is not *completed* within a reasonable time (section 44).

Apart from these statutory arrangements, a planning permission cannot normally be lost as the result of the landowner's conduct. In *Pioneer Aggregates Ltd* v. *Secretary of State* (1985), the previous owners of the site had received planning permission for mining operations. They had decided to discontinue the working. The present owners later acquired the site and wished to resume mining. They committed a token act of blasting so as to challenge the local planning authority to take enforcement action. The House of Lords held that the owners were entitled to the benefit of the planning permission and that a planning permission cannot be generally abandoned by the voluntary conduct of the landowner. The House of Lords recognised that there are exceptional cases where the benefit of a planning permission might be lost. These are as follows:

(i) Where a landowner holds two or more inconsistent permissions. A person can apply for and obtain as many permissions as he wishes. If he implements one, then the benefit of the others is lost to the extent that they cannot physically be implemented together. This is a matter of interpreting the scope of the relevant permissions. A local planning authority can take advantage of this principle by imposing a condition that a new planning permission cannot be implemented in conjunction with another permission, or that the benefit of an earlier permission must be forfeited (*Kingston upon Thames Royal London Borough* v. *Secretary of State* (1974)). The authority can also restrict rights conferred by the Act itself. For example, a condition can forbid changes of use that are not development (*City of London Corporation* v. *Secretary of State* (1971)).

Even where there is no express condition, the benefit of a permission is lost once a physically inconsistent permission is implemented (see *Pilkington* v. *Secretary of State* (1973)).

(ii) As we have already seen, a *use* can be lost by abandonment, or by a change to another use. Some writers argue that because a planning permission lasts permanently, then a use *with* planning permission can never be abandoned or lost. It is submitted that this is wrong and that it is irrelevant whether or not the use in question has planning permission. The argument seems to be based upon a misunderstanding of the nature of a change of use and upon a misreading of the *Pioneer Aggregates* case. *Pioneer Aggregates* did not concern a use, but a permission *that had not been fully implemented*. Lord Scarman expressly stated (at p. 365) that the abandonment of a use has nothing to do with the extinguishment of a planning permission. Planning permission, it will be recalled, is for a specific *change* of use and not for the use as such. Furthermore, the various special exemptions provided by the Act for the benefit of persons reverting to certain previous uses (see below) make no sense if it is assumed that a use permission is never lost. (See also *White* v. *Secretary of State* (1989).) Even in the case of operational development, once a building is completed the question of abandoning the planning permission becomes irrelevant. For example, if the building is burned down by accident, planning permission is needed for the new operation of restoring it.

(iii) A fundamental physical change made to the land apparently destroys existing planning rights. This is called the 'new chapter in the planning history' doctrine. The change must be great enough to justify the planning authority taking the view that an entirely new planning situation has arisen so that the slate should be wiped clean. This doctrine is very exceptional. For example, the subdivision of a site does not in itself create a new chapter (*Winton* v. *Secretary of*

State (1982)). Nor does the erection of a new building, unless perhaps the whole site is covered. Where a new building covers only *part* of a site, existing use rights both within and around it are preserved unless, of course, the planning permission states otherwise. It may be that this 'new chapter' doctrine is essentially a variation of the 'inconsistency' doctrine discussed earlier. See *South Staffordshire District Council* v. *Secretary of State* (1987), *Jennings Motors Ltd* v. *Secretary of State* (1982), *Hilliard* v. *Secretary of State* (1978) for illustrations. There is also a short discussion of the doctrine in *Newbury District Council* v. *Secretary of State* (1981).

(iv) A planning permission can also be formally revoked or modified before it is implemented (section 45). Compensation must be paid, and unless the proposal is unopposed the Secretary of State must confirm it (section 46). Once a permission has been implemented, the authority can remove it by means of a discontinuance order under section 51 (see above).

AUTOMATIC PLANNING PERMISSION

Planning permission can be conferred automatically by several devices.

DEVELOPMENT ORDERS (section 24)

The General Development Order 1988 applies to designated kinds of development throughout the country, but can be withdrawn in particular cases provided that this is done before the development has commenced (Art 4; see *Strandmill Ltd.* v. *Secretary of State* (1988)). The General Development Order is highly pragmatic. It covers a range of domestic, industrial, recreational and agricultural activity, temporary and recreational activity, and a considerable amount of development carried out by public authorities.

There are also '*Special Development Orders'* made by the Secretary of State. These apply to particular projects, usually large-scale developments or development by public bodies such as Urban Development Corporations. Special Development Orders are listed in the *Encyclopaedia of Planning Law and Practice*.

Development and planning permission

DEVELOPMENT DESIGNATED BY 'ENTERPRISE ZONE SCHEMES' OR 'SIMPLIFIED PLANNING ZONE' SCHEMES

These schemes create special areas, usually in respect of disused or underused urban land where development is particularly desirable. *Enterprise zones* are designated by the Secretary of State under the Local Government, Planning and Land Act 1980. Designation confers tax and other benefits as well as planning privileges. Simplified Planning Zones were introduced by the Housing and Planning Act 1986 and are designated by the local authority itself (section 24A-E). Certain categories of land such as national parks and green belt land cannot be designated as a simplified planning zone. Nor can land or development excluded by the Secretary of State (see section 24E).

Within the zones, the scheme itself can grant planning permission for all or any development either unconditionally or subject to conditions. The scheme can also designate activities for which applications for planning permission must be made in the ordinary way.

DEEMED PLANNING PERMISSION

There are miscellaneous cases where planning permission is deemed to be granted by virtue of the developer complying with some other procedure. The main cases are:

(i) Development by local planning authorities.
(ii) Development by a public authority that requires and obtains the consent of a government department (section 40)
(iii) The display of advertisements complying with special advertisement regulations (see below).

EXEMPTIONS FROM THE NEED FOR PLANNING PERMISSION

There are miscellaneous cases where development can take place without the need for planning permission. These must not be confused with;

(a) cases where automatic planning permission exists under the general law (above);
(b) cases which for some special reason do not qualify as development, e.g. under the Use Classes Order 1987 (see above);
(c) development which is immune from enforcement because of the time limits which apply to the issue of an enforcement notice (see below).

These are often lumped together as 'existing rights' but they have different legal consequences. In particular, acts which have planning permission or which do not require planning permission are lawful whereas acts which are time-barred from enforcement remain unlawful.

The exemptions from the need for planning permission are as follows:

(a) Development by or on behalf of the Crown, but not development by other people in land owned by the Crown, although this has certain privileges (see below).
(b) A list of cases in section 23. These are mainly intended to deal with technical problems arising because development is an *activity* or a *change* and not a building or use as such (above). The list is as follows:

   (i) The resumption before 6 December 1968 of the *normal* use of the land as it was on 1 July 1948 following a temporary use (section 23(2)). This may still be relevant because an enforcement notice can issue in respect of a change of use taking place after 1963.
   (ii) Where an occasional use of the land took place before 1 July 1948 and the occasional use was resumed on a similar basis between then and 6 December 1968. Once this condition is satisfied, uses for the occasional purpose after 6 December 1968 are also exempt (section 23(3)).
   (iii) Reversion to the last use where the land was unoccupied on 1 July 1948, but was occupied at some time after 1 January 1937. (All relevant dates are those in which major changes in planning law came into effect.)
   (iv) Resumption of the normal use of the land after the expiry

Development and planning permission

of a temporary planning permission (section 23(4)). In the case of a caravan site, there is no exemption unless the site has been used at least once during the two years up to 9 March 1960 (the date special caravan site legislation took effect).

(v) Resumption of the *normal* use of land following a planning permission granted *subject to limitations* by a development order (section 23(8)). *Cynon Valley* v. *Secretary of State* (1986) illustrates this. Premises had GDO permission as a shop subject to a 'limitation' as to the kind of shop. The premises then reverted to a previous use as a hot food takeaway. It was held that this would have required planning permission (see above) but that the exemption in section 23(8) applied. We shall see later that there is some uncertainty as regards what is meant by a 'limitation' (see below).

(vi) Resumption of the preceding *lawful* use of the land when complying with an enforcement notice (section 23(9). If an unlawful use is stopped *before* an enforcement notice takes effect, planning permission *is* needed to restore the previous use. This exemption will be discussed more fully later.

(c) Development which took place on or before 1 July 1948 does not need planning permission (Schedule 24, para. 12). This was the date on which the present planning system was introduced. For the purpose of these exemptions, a use is not 'normal' unless it either had planning permission or did not need planning permission (section 23(5)). Similarly, a use is not 'lawful' except under the same conditions (*LTSS Print and Supply Services Ltd* v. *Hackney London Borough Council* (1976)).

INTERPRETATION OF A PLANNING PERMISSION

Interpretation of a planning permission is all important. For this purpose, the planning permission is not the resolution made by the council or planning committee or the officer's decision, but is the document which formally notifies the applicant of the decision. Unless this is completely inconsistent with the resolution or decision, it must be taken for all purposes as representing the planning

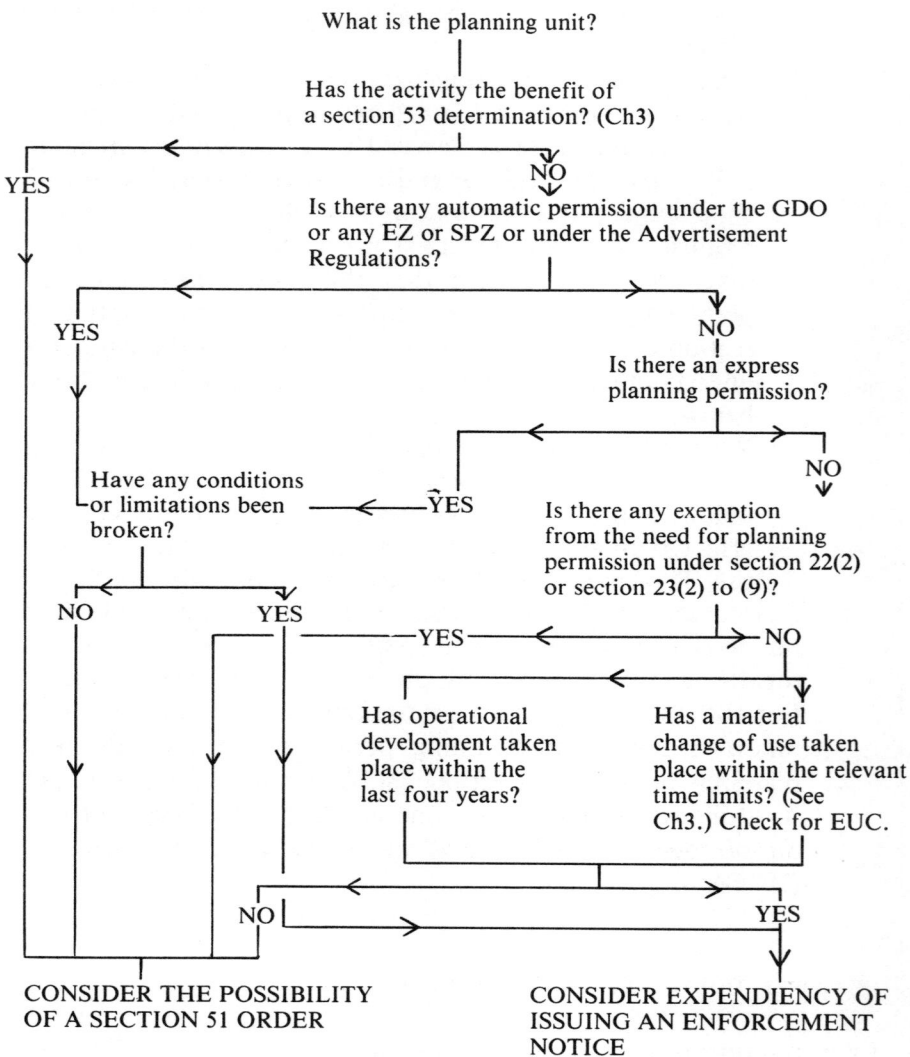

Fig. 1. Taking enforcement action: factors to be considered.

permission. (See *R* v. *West Oxfordshire District Council ex parte Pearce Homes* (1986), *Norfolk County Council* v. *Secretary of State* (1973).) Other documents such as the application and any plans or letters can be looked at if they are expressly mentioned in the notification letter. (It is usual practice to mention them, but see *Wilson* v. *West Sussex County Council* (1963).)

A planning permission should be read broadly in a commonsense way taking account of the authority's planning policy as stated in the development plan and the landowner's knowledge of the state of the land, its neighbourhood and the history of the site. It should be interpreted in favour of it being valid and workable in practice (*Fawcett Properties* v. *Buckinghamshire County Council* (1961)). However, the fact that a condition cannot be enforced in practice has no bearing on its legal validity (*Bromsgrove District Council* v. *Secretary of State* (1988) – condition that only meat reared in certain farms be sold from a farm shop.) On the other hand, a permission that is so vaguely worded as to be meaningless or to provide no clue as which of several meanings it might have is invalid (*Shanley* v. *Secretary of State* (1982) – 'first opportunity' to buy houses should be given to local people). As we shall see, a similar test applies to enforcement notices themselves.

Conclusion

Before deciding whether it is 'expedient' to issue an enforcement notice, the authority should ideally consider the questions in Fig. 1.

Chapter 3

The decision to take enforcement action

The discretionary power

Enforcement is discretionary. Even when there has been a clear breach of planning control there is no obligation to take enforcement action. Indeed an LPA would be unlawfully fettering its discretion if it adopted a policy of automatically issuing an enforcement notice whenever it discovered a breach of planning control. Thus 'where it appears to the local planning authority that there has been a breach of planning control (after certain dates' (see below)) the authority *may* issue an enforcement notice 'if they consider it expedient to do so having regard to the provisions of the development plan and to any other material considerations' (section 87(1)(2)).

The breach of planning control must appear to *have taken place*. There is no power to take enforcement proceedings in advance as a precautionary measure. However, in an extreme case, for example where permanent damage to the environment is threatened, an authority could apply to the court for an injunction to prohibit an anticipated breach of planning control (see Chapter 8).

The breach of planning control need not *actually* have occurred. The Act requires only that it *appears to the authority* to have occurred. If the authority is wrong – suppose, for example, that the allegations do not amount to a breach of planning control, or the breach as described in the notice never happened, or it happened outside the time limits – the remedy normally lies only in the statutory right of appeal to the Secretary of State. This must be exercised before the notice takes effect (see below). If a valid appeal is not launched or an appeal fails, then the enforcement notice takes effect and the authority's error cannot be raised as a defence except in special cases (see below). This happened in *Jeary* v. *Chailey Rural District Council* (1973). The applicant's land had been used as a breaker's yard since before 1948. Planning permission was therefore

The decision to take enforcement action 35

not needed. Nevertheless, the local planning authority served an enforcement notice. The applicant failed to appeal to the Secretary of State and the Court of Appeal held that the enforcement notice could validly require the yard to be closed.

In *Jeary* the authority's belief that the breach was more recent was not unreasonable. Where the authority acts in bad faith or without any rational basis for its belief at all – for example, if it fails to provide any evidence – the enforcement notice will be completely void and ineffective for any purpose. In such a case the citizen need not appeal to the Secretary of State but can raise the matter in the ordinary courts. The same applies if the authority takes irrelevant factors into account or fails to take relevant factors into account, or if the wrong person has issued the notice. The distinction between a void enforcement notice and a notice which can be challenged only on appeal is fundamental and should be borne in mind throughout. It will be discussed more fully in Chapter 6.

The authority can therefore issue an enforcement notice if it has some rational foundation for an honest belief that a breach of planning control has taken place. For this purpose the authority is entitled to rely upon whatever evidence is available in its records and need not at this stage prepare full supporting evidence and argument.

The courts have consistently endorsed this. For example, in *Nelsovil* v. *Minister of Housing* (1962), Mr Justice Widgery emphasised the practical difficulties faced by local authorities in discovering when a breach of planning control had taken place, and in *Ferris* v. *Secretary of State* (1988) Mr Graham Eyre QC held that in deciding whether to issue a notice a local planning authority did not have to satisfy itself that a breach of planning control had definitely taken place, nor did it have to consider possible grounds of challenge to its notice. Again, the court's reasoning emphasised the practical impossibility of monitoring possible breaches of planning control.

However, when it comes to central government policy, which is what matters in an appeal, a much stricter approach is currently being taken (see below).

EXPEDIENCY

The authority must consider it 'expedient' to issue an enforcement notice and must state reasons for this in the notice (see overleaf).

The following factors may be particularly relevant:

(1) The harm caused or likely to be caused by the offending development. This embraces a wide range of matters. For example, in *Lilo Blum* v. *Secretary of State* (1987), an enforcement notice alleged a material change of use from a livery stable to a riding school. It was held that the authority was entitled to take into account considerations of purely visual amenity, and the expense of maintaining bridleways, etc. The current pattern of uses in the area and its overall character are, of course, vital factors. The relevance of the development as a precedent is also important.
(2) The Development Plan in force in the area. Again, this must not be treated as absolutely binding. Inconsistency with the plan does not automatically justify enforcement proceedings. (See Circular 14/85, para 3.13.)
(3) Central government policies embodied in circulars (see below).
(4) The practical problems of enforcement.
(5) The developer's personal circumstances, such as hardship, will only exceptionally be relevant for the purpose of deciding whether or not to take enforcement action but are more likely to be relevant as regards the timescale for enforcement. (See Circular 22/80, Annex B, para 1.) On the other hand, individual interests related to the use of land, such as safety and noise levels, are relevant.
(6) Local opinion and the political policy of the authority. Unlike the case with applications for planning permission, a local planning authority has no duty to consult with any other body before taking enforcement action.
(7) The developer's 'fall back' position.

The developer may revert to the immediately preceding lawful use of the land or take up any alternative planning permissions for operational development. Other *use* permissions will no longer be in force (see above). The authority must take these possibilities into account to see if they are worse than the development which it is proposed to enforce. In *Lewstar Ltd* v. *Secretary of State* (1984) an enforcement notice was served in respect of a change of use in London's Soho to a sex-orientated coin-operated peep show. The appellant argued that given the unpleasant character of the

The decision to take enforcement action

area there was no point in taking enforcement action because likely alternative uses were equally undesirable. It was held that possible fall back uses need only be taken into account if the fall back use was *worse* than the use to be enforced against. The authority may also adopt a policy in favour of preserving the previous use provided that on 'balance of probabilities' – or possibly if there is 'a fair chance' – the previous use would be restored. (See *Westminster City Council* v. *British Waterways Board* (1984).)

Expired planning permissions may also be taken into account as indications of possible alternative uses, but must be given less weight than live permissions (*South Oxford District Council* v. *Secretary of State* (1981)).

(8) In some cases alternative sites for the offending development should be taken into account. This seems to be the case where the development to be enforced against meets a social or economic need but causes substantial and unavoidable environmental harm and where the supply should be rationed. (See *Greater London Council* v. *Secretary of State* (1986).) Examples include power stations, coalmining, gypsy camps, and hotels but not usually dwelling houses, offices or superstores. In these cases an authority can enforce against a development for which there is an accepted need if they consider that the need can be better met elsewhere, even if there is no definite alternative site in view (see *Trusthouse Forte Hotels Ltd* v. *Secretary of State* (1986).) In general, however, planning permission cannot be refused solely because there may be a better site or because there is another better use for the site in question. The DoE has recommended that in appropriate circumstances the authority should help the developer to find an alternative site. (See PPGN(I), para. 30 (1988).)

CENTRAL GOVERNMENT POLICY

Every appeal against an enforcement notice is deemed to be an application for planning permission to the Secretary of State (section 88B(3)).

We have already seen that published central government policy must be taken into account but must not be treated as absolutely binding (see above). Short of fettering discretion completely, the weight to be given to any particular factor is a matter of policy and not usually the concern of the courts. (See, for example, *ELS Wholesales (Wolverhampton) Ltd* v. *Secretary of State* (1987).) On the other hand, a local planning authority that fails to follow central government policy may lose an appeal to the Secretary of State unless it can show strong reasons why an exception should be made to the policy. Nor can a central government policy make a factor relevant that is lawfully irrelevant, or vice versa.

Current central government policy set out in circulars is to emphasise that enforcement proceedings are a last resort and should be taken only where there are clear planning objections to the activity and where a satisfactory resolution cannot be achieved by negotiation (circular 22/80, para 15; PPGNI, para 30). There is a general presumption in favour of granting planning permission (Circular 14/85, para 3). In order to succeed at an appeal, the authority has to satisfy the Inspector that development 'causes demonstrable harm to interests of acknowledged importance' which cannot be mitigated by a condition or through an agreement. Local planning authorities are advised to warn developers in advance of the possibility of enforcement and to encourage negotiation (Circular 20/85, Welsh Office 49/85, Appendix 1). The policy of encouraging 'small business' is particularly stressed (Circular 22/80, Annex B).

The policy of encouraging negotiations between developers and local planning authorities has not been encouraged by the case of *R* v. *Richmond Borough Council ex parte Macartney and Stones (Developers) Ltd* (1989). Mr Justice Popplewell held that a local planning authority could lawfully make a charge of £25 for a meeting between planning officers and a developer in respect of a proposed application for planning permission. This was because of section 111(1) of the Local Government Act 1972 which authorises local authorities to do anything... 'which is calculated to facilitate or is conducive or incidental to, the discharge of any of their functions'. This seems equally applicable to negotiations arising out of enforcement proceedings.

As regards conditions, the central government applies tests similar to but not exactly the same as those required by the law. Thus:

'Conditions should only be imposed when they are necessarily relevant to planning, relevant to the development to be permitted, enforceable, precise, and reasonable. ... One key test is whether planning permission would have to be refused if the condition were not to be imposed. If not then such a condition needs special and precise justification.'

As regards legal validity, a condition must certainly be relevant and reasonable but need not be enforceable or necessary. (See *Bromsgrove District Council* v. *Secretary of State* (1988).) Furthermore, for purposes of legal validity, a condition will be unlawful for unreasonableness and uncertainty only in extreme cases. The onus is on the challenger to establish these factors. By contrast, the Inspector on appeal may set aside a condition solely because he regards it as undesirable. A previous appeal decision in which the same condition was upheld may be taken into account but is not binding (see above). The subjective nature of planning judgments coupled with the opportunity to raise the same matter over and over again is one of the fundamental flaws in our development control system.

In appeal proceedings, costs may be awarded against the local planning authority if the Inspector or Secretary of State, as the case may be, takes the view that the local planning authority has acted unreasonably. Examples of unreasonable conduct include issuing an enforcement notice without adequate grounds, failing to negotiate, or causing delay. (See Circular 4/87, Welsh Office 5/87; *Manchester City Council* v. *Secretary of State* (1987).) Costs are not automatically awarded to the winning party.

Obtaining information

There is no systematic method by which a local planning authority can monitor its area and obtain the information it needs in order to decide whether to take enforcement action. It may be particularly difficult to discover the identity and addresses of all those with interests in the land. Title to land can readily be moved around through a network of companies and individuals. It may also be difficult to discover the planning history of the site which in some cases must be determined as far back as 1948, and the location, duration and interrelationship of the various uses of the site 'Intensification' also raises problems in deciding when the level of activity crossed the threshold of legality.

The Local Planning Authority has certain statutory powers to obtain information.

(i) Under section 280, a person with the written permission of the Secretary of State or of the local planning authority may at any reasonable time enter any land for the purpose of surveying it in connection with a 'proposal' to take enforcement proceedings and for various other purposes.

It is not clear how much evidence is required to justify an entry to land under section 280. Unlike police powers of entry, the planning authority does not have to show 'reasonable grounds' for issuing an enforcement or stop notice (section 280 1(c)). It seems to follow that the test is that generally appropriate to the exercise of a discretionary power, i.e. the authority must show some rational basis for deciding to enter. It cannot therefore carry out a random survey. There is also power to enter land to determine whether an enforcement notice has been obeyed (section 280(8)).

Twenty-four hours' notice must be given to any occupier and compensation must be paid for any damage (section 281).

(ii) The Secretary of State or local planning authority can by notice in writing require the occupier and 'any person who either directly or indirectly receives rent in respect of any premises' to provide certain information in writing within 21 days (section 284). However, this power can be used only following a decision to take enforcement action. This information includes the following (section 284(1A)):

(a) the nature of the interest in the premises of the person served;
(b) the name and address of any other person known to him as having an interest in the premises;
(c) the purpose for which the premises are being used;
(d) the time when that use began;
(e) the name and address of any person known to him as having used the premises for that purpose;
(f) the time when any activities being carried out on the premises began.

It is an offence wilfully to obstruct an official exercising the right of entry (section 281(2)), and also to refuse to give the information required by a section 284 'information notice' without reasonable excuse or to give false information. The latter carries up to two years' imprisonment (section 284(2)(3)). It is not clear what 'reasonable excuse' means in this context. It might be possible, for example, to refuse to give information on the ground that it is confidential, either because of some special relationship or in the public interest.

The information required under section 284 is by no means comprehensive. For example, it does not extend to previous uses of the premises. Nor does it include the time when building operations took place unless these are still continuing. However, a section 284 notice may serve as a useful warning to the developer that enforcement action is being contemplated.

(iii) There is power under the Local Government (Miscellaneous Provisions) Act 1976, section 16, to require information within 14 days. However, this only concerns the names and addresses of persons with interest in the land.

(iv) By virtue of section 129 of the Land Registration Act 1925, the Land Registry may provide information to local authorities and the Secretary of State on request. However, this only includes information which the authority are entitled to receive directly from the landowner under other statutory powers. This information is less comprehensive even than that obtainable under the other powers. Firstly, it does not relate to the physical description of the land and its use but only to the names of persons with interests in the land. Secondly, leases for less than 21 years do not necessarily appear in the register. Nor do interests arising under trusts, nor informal rights of occupation. Thirdly, by no means all title to land is within the Land Registry system.

(v) The Land Registration Act 1988 confers a public right to inspect the register of which local authorities and Urban Development Corporations can take advantage. This has not yet been implemented.

The powers conferred by sections 280 and 284 apply to Urban Development Corporations but not the powers under the 1976 Act or the Land Registration Act. This is because Urban Development Corporations are not local authorities for the purpose of local government legislation (see above).

Other sources of information include:

- Registers of planning permissions, local land charges, enforcement and stop notices maintained by the local planning authority. The register of enforcement notices only goes back to 27 November 1981. The register also includes 'section 53 determinations' (see below) and certificates of established uses. It contains information as to whether the steps required by the notice have been taken (section 92A).
- The Companies Register containing the names of directors and officers, although these are not necessarily helpful.
- Similar registers relating to Industrial and Provident Societies, Friendly Societies and Charities.
- The Electoral Register and the Rating Valuation list.
- The planning authority's records of previous planning appeals, correspondence, plans, etc.
- Records compiled by other departments and authorities including building regulation records, public health records, police records and vehicle licensing records.

Informal information on the basis of which enforcement action can legitimately be contemplated includes complaints from the public or from councillors, press reports, advertisements and the like. In practice, local planning authorities rely mainly on complaints from the public. This is open to obvious objections because of its capriciousness and in 1981 was criticised by the Commission for Local Administration (see Jowell and Millichip (1986)).

Breach of planning control

The authority must be clear exactly how the different kinds of breach of planning control relate to each other and the different legal consequences of each. As we shall see, the enforcement notice must describe the alleged breach of control and to some extent place it in its correct legal pigeonhole. There are two kinds of breach of control. These are:

(1) Development without planning permission.
(2) Breach of a condition or limitation subject to which planning permission was granted (section 87(3)).

DEVELOPMENT WITHOUT PLANNING PERMISSION

Development without planning permission must be subdivided into (i) operational development and (ii) material change of use, although as a matter of drafting the enforcement notice itself probably need not make this distinction (see below). However, if the draftsman attempts to make the distinction and gets it wrong, the notice is liable to be quashed or amended on appeal (see below). There are standard model enforcement notices for each of these kinds of development (DoE Circular 38/81 WO 57/81: see appendix). The main reasons for distinguishing between operational and change of use development are that the time limits for enforcement differ (see below) the sanctions differ (see below) and stop notice law differs (see below). We devoted Chapter 2 to the meaning of the crucial term 'development' and shall deal with conditions and limitations here.

There are also cases where the terms of a planning permission have been violated, e.g. building a house which is not in the exact location specified in the application, or using the wrong materials. This counts as development without planning permission (see below).

CONDITIONS AND LIMITATIONS

Breach of condition or limitation raises problems because the Act does not define what is meant by a limitation. In drafting an enforcement notice, the terms 'condition' and 'limitation' can be used interchangeably (section 243(5)), but this does not solve all possible problems. Conditions and limitations differ in their legal effect. Furthermore, breach of a 'limitation' may have to be distinguished from development without planning permission, and the notice must be drafted with this in mind (see below).

In *Peacock Homes Ltd* v. *Secretary of State* (1984), Lord Justice Dillon said that the term 'limitation' seems to be superfluous except possibly in the sense of time limit. But in *Cynon Valley District Council* v. *Secretary of State* (1986), the Court of Appeal held that a GDO permission for retail uses excluding certain kinds of shop was a permission subject to limitations. The same seems to apply to express planning permissions, e.g. *Carpet Decor* v. *Secretary of State* (see below).

A limitation therefore seems to be a functional restriction on a use.

The same result could equally be achieved by a condition, so the matter depends entirely on the language of the planning permission.

A view which is often put forward is that 'time limits' upon a planning permission are limitations. However, the time limits imposed by the Act itself (section 41) are expressed as conditions and in *Miller-Mead* v. *Minister of Housing* (1963) it was held that a use which exceeded the 28 days' planning permission conferred by the GDO Class IV is correctly described as development without permission.

The GDO previously referred to permission subject to 'limitations'. These related to the physical dimension or location of buildings and structures and the description of a use. Nevertheless, it has been held that an operation which exceeds physical restrictions – too high, etc. – is development entirely without permission, and not breach of a limitation. The entire building can therefore be enforced against (*Copeland Borough Council* v. *Secretary of State* (1976); *Garland* v. *Minister of Defence* (1968); *Rochdale Metropolitan Borough Council* v. *Simmonds* (1980)). The GDO 1988 avoids applying the term 'limitation' to any kind of planning permission.

What, then, are the differences between conditions and limitations? Firstly, a limitation can be implied into a planning permission by reason of the surrounding circumstances. In *Kwik-Save Discount* v. *Secretary of State* (1981), a garage and an associated motor parts shop were split up. The shop was sold to Kwik-Save with planning permission for retail use. It was held that the planning permission was only intended to apply to retail sales in association with the adjacent garage and did not authorise use as a supermarket, even though the permission did not actually state this restriction. The result depended on the interpretation of the permission document as a whole against the background of the physical nature of the site.

Secondly, a *condition* can prevent a further change of use even if that change is not in itself development (*City of London Corporation* v. *Secretary of State* (1971), condition that premises be used only as an employment agency). A limitation cannot do this. In *Carpet Decor (Guildford) Ltd.* v. *Secretary of State* (1981), underground vaults were used for the storage of building society and later bank documents. Planning permission was granted 'as a store for papers'. Under the Use Classes Order, the storage of any goods would be permissible. It was held that, despite the limitation in the permission, the appellant could take advantage of the UCO and change the use of the vaults to the storage of carpets. Sir Douglas Frank QC held that an express condition but nothing less was required to exclude the UCO. It will be recalled that the effect of the UCO is to prevent certain changes of use being development (see above). In the case of a limitation it is sometimes wrongly thought that a limitation by defining the use can make any change from that use development. In fact, a two stage test must be applied:

(1) Is the new use within the language of the permission? If so, that is the end of the matter.
(2) If the new use is outside the permission, it must then be asked whether the change is development *on general principles* (*Waverley District Council* v. *Secretary of State* (1982) – permission for 'cattle transport depot', change to 'general haulage'). This has the odd result that breach of limitation *in itself* does not appear in practice to be enforceable despite section 87(3).

The whole question of limitations needs a thorough rationalisation. As the law stands, if a planning authority seeks to exercise detailed control over a use it is preferable to use an express condition.

Bars to enforcement action

Having decided which category of breach of planning control is involved, the authority must next consider whether there is a legal bar to enforcement action. There are two possibilities. Firstly, there might be a 'section 53 determination', in force that planning permission is not required. Secondly, enforcement might be time barred.

SECTION 53 DETERMINATIONS

Under section 53, a person who proposes to carry out operations or to make a change of use can apply to the local planning authority (with an appeal to the Secretary of State) for a determination whether planning permission is required. Any determination made under section 53 is binding on the authority and is registrable in the register of planning permissions. Application must be made formally in writing. As we have seen, informal statements by officers are not usually binding (see above). However, an application for planning permission has been held automatically to include an application to the authority to decide under section 53 that planning permission is not required (*Wells* v. *Minister of Housing* (1967) – a much criticised case). Because of this, an authority might inadvertently tie its hands for the future. On the other hand, if the authority grants planning permission in a case where permission is not required the landowner can ignore the permission (*Newbury District Council* v. *Secretary of State* (1981)).

A section 53 application cannot be made once the development has taken place. Nor can section 53 apply to the question whether the development is within the terms of a grant of planning permission on a previous application. Section 53 determinations concern whether the proposed activity is development at all, and if so, whether it has permission under the General Development Order, any enterprise zone or a simplified planning zone scheme (section 53(1) as amended). If the developer wishes to rely on an express planning permission he may raise the matter on appeal to the Secretary of State. Alternatively, *but before an enforcement notice is issued*, he may seek a declaration from the Court (see below).

TIME LIMITS

Development before 1948 is not a breach of planning control at all (see above). Apart from this, the matter depends upon whether operational development or material change of use is involved.

OPERATIONS

In the case of operational development, an enforcement notice must be issued within four years of the date of the breach (section 87(4)). Operations are a continuing process which may last for months or years. In the case of building and probably engineering operations, the whole enterprise, e.g. building a house, is a single operation (*Copeland Borough Council* v. *Secretary of State* (1976)). An enforcement notice can be issued once the work has started.

Nevertheless, it appears that time only runs from when the work is 'substantially completed'. (See *Ewen* v. *Secretary of State* (1984).) It follows that the whole of an operation can be prohibited, not just the part which took place within the last four years. In the case of mining operations, each separate extraction of minerals – every bite with the shovel – has been treated as a separate operation so that while the mine is active time never expires (*Thomas (David) (Porthcawl) Ltd* v. *Penybont Urban District Council* (1972)).

MATERIAL CHANGE OF USE

In the case of a material change of use an enforcement notice can be issued if the breach took place after 1963 (section 87(1)). There is one exception to this: change of use of a building *to* use as a single dwelling house must be enforced against within four years (section 87(4)c). A use protected by these rules is called an 'established use'.

If an operation is an integral part of a change of use it can be enforced against outside the four year period. This is because the local planning authority may require operations to be prohibited or buildings to be removed or altered as part of the steps required for the discontinuing of a use (see below). (See *Murfitt* v. *Secretary of State* (1980), *Ewen Developments* v. *Secretary of State* (1980).) Similarly, a use which was begun before 1964 can be prohibited if it is inextricably related to a post-1963 change of use (*Denham* v. *Secretary of State* (1984)).

The courts seem prepared to apply the time limit provisions flexibly in favour of the local planning authority. In *Perkins* v. *Secretary of State* (1981), the judge thought that a pre-time-limit activity could probably be required to cease even if it is not an integral part of the use enforced against, provided that it is a step required to restore the land to its condition before the breach took place.

A change of use takes place where there is some act carried out which is evidence of the new use, e.g. conversion work on a building from office to dwelling house. The use does not commence only when the dwelling is occupied. In *Backer* v. *Secretary of State* (1983), a dwelling house was completed more than four years ago but not occupied until within the four year period. It was held that the authority could not enforce.

The immunity given to a pre-1964 change of use includes, of

course, any subsequent change of use that is not development. If the pre-1963 use is later abandoned or a subsequent material change of use is made, the original use is lost.

The time limit provisions can normally be raised only by appealing to the Secretary of State (see below). Once an enforcement notice takes effect its language is conclusive. Even established uses can therefore be prohibited if they fall within its language (*South Staffordshire District Council* v. *Secretary of State* (1987), *Nash* v. *Secretary of State* (1986)). In such cases there may effectively be no use other than agricultural use (which is not development) to which the land can be put (see below).

CONDITIONS AND LIMITATIONS

If the breach of control takes the form of a breach of condition or limitation, the Act is a little obscure. Under section 87(4)d 'the failure to comply with a condition which prohibits or has the effect of preventing a change of use of a building to use as a single dwelling house' attracts the four year time limit and so does 'the failure to comply with any condition or limitation which *relates to* the carrying out of [building, engineering, mining or other operations] and subject to which planning permission was granted for the development of that land' (section 87(4)d).

Does this include any condition relating to the operation, e.g. permission for the erection of a building subject to a condition that it be occupied only by agricultural workers? Or does it apply only to a condition which regulates the operation itself, e.g. as to the landscaping, etc.? In *Peacock Homes* v. *Secretary of State* (1984), the Court of Appeal held that a condition attached to planning permission for the erection of a warehouse which required the warehouse to be later demolished did sufficiently relate to the erection of the building and must therefore be enforced within four years. The court did not decide that *all* conditions attached to an operational permission would do so. For example, a condition that land adjacent to a building be used as a car park might escape the four year rule.

A special rule applies to conditions or limitations attached to mining operations. These may be enforced within four years from when the authority finds out about the breach (Town and Country Planning (Minerals) Regulations 1971, Reg 4).

ESTABLISHED USE CERTIFICATES

It may be difficult to establish whether or not a change of use occurred before the end of 1963. The Act provides special machinery for this purpose in the form of an 'established use' certificate (section 94). This applies to any use of land except use as a single dwelling house (section 94(2)). Any person with an interest in the land may apply to the local planning authority for an EUC relating to all or part of the land. An 'established use' includes:

(a) a use begun before 1964 without planning permission and which has continued uninterrupted until the present day; or
(b) a use which began before 1964 in breach of conditions or limitations which have either never been complied with or have not been complied with since the end of 1963; or
(c) a use begun after 1963 as the result of a change of use not requiring planning permission and where there has been since the end of 1963 no change of use requiring planning permission (section 94(1)).

The use must still be in existence (section 94(3)). However, an ECU can relate to a lesser use (*Bristol City Council* v. *Secretary of State* (1988)).

If a use was given planning permission at any time even temporarily, an EUC cannot be obtained (*Bolivian Tin Trust Co* v. *Secretary of State* (1972)). Nor can an application for an EUC be made if a valid enforcement notice has already taken effect against the use in question, even if the notice has not been implemented (*Vaughan* v. *Secretary of State* (1986)). The reason for this is that the terms of an enforcement notice must be conclusive because an enforcement notice binds the land permanently. To allow an EUC or any established use to prevail over an earlier enforcement notice would be to allow a backdoor appeal outside the time limit. An appeal against an enforcement notice must be launched before the notice takes effect, usually within 28 days.

It is sometimes said that an EUC cannot be obtained in respect of any 'illegal' use. Indeed it is argued that an illegal use cannot claim the benefit of the time limits at all. In this context 'illegal' seems to mean criminal in any respect (e.g. *Glamorgan County Council* v. *Carter* (1963) – breach of caravan site regulations). This view is dangerously wide and bears little relationship to planning concerns.

Given the limitations upon an EUC, what is its purpose? An EUC is relevant *only* in an appeal to the Secretary of State against an enforcement notice. A statement in an EUC that a use is established is conclusive for the purpose of an appeal to the Secretary of State against an enforcement notice issued after the date of the application (section 94(7)). Possession of an EUC is therefore convenient proof of the existence of an established use for this purpose. It does not mean than an established use cannot be proved without an EUC.

In all other proceedings and, as we have said, against an earlier enforcement notice, an EUC is irrelevant. For example, in *Moran* v. *Secretary of State* (1988) the applicant had an established use certificate for storage purposes. He wished to use the land for long-term car parking and applied for a section 53 determination that planning permission was not required. He argued that the terms of the EUC were relevant to this. Not surprisingly it was held that the EUC was completely irrelevant and that the LPA were entitled to apply ordinary change of use principles in order to see whether the particular change in view was development.

By contrast, where it does apply, the language of an EUC is conclusive. If the use is within its terms the enforcement notice must be quashed on appeal even if development took place after 1963. For example, in *Broxbourne Borough Council* v. *Secretary of State* (1979) an EUC described the use as 'storing, sawing, resawing and disposing of timber in the round and for storing, maintenance, repair and overhaul of vehicles and plant incidental to that use'. The site was originally used for low-density 'rural' timber storage. From 1975 it became used for high-intensity bulk storage for industrial purpose with a substantial impact on the neighbourhood. An enforcement notice was served, the local planning authority arguing that the change made after 1963 was development needing planning permission and that therefore the use was not an established use (see above). The court held that this was irrelevant. The EUC was drafted so loosely as to include the increase in activity that had taken place. The Secretary of State must therefore quash the notice. The court advised planning authorities to draft EUCs more carefully, for example by specifying the location and density of the use.

An EUC is sometimes regarded as the same as a planning permission. The *Broxbourne* case makes this analogy plausible but because the EUC is only relevant in the context of an enforcement appeal the analogy is misleading and should be discarded.

The decision to take enforcement action 51

However, under section 95(1) the Secretary of State can 'call in' an application for an EUC to decide himself, and the applicant may appeal to the Secretary of State against a refusal by the LPA to grant an EUC section 95(1). By virtue of section 95(6) the Secretary of State may automatically grant planning permission for the use in question. It is for this reason that in the *Vaughan* case (see above) the court refused to allow an application for an EUC in respect of a use which was already the subject of an enforcement notice. The applicant wanted to use the EUC procedure as a way of belatedly appealing against the notice. This is one context where the court has set its face against attempts to have repeated bites at the cherry, a practice which the development control system seems to encourage.

(For procedures governing EUCs and their registration, see Schedule 14 and GDO 1988, Art 9.)

Chapter 4

Drafting an enforcement notice

Introduction

The purpose of an enforcement notice is to inform those using the land that a breach of planning control has taken place and to require the breach to be put right. Once a valid enforcement notice has taken effect it remains permanently binding unless and until replaced by a grant of planning permission. Once it has taken effect an enforcement notice cannot generally be challenged on the ground that no breach of planning control has taken place, nor that the facts it alleges have not occurred, nor that the breach is immune from enforcement because of lapse of time (see below).

The drafting of an enforcement notice is likely to come in for scrutiny where there is an appeal to the Secretary of State albeit with the 'safety valve' that the Secretary of State may be able to correct or vary the notice (see below). The matter may also arise in a criminal prosecution if the accused argues that the notice is so badly drafted as to be a nullity.

Since the leading case of *Miller-Mead* v. *Minister of Housing* (1963), the courts have shown considerable sympathy for the drafting problems of local planning authorities. Except in extreme cases where an enforcement notice has serious omissions or is incomprehensible, the courts have refused to invalidate enforcement notices because of drafting irregularities, preferring to let the matter be dealt with by the Secretary of State. A dictum of Lord Justice Upjohn in *Miller-Mead* (see above) has consistently been applied: 'Does the notice fairly tell [the recipient] what he has done wrong and what he must do to remedy it?' The recipient is taken to know all the background facts including the state of the land and its history, even if the authority does not.

For example, an enforcement notice can require the land to be restored 'to its former state' without setting out what that was (*Bath City Council* v. *Secretary of State* (1984)). Furthermore, in an appeal the onus is on the landowner to show that his acts are not a breach of planning control. The courts are also very sympathetic to the problems of a local planning authority in obtaining relevant information and in implementing the enforcement system generally. (See above and *Ferris* v. *Secretary of State* (1988).)

But in *Warrington Borough Council* v. *Garvey* (1988), a stricter approach was taken. This was a prosecution in the Crown Court for disobeying two enforcement notices alleging breaches of conditions relating to infilling operations. Judge Woolley took the view that because this was a criminal case the court should *not* interpret the enforcement notices benevolently in favour of the authority and in favour of making the planning system work. He thought that although a benevolent interpretation may be appropriate in civil cases where enforcement notices are directly challenged in the courts, in a criminal case the accused should be given the benefit of the doubt. His Lordship then held that one notice was a nullity because, due to difficulties in obtaining accurate evidence, it did not specify the boundaries of land sufficiently precisely for the purposes of a criminal case. He held that the other notice was void because the conditions alleged to be broken were not expressly set out in the notice but had to be inferred by reading a letter accompanying the planning permission. His Lordship emphasised that he was applying a different and stricter test than has been applied in non-criminal cases.

If *Garvey* is correct then an enforcement notice which is upheld on appeal by the Secretary of State and by the High Court could be struck down in criminal proceedings. *Garvey* was a Crown Court decision and not of binding authority. It is suggested that it be treated with caution since it runs counter to a primary objective of the appeal system, which is to ensure that planning issues are decided within the planning system rather than by the courts.

An enforcement notice must contain certain information but there is no legally prescribed form of enforcement notice. Model forms of notice have been recommended by the DoE dealing with allegations of operational and change of use development without planning permission (Circular 38/81; see appendix). There is no official model for a notice alleging breach of condition or limitation (see Bourne, *Enforcement and Stop Notice: A Practical Guide*, page 170).

The contents of an enforcement notice

The Act requires every enforcement notice to contain the following information:

(1) A description of the nature of the alleged breach of planning control (section 87(6)).
(2) The steps to be taken to remedy the breach (section 87(7)).
(3) The date on which the notice is to take effect (section 87(13)). This is also the date *before which* an appeal must be received by the DoE and must be at least 28 days after all copies of the notice have been duly served (see Chapter 6). The authority cannot withdraw the notice after this date.
(4) A period for taking the steps required by the notice to run from the date on which it takes effect (section 87(8)). This is a matter for the authority's discretion. Different times can be specified for taking different steps.
(5) The Secretary of State may make regulations requiring further matters to be specified in an enforcement notice (section 87(12)). He has exercised this power to impose two requirements (Town and Country Planning (Enforcement Notices and Appeals) Regulations 1981 (S1 1981 No 1742)).
 (i) The authority must state the reasons why it deems it expedient to issue the enforcement notice.
 (ii) The precise boundaries of the land to which the notice relates must be specified. This need not necessarily be the planning unit in its technical sense and the enforcement notice can relate to a smaller area of land within a unit (see below). However, as we have seen, it is vital for the authority to have a reasonable basis for identifying the planning unit.
(6) The Secretary of State may also require that every copy of an enforcement notice be accompanied by an explanatory note giving information about the right of appeal to the Secretary of State (section 87(12)b). The present regulations require that sections 87 to 88B of the Act be set out or summarised, specifically mentioning the relevant time limits and the obligation to notify the Secretary of State of grounds of appeal and supporting facts (Enforcement Notice etc. regulations (above), Reg 4; see below). A copy of the DoE guide to

Drafting an enforcement notice

planning appeals, is normally sent with every enforcement notice in order to comply with these requirements.

We shall look at each of these matters in turn. From a drafting point of view, the understanding of the ordinary person familiar with the land is the crucial test. Attempts to use legal or planning jargon could backfire. The authority must strike a happy medium between digging a pit for itself with excessive detail and not including sufficient information to make the notice comprehensible. For example, the essential facts which are alleged to contribute a breach of planning control must be set out but a precise legal analysis need not be provided. Indeed in a change of use case there is no need even to state the previous use of the land (*Ferris* v. *Secretary of State* (1988)). That matter can be left for argument at the appeal stage and it is foolish for an authority to commit itself unnecessarily.

The nature of the breach

The notice must firstly describe the facts that are alleged to constitute the breach of planning control. *Richmond-upon-Thames London Borough Council* v. *Secretary of State* (1988) illustrates the pitfalls of excessive detail. The enforcement notice alleged that there had been a material change of use of the first floor of certain premises to an office. On appeal the inspector decided that this description was inadequate because office use might include an office that was ancillary to other existing activities and which could not therefore be enforced against. He thought that the notice should specify 'a material change of use either from mixed use for shop and residential purposes, or from use for residential purposes only, to mixed use as a shop and builders yard'.

The council contended in the court that the inspector was under a misapprehension as to what the main uses of the premises were. The Secretary of State contended in reply that the office use as such was not in law a use at all being merely ancillary to whatever other uses existed. Mr Graham Eyre QC cut across all this, holding firstly that the Act did not require the planning unit in its legal sense to be specified. An enforcement notice must specify the land aimed at, but this can be any area within the unit, in this case the first floor. The importance of the planning unit is as part of the chain of reasoning needed to establish whether there has been development (see above). 'Of course, any prudent authority would ask itself that question before [the notice] was issued' but as far as the wording of the notice itself was concerned all that mattered was that the recipient be clearly told what were the physical facts complained of – in this case, the use of the first floor as an office. Whether the particular office was ancillary to something else is a question to be determined at the appeal. The language required by the inspector may have been legally correct but was factually meaningless to the ordinary reader. Mr Graham Eyre QC also criticised the fact that three enforcement notices were issued when one would suffice.

The notice must secondly state which of the two limbs of breach of planning control is involved, i.e. it must state whether the allegation is of development without permission or of breach of condition or limitation. If a notice fails even to attempt to specify which limb is alleged it is completely void (*Miller-Mead* v. *Minister of Housing* (above); *Eldon Garages* v. *Kingston-upon-Hull Borough Council* (1974)). If the notice tries to pigeonhole the breach but gets it wrong, it can be quashed or perhaps corrected by the inspector on appeal (see below).

Mistakes of this kind are often made in the case of caravans or where the developer has built to an excessive height or width or with unauthorised materials. In these cases the whole development counts as development without permission (*Copeland Borough Council* v. *Secretary of State* (1976) – wrong kind of roof tiles). On the other hand, if a *use* contravenes the specific description in a planning permission this may be breach of a limitation (*Carpet Decor Ltd* v. *Secretary of State* (1981); see above). Whether it is also development is a separate issue.

Indeed the same facts can be both a breach of condition and development. In *West Oxfordshire District Council* v. *Secretary of State* (1988), planning permission was granted for the use of a house as a home for Christians. A condition was attached that the building must be used for no other purpose. The building was used as an ordinary school with consequent complaints from the neighbours. The enforcement notice alleged that a breach of condition had taken place. However, on the facts the change of use was certainly development. The inspector seemed to think that the two limbs were mutually exclusive and quashed the notice. Mr Graham Eyre QC held that, provided the essential facts were clearly stated, it did not matter whether the notice described it as breach of condition or as development without permission. Both descriptions were correct on the facts.

In *Kerrier District Council* v. *Secretary of State* (1981), planning permission was granted for the erection of a bungalow. This was built with an unauthorised basement. There was a condition attached to the planning permission limiting occupation of the bungalow to agricultural workers. The LPA served an enforcement notice in respect of the condition. The developer argued that since he had developed without planning permission (because of the basement) the condition did not apply to the bungalow at all. The court was not persuaded. It was held that the developer had developed without planning permission *and* that he was in breach of condition. By building the bungalow the developer had relied on the permission. He was therefore bound by the condition. Provided that the LPA clearly specified which of the two they were alleging, they could go for either or both.

In general the courts have taken a relaxed approach to the description of the development. This has shown itself in the following ways:

(i) The notice need not use technical language or, as Mr Justice Templeman put it in *Eldon Garages* v. *Kingston-upon-Hull Borough Council* (see above), it need not resort to 'ritual incantations'. As long as read as a whole it is clear that it is concerned with development or breach of condition as the case may be, the notice is valid.

(ii) The notice need not state whether the breach consists of operational or change of use development nor which kind of operational development is involved (*Scott* v. *Secretary of State* (1983)). However, the DoE has recommended standard forms of enforcement notice for change of use and operational development (Circular 38/81; see appendix). If the wrong kind of breach is chosen the notice can be corrected on appeal (*Harrogate Borough Council* v. *Secretary of State* (1986)).

(iii) The notice need not state whether or not the alleged breach of control took place within the appropriate time limit. It is up to the developer on appeal to raise this question (*Harrogate Borough Council* v. *Secretary of State* (see above).

However, the time factor may sometimes be crucial to the development itself. For example, where development by way of *intensification* is alleged (see above) the authority must select a date on which the alleged increase in activity had become large enough to constitute development. If this is practicable, the notice must specify such a date (*de Mulder* v. *Secretary of State* (1974)). However, if a date cannot be specified it may suffice to refer to the level of activity that existed at the end of 1963, assuming that a sufficient increase had taken place since then (see *Trevors Warehouses* v. *Secretary of State* (see below)). It would then be for the developer to challenge this on appeal by showing that there was no increase in activity substantial enough to count as development after that date. In *de Mulder*, the court emphasised that when it comes to a prosecution the court should be alive to any injustice that might arise in this kind of case. In a prosecution the authority would have to prove that the present level of activity is above that which existed on the date selected by the notice.

(iv) In change of use cases the notice need not state what was the 'base use', i.e. the use which existed before the alleged change of use took place and against which the change must be measured (*Ferris* v. *Secretary of State* (1988)).

(v) Contrary to the conventional wisdom, some judges have expressed doubt as to whether it is even necessary to state which kind of breach of control is alleged at all, preferring to leave the matter to the inspector's discretion on appeal (see *Rochdale Metropolitan Borough Council* v. *Simmonds* (1980)). However, this remains a speculative view and is contrary to dicta in *Miller-Mead* v. *Minister of Housing* (1963), which remains the leading case.

There is something to be said for requiring the authority to attempt to specify the kind of breach of control involved as evidence that it has considered this vital matter. If it makes the attempt and gets it wrong, the Inspector may then be in a position to correct the notice on appeal (see below). In *West Oxfordshire District Council* v. *Secretary of State* (see above), Graham Eyre QC drew attention to the inconsistent cases on the point but refused to express a view. He did, however, express strong disapproval of using technical arguments to bring down enforcement notices.

The moral for draftsmen seems to be that excessive detail, standardised formulae and legal jargon should be avoided. The facts as they appear to the authority on the information before them should be clearly stated in as straightforward a way as possible using ordinary everyday language. However, it should be stated whether the allegation is of development or of breach of condition. If the standard form notices are used the authority must also be clear that the development is an operation or a change of use, as the case may be.

Time limits

The notice must specify the date on which it is to take effect. This must be at least 28 days after the last person to be served with a copy of the notice was in fact served. During this period an appeal to the Secretary of State may be launched and the local planning authority can have second thoughts and withdraw the notice. If an appeal is launched the notice cannot take effect until the end of the appeal process, including any further appeal to the courts (see below). The notice must also specify the period for compliance. This can be challenged on appeal on the ground that it is too short.

The steps required to remedy the breach

The notice must specify the steps that are required to remedy the breach of planning control. As with the description of the breach, these must be stated with reasonable certainty so that a person knowing the physical conditions of the land will be aware what he must do to escape conviction. In this context it is important to remember that in criminal proceedings the authority will have to prove that the enforcement notice has been disobeyed. At that stage its language is all-important and there is no possibility of varying or correcting it. The Secretary of State can vary or correct it on appeal but after that the notice defines the extent of the landowner's rights.

The courts' standards are liberal in favour of the authority (but see above). However, a notice which is too uncertain is a complete nullity – so much waste paper which can be ignored. There is no need to appeal to the Secretary of State (*Miller-Mead* v. *Minister of Housing* (1963)). An enforcement notice is uncertain only if its requirements are completely meaningless. It will be construed in the light of the local planning authority's policy and the condition of the land. The recipient is taken to be fully informed of these matters.

Some examples from the cases may be helpful.

(1) In *Trevors Warehouses* v. *Secretary of State* (1972), the notice complained about a change of use to a retail supermarket from 1 May 1970. Before then the building had been used as a wholesale fruit and vegetable warehouse with some retail sales. It was not clear for how long retail sales had previously existed. The notice as amended by the Secretary of State required the discontinuance of the use of the building for retail sales 'except to the extent to which such use was carried on prior to 1 January 1964'. This date was selected simply because no better alternative was available, uses before that date always being immune from enforcement.

It was held that the notice was valid. It was clear in itself and was not invalidated because of practical difficulties in discovering the extent of retail sales at that date. However, the change of use was based upon events which took place in 1970. The notice was therefore remitted to the Secretary of State to consider whether to substitute the later date. Only if no specific date for the change of use is established should an authority revert to the general cutoff point of 1964. The citizen has some protection because if the authority is unable to prove what the level of activity before the cut off date actually was, a prosecution could not succeed.

(2) In *Lipson* v. *Secretary of State* (1977), notices alleged a material change of use of a row of houses to 'use for the purpose of multiple paying occupation'. The notice as amended by the Secretary of State required that the use should be restored to its condition before the development complained of had taken place. It was argued that no one knew what this had been. It was held that this did not invalidate the notice, but merely meant that no one would be able to prosecute the landowner until better information was available. This reasoning would also apply in cases where 'intensification' is alleged and where the authority cannot prove what the lawful pre-intensification level actually was (see above).

Both these cases illustrate that practical problems do not as such make a notice invalid.

Drafting an enforcement notice

(3) In *Metallic Protectives* v. *Secretary of State* (1976), an enforcement notice was held to be void which required the occupier to install 'satisfactory' soundproofing and to take 'all possible action' to minimise the effects of acrylic paint.

(4) In *Hounslow Borough Council* v. *Secretary of State* (1981), a notice requiring powers to 'comply or seek compliance' with a condition was also declared to be a nullity. It may be possible to avoid this kind of uncertainty by including in the notice some kind of machinery for resolving uncertainties. For example, the soundproofing in *Metallic Protectives* could be made subject to the approval of a designated official.

(5) In *Pittman* v. *Secretary of State* (1988), thirteen enforcement notices were served in respect of a caravan site. They alleged a change of use from agriculture to use as a 'leisure plot'. It was held that 'leisure plot' was a sufficient description. (*Sykes* v. *Secretary of State* (1981) – allegation of use as 'paddock' invalid.) This was because unlike 'leisure plot' the word paddock is not descriptive of any particular function but is a method of enclosure.

(6) In *Dudley Bowers* v. *Secretary of State* (1986), an enforcement notice prohibited a weekly Sunday market during 'summertime'. This was held void because it was impossible by reading the notice to ascertain what was meant by 'summertime'.

(7) In *R* v. *Runnymede Borough Council* (1987), a notice that prohibited religious ceremonies in a building except those incidental to domestic use was upheld.

(8) Similarly, in *Ivory* v. *Secretary of State* (1985) an enforcement notice required that the use of the land 'for showjumping and other equestrian events' be discontinued. The court held this to be valid, emphasising that an enforcement notice should not be invalidated merely because borderline or doubtful cases can be envisaged. A notice will not be invalidated on the ground that it is vague and ambiguous but only if it is completely meaningless. Questions of ambiguity or the application of the notice to borderline cases are treated as questions of fact.

'OVERENFORCEMENT'

An enforcement notice might validly prohibit even lawful activities if they are closely bound up with the steps required to restore the land to its state prior to the unlawful development (see above). For example, in *Somak Travel* v. *Secretary of State* (1987) it was held that an enforcement notice could require the developer to remove a spiral staircase in connection with an enforcement notice requiring the discontinuance of an unlawful use as a shop. This was so even though the building of the staircase was not development. Indeed, the staircase could be erected again without contravening the notice provided that this was not connected with a shop use.

Apart from this, the notice must not prohibit lawful activities and if it does so it can be set aside on appeal. The problem arises particularly in the case of ancillary uses which have expanded to become independent of their parent use, and to cases of displacement and intensification. All of these involve a use expanding from a lawful base level. It is generally thought that an enforcement notice must expressly preserve these use rights by using language such as 'except as ancillary to a given use' or 'to reduce the use to its level at a given date' (see above).

This rule is often called the *Mansi* rule after the case of *Mansi* v. *Elstree Rural District Council* (1965). There a site was used as a plant nursery, with a glasshouse being used as a retail shop ancillary to the nursery. The glasshouse later became a retail use in its own right. An enforcement notice prohibited use of the glasshouse for the sale of goods. It was held that the Minister must amend the notice so as to safeguard the appellant's right to carry out retail trade as a use subsidiary to the plant nursery. Violation of the *Mansi* rule does not therefore make the notice invalid as such. There are many examples of the *Mansi* rule in action (e.g. *Cleaver* v. *Secretary of State* (1981); *Cord* v. *Secretary of State* (1981); *North Sea Land Equipment* v. *Secretary of State* (1982); *Runnymede Borough Council* v. *Singh* (1987)).

In *Swinbank* v. *Secretary of State* (1987), Mr David Widdicombe QC held that an enforcement notice need not expressly preserve *Mansi* uses at all. A notice can simply be construed as not being intended to cover them so that a prosecution would fail. This is at first sight attractive but has its problems and may not be correct. Any allegation that the matters alleged are not a breach of planning control or are time barred can be raised only in appeal proceedings before the Secretary of State (section 243(1); see below). Apart from that, the language of an enforcement notice is conclusive (*South Staffordshire District Council* v. *Secretary of State* (1987)).

However, the *Swinbank* reasoning seems appropriate to the case of an ancillary use. It will be recalled that an ancillary use has the legal character of its parent use. Suppose, for example, an enforcement notice prohibits retail sales. This would not include retail sales ancillary to, say, horticulture because the correct description of that use would be 'horticulture' so that the retail sales in question are not within the language of the notice. This analysis cannot apply to time barred uses nor to cases of intensification. In these cases it is suggested that the enforcement notice must expressly preserve the lawful use.

'UNDERENFORCEMENT'

The enforcement notice must specify 'any steps required by the authority to be taken in order to remedy the breach' (section 87(7)a). This means:

> '...according to the particular circumstances of the breach steps for the purpose (a) of restoring land to its condition before the development took place; or (b) of securing compliance with the conditions or limitations subject to which planning permission was granted' section 87(9).

Read literally, this language does not seem to allow the authority a discretion to 'underenforce', that is, to require something less than full restoration; for example, to reduce the level of a prohibited activity or to remove part of a building. This seems unduly restrictive and, if correct, would require the developer to appeal and be granted planning permission by the Secretary of State (see below) or to make a fresh application for planning permission.

The cases are inconclusive and have not addressed the issue directly. In *Copeland Borough Council* v. *SoS* (1976), an enforcement notice was quashed which related only to part of a development. As we have seen, this was because the notice described the development incorrectly (see above). Lord Widgery CJ refused to decide the separate question as to whether a notice can require less than the whole breach to be remedied. However, his Lordship expressed the view that commonsense should permit some tolerance or latitude. In *Iddenden* v. *Secretary of State* (1972), Lord Denning MR was more forthright. He thought that an authority should always have a discretion as to the extent of enforcement except that it cannot require more to be done than is necessary to remedy the breach. However, this was not necessary for the decision because the offending act – the demolition of a shed – was not a breach of planning control at all.

The Act provides a certain amount of flexibility. Section 87(10) permits the authority to require steps to be taken for the purpose of (a) making the development comply with any planning permission, or (b) removing or alleviating any injury to amenity which has been caused by the development. Section 87(11) applies to development involving the making of refuse or waste deposits. The notice can require that the contours of the deposit be modified by altering the gradient or gradients of its sides.

DESCRIPTION OF THE LAND

An enforcement notice need not define the planning unit in its legal sense. Such a requirement would place a heavy burden upon an authority in relation to investigating the condition of the site. It is up to the developer on appeal to show that the wrong planning unit has been chosen and that this affects the legality of his activities. However, the notice must specify the precise boundaries of the land to which it actually relates (Town and Country Planning (Enforcement Notice and Appeals) Regulations 1981 (S1 No 1742, Reg 3)). This is most conveniently achieved by means of a plan (see Circular 38/81; WO 57/81).

A notice can be restricted to a smaller area within the planning unit or can embrace a whole unit even if multiple ownership is involved (*Rawlins* v. *Secretary of State* (1989)). However, a developer is *prima facie* entitled to distribute a use where he likes within the unit. A planning authority cannot therefore arbitrarily divide a unit into parts and issue separate notices against each part if the effect of doing so is more restrictive than if a single notice were issued.

For example, in *de Mulder* v. *Secretary of State* (1974) the site was used (1) as a slaughterhouse, and (2) for car repairs and sales. A factory was erected on the site for the slaughterhouse business which first increased but then seriously declined due to problems with the foundations of the factory. As a result, the car business expanded to cover the whole of the premises. Three enforcement notices were served against the car business. The first related to the factory, the second to a compound near the factory and the third to a driveway. Each required the level of business to be reduced. It was held that the notices should be referred back to the Secretary of State. If one notice had been served the landowner would have been entitled to concentrate his use anywhere on the site. As it was, the arbitrary subdivision meant that the use had to be spread thinly over the whole site. If a local authority wishes to achieve this result it must do so by means of an appropriate planning condition.

EXPEDIENCY

As we have seen, the authority must include in the notice a statement as to why they consider it 'expedient' to issue it. This statement usually takes the form of an annex (see Circular 38/81) but is nonetheless part of the notice. If it is missing or incomplete, the notice is probably void.

It is not sufficient merely to recite that there has been a breach of planning control or even that the activity is contrary to some general policy, although in practice many statements of reasons confine themselves to this. The authority must give *specific* reasons related to the actual or potential harm caused by the activity. However, these need not be given in detail and supporting evidence is not necessary (see appendix).

Chapter 5

Service of an enforcement notice

'A copy of an enforcement notice shall be served not later than 28 days after the date of its issue and not later than 28 days before the date specified in the notice as the date on which it is to take effect' (section 87(5)). It must be served (a) on the owner and occupier of the land to which it relates, and (b) on any other person having an interest in that land, being an interest which in the opinion of the authority is materially affected by the notice (ibid).

These provisions were introduced in 1981. Before then, no distinction was made between the enforcement notice itself and copies of it. Each person had to be served with a valid notice and all at the same time. Given the uncertainties of the postal system, this led to considerable problems. The present law avoids these problems by distinguishing between the enforcement notice itself which is 'issued', and copies of the enforcement notice. Separate copies of it must be served on the persons concerned within 28 days, bearing in mind that there must also be at least 28 days between the date the last person is served and the date specified in the notice on which it is to take effect. As we shall see, a failure to serve can usually be challenged only on appeal to the Secretary of State although a person who was not served has certain additional rights (see below). The authority is, of course, free to serve copies of the notice on anyone else it wishes.

Persons to be served

i) *Owner* for this purpose has the meaning given by the definition section of the Act (section 290(1)) as:

> '...a person other than a mortgagee not in possession, who, whether in his own right or as trustee for any other person, is entitled to receive the rack rent of the land or where the land is not let at a rack rent would be so entitled if it were so let.'

A rack rent is a market rent, ignoring for this purpose the effects of rent control legislation. The freeholder will usually be the owner. However, in *City of London Corporation* v. *Cusack Smith* (1955) the House of Lords held that if the land is in fact let at a rent less than the rack rent the lessor is not the owner although the lessor is the owner if the land is not let at all. Similarly, a lessee or sub-lessee who sublets at a rack rent is the owner, as is any lessee or sub-lessee who does not let at all. There may therefore be more than one owner at any given time. A person with an equitable interest under a trust is not an owner for this purpose.

ii) The occupier may, of course, be a lessee and therefore entitled to be served in the capacities of owner and occupier. However, the term *occupier* embraces anyone who is actually in control of the land and who is not merely transient. It is irrelevant whether or not the occupier has a proprietary interest in the land provided that the necessary element of permanence is established. A person who is occupying under an informal permission (a licensee) may be an occupier for this purpose including, for example, caretakers or dwellers on a caravan site (see *Stevens* v. *London Borough of Bromley* (1972)). A squatter or trespasser might also be an occupier (*Scarborough Borough Council* v. *Adams & Adams* (1983)). Practical problems may arise in identifying occupiers because the 'information notice' procedure (see above) does not adequately cater for persons who have no legal interests in the land.

In the case of other persons with interests in the land, the authority must serve a copy of the notice if it is of the opinion that that person's interest is materially affected. As we shall see, the right of appeal is not limited to persons served, and if in doubt the authority should serve a copy. They can if they wish serve a copy of the notice on anyone. A person who has not been served and who should have been served may raise the matter if prosecuted (see below). It may be difficult to discover who has an interest in the land. This is particularly the case where persons have made contributions to the purchase or the improvement of the property. This gives them an equitable interest in the land which may not appear in any written documents.

If part of the land appears to the authority to be unoccupied, the notice can be served on any owner or occupier of that part by being addressed 'to the owners and any occupiers' and affixed conspicuously to some object on the land (section 283(3)).

Method of service

'Service' means either:

(a) personal delivery; or
(b) leaving a copy of the notice at the recipient's usual or last known place of abode; or
(c) posting a copy of the notice by prepaid registered post or recorded delivery at the usual or last named place of abode, or an address for service given by the recipient; or
(d) if the recipient is a company, delivery in these ways to the secretary or clerk of the company at the company's registered or principal office (section 283).

In the case of a partnership, the notice should be addressed to a partner or a person having control or management of the business at the partnership address or its principal office (LGA 1972, section 233).

Service is deemed to be effective in postal cases at the time at which the letter would be delivered in the ordinary course of post (Interpretation Act 1978, section 7). It seems that evidence cannot be brought to show that the notice arrived later than this (*Moody* v. *Godstone Rural District Council* (1966)). However, evidence can be brought to show that the notice did not arrive at all (*Hewitt* v. *Leicester Corporation* (1969)).

In the case of personal service the law also favours the authority. It is sufficient to hand the notice to another person who promises to give it to its proper recipient (*Borough of Morecambe and Heysham* v. *Warwick* (1958)).

It may be that the name of the proper recipient cannot be discovered. In this case the procedure is as follows:

(1) having made reasonable enquiries, the authority can deliver or post it addressed to 'the owner' or 'the occupier' in the manner described above. *Or*
(2) the authority can *either* send it by prepaid registered or recorded delivery post to the premises in question, in which case it must not be returned, *or* deliver it to a person on the premises, *or* affix it conspicuously to some object on the premises; in all these cases the envelope and the notice must be

Service of an enforcement notice

marked 'Important – this communication affects your property' (Town and Country Planning General Regulations 1976, Reg 15 (SI 1976 No 1419)).

Slightly more relaxed rules for service of local authority documents are prescribed by section 233 of the Local Government Act 1972. Because this Act is later than the 1971 Act, they arguably supercede it. They involve ordinary posting to the recipient's address, or, if the name or address is unknown, leaving it in the hands of a person who appears to be resident or employed on the premises, or affixing it conspicuously to a building or object on the land. It is an offence for an occupier wilfully to refuse to give the name of the owner or lessee.

The effect of a failure to serve a notice

An appeal to the Secretary of State can be brought on the ground that an enforcement notice was not served as required (section 88(2)f). The appellant may, for example, claim that he or other persons were not served. Because this specific method of challenge is provided, an enforcement notice is not invalidated by a failure to serve, unless the Secretary of State quashes it on appeal. If he does not do so or no appeal is brought, the matter cannot usually be raised in any other proceedings (section 243(1) and see *R* v. *Greenwich London Borough Council ex parte Patel* (1985) see below). There are exceptions to this where service is essential for criminal liability (below).

The Secretary of State may disregard a failure to serve if neither the appellant nor the person affected has been substantially prejudiced by the failure to serve (section 88A(3)).

It cannot therefore be argued that the enforcement notice is a nullity merely because of a failure to serve or a defective service, even though a failure to serve raises issues about fairness and natural justice which in other contexts may be fatal to the validity of government action. However, a failure to serve *is* sometimes relevant to the criminal offences involved in disobeying an enforcement notice and also to the local authority's power to enter the land and carry out remedial work. These matters are discussed in the next chapter (see below). There is an overriding rule that if a person has actually appealed to the Secretary of State against the enforcement notice then neither that person nor anyone else can in *any* other proceedings complain that the notice was not duly served on the person who appealed (section 110(2); see below).

Defective service

Difficulties may arise where all persons entitled to be served have been served but in one or more cases service is defective. An example of this is where a copy of the notice is not served at least 28 days before the notice takes effect as required by the Act. It is clear that this defect can only be challenged by way of appeal to the Secretary of State (section 243(1)). However, the appellant may be short of time to appeal because an appeal must be lodged before the notice takes effect and the Secretary of State has no power to waive or extend this time limit (section 88(1)). Suppose an appeal is validly lodged: the Secretary of State's discretionary power to disregard a failure to serve does not apply since this can be used only where a person was not served at all.

On this view, the notice *must* be quashed by the Secretary of State even though the defect is less serious than a total failure to serve. A possible solution may be that the Secretary of State can use his discretionary power to *vary* the enforcement notice by extending the time for compliance (section 88A(2)). This solution was accepted in one first instance case (*Porritt* v. *Secretary of State* (1988); see below).

Service and the right of appeal

The relationship between service and the right of appeal is fragmented and complicated. Curiously, not everyone who is actually served with a copy of the enforcement notice has a right to appeal to the Secretary of State. Only a person having an interest in the land may appeal (section 88(1)) but, as we have seen, occupiers must be served whether or not they have an interest in the land. An occupier served with a copy of the notice who has no interest in the land cannot appeal but is still subject to section 243(1) which prevents anyone from challenging the notice on grounds which fall within the statutory grounds of appeal. Such a person can allege that the notice is a complete nullity or that he has not disobeyed it, but cannot challenge the planning merits nor the basic assumption that an enforceable breach of planning control has taken place. (See *Scarborough Borough Council* v. *Adams & Adams* below.)

Some people using the land, such as temporary licencees or contractors, are not entitled to be served. Nor do they have an interest in the land which entitles them to appeal. However, the rigours of section 243(1) are slightly mitigated where persons who were not served are prosecuted for offences in breach of an enforcement notice (see below).

R v. *Greenwich London Borough Council ex parte Patel* (1985) illustrates these points. The owner of premises was living in the USA and the premises were occupied by his sister-in-law. She erected a building in breach of planning control. An enforcement notice was mistakenly served on her as owner but not served on the real owner. It followed that:

(1) The owner had no opportunity to appeal but could not be prosecuted because he had not been served (see below).
(2) The sister-in-law as occupier could not appeal because she had no interest in the land. However, she could not be prosecuted either because the offence in question – not removing the building – can be committed only by an owner (see below).
(3) However, the authority could enter the land and carry out the work itself at the owner's expense. Section 243(1) prevented any challenge arising out of the failure to serve.

In *Scarborough Borough Council* v. *Adams & Adams* (1983), occupiers were prosecuted for using land as a caravan site contrary to a notice. They were squatters and although they had been served they had no right of appeal. The owner of the land should have been served but this could have been raised only on appeal. They were therefore validly convicted.

Although the law relating to the serving of an enforcement notice has been improved in recent years, further rationalisation is desirable. In particular, it is arguable that any person served with a copy of the notice should have a right of appeal in addition to other persons with an interest in the land.

Chapter 6

Challenging an enforcement notice

General principles

The law governing challenge to an enforcement notice is excessively technical and full of pitfalls for the unwary. Different forms of challenge apply to different kinds of defect. In particular, the developer is faced with the question whether he must take active steps to challenge the enforcement notice by appealing to the Secretary of State within a strict time limit or whether he can sit back and ignore the notice and then raise a defence when and if the local planning authority decides to take action against him. The law has developed piecemeal with periodic attempts at rationalisation, but arguably needs a complete overhaul.

There are four methods by which the validity of an enforcement notice can be challenged. Firstly, there is a right of appeal to the Secretary of State under section 88, with a further right of appeal against his decision to the High Court on a question of law (section 246). Secondly, a person with 'sufficient interest' can seek judicial review of the enforcement notice in the High Court. This also applies in certain cases to the Secretary of State's appeal decision. Thirdly, the notice can be challenged by way of a defence to a prosecution for disobeying it. Fourthly, the landowner can sue the local planning authority for trespass if the local planning authority attempts to enter his land in reliance on an invalid enforcement notice.

With the exception of challenges to the Secretary of State's appeal decision, any attempt to challenge the notice in the court presupposes that the notice is so seriously defective as to be a nullity. We shall discuss later what this means. By contrast, under section 88, appeal against the enforcement notice to the Secretary of State lies on eight defined grounds. These are a pragmatic mixture of legal, factual and policy questions. They include the basic issue of whether the developer's activities are a breach of planning control.

There is one overriding principle. This is provided by section

243(1)(a): '...the validity of an enforcement notice shall not, except by way of an appeal [to the Secretary of State under section 88] be questioned in any proceedings whatsoever on any of the grounds on which such an appeal may be brought.'

This provision makes it clear that the spheres of appeal and of the other methods of challenge are distinct. There are certain limited exceptions to section 243(1) which will be discussed in the next chapter. They relate to persons not served with a copy of the notice who are prosecuted for disobeying it. In the main, the subsection is comprehensive and strict. It applies to all other proceedings including a criminal prosecution and judicial review. It is normally irrelevant that the person concerned has not appealed or could not appeal. In other contexts statutory provisions attempting to oust challenge in the courts have been skilfully circumvented by judicial sophistry, but section 243(1) has proved successful in its aims. It is designed to ensure that technical questions of fact, drafting, and planning policy are decided within the planning system rather than by the ordinary courts. The introduction in 1960 of the predecessor to section 243(1) persuaded the courts to adopt their present policy of reluctance to upset enforcement notices. (See *Miller-Mead* v. *Minister of Housing* (1963).)

Square Meals Frozen Foods Ltd v. *Dunstable Corporation* (1974) shows section 243(1) in action. The local planning authority alleged that the plaintiffs' proposal to use a warehouse for a cash and carry business was outside the terms of an existing planning permission which limited use of the premises to use as a wholesale warehouse or repository. The authority warned the plaintiffs that they proposed to take enforcement action. The plaintiffs immediately applied to the court for a declaration that their activities did not require planning permission. Before the case was heard, they commenced their use and an enforcement notice was issued.

It was held that the legal proceedings must be stayed because they were started in anticipation of the enforcement notice and were therefore caught by section 243(1). Lord Justices Stamp and Scarman went further. They thought that any proceedings started before a notice was issued must be stopped once the notice has actually been issued.

But suppose no enforcement notice is issued. In *R* v. *Basildon District Council* (1987), the LPA resolved to issue an enforcement notice but the actual issue was postponed pending an application to the High Court. The application concerned the interpretation of a previous planning permission. Mr Justice McOwen held that the court proceedings were properly brought and that section 243(1) only applied once a notice has been issued. In Scotland a stricter approach has been taken. It has been held that the Scottish equivalent of section 243(1) prevents challenge even to an anticipated enforcement notice (*James Barrie (Sand & Gravel) Ltd* v. *Lanark District Council* (1979)).

In the *Basildon* case, the point in issue was one of law – what did a planning permission mean? Where factual and policy issues are involved, as may be the case where the question of development is in dispute, the court may refuse to intervene in its discretion until the local planning authority has made its decision on the facts (see *Square Meals* (above)).

Other examples of the strictness of section 243(1) are discussed later (see below).

An enforcement notice cannot be a nullity on any of the grounds of appeal to the Secretary of State. For example, a person not served with a copy of the notice and who was therefore denied the chance to appeal still cannot challenge it (see below). Conversely, if an enforcement notice is a nullity the Secretary of State has no power to hear an appeal. The distinction between nullity and an appealable defect is therefore crucial.

An enforcement notice is a nullity only in extreme circumstances where, for example, it is incomplete or its meaning is completely uncertain. This will be discussed later.

We shall discuss the right of appeal and judicial review in this chapter. We shall also outline the other methods of challenge. However, defences and actions for trespass relate to particular offences and powers of entry in the hands of local planning authorities, and will be discussed more fully in the next chapter.

Appeals to the Secretary of State

PROCEDURE

Any person with an interest in the land may appeal to the Secretary of State. An appeal must be lodged in writing by the date on which the enforcement notice takes effect (section 88(1)(3)). This is usually 28 days from the date on which the last person to be served with a copy

Challenging an enforcement notice

of the notice can be expected to receive it. Every enforcement notice should be accompanied by a DoE leaflet explaining the scope of the right of appeal and how to exercise it. Notice of appeal must be sent in writing to the DoE. The time limit is strictly applied (*Howard* v. *Secretary of State* (1975)). The notice of appeal must *reach* the DoE at the latest by the day before the notice takes effect. Loss in the post is no excuse (see *R* v. *Secretary of State ex parte Jackson* (1987)).

In *R* v. *Secretary of State ex parte JBI Financial Consultants Ltd* (1989), it was held that delivery by hand on the day the notice took effect was too late. However, delivery on the day before (a Sunday) by putting the appeal through the DoE's letter box would be valid. (Despite *DoE Guide to Appeals* DoE 14069 (rev 1985).) Even though the building was empty on a Sunday, dropping the document through the letter box is deemed to be sufficient delivery and receipt for this purpose.

Incidentally, this does not apply to documents which have to be served in connection with *court* proceedings. The principle there is that if the court office is closed on the deadline day, the time limit is extended until it is open.

The appeal is almost always decided by an inspector appointed by the Secretary of State, and the parties are entitled to a hearing (section 88(7)). This usually takes the form of a public local inquiry before an inspector appointed by the Secretary of State. With the parties' consent the appeal can be heard by written representations. The inspector usually makes a site visit either alone or accompanied by both parties. He is *not* allowed to discuss the merits of the case during the site visit, nor at any time to consider evidence without giving both parties a chance to comment on it and, if relevant, to cross examine.

In most cases the inspector decides the appeal, but in large or controversial cases the decision may be made by the Secretary of State himself or by a senior officer in his department. Where this is so the inspector who holds the inquiry sends a report to the Secretary of State stating his findings of fact, conclusions and recommendations if any. A copy of this report is sent to the parties along with the decision letter. Reasons must be given in writing for all appeal decisions.

Where the inspector makes the decision, a single letter is sent to the parties and to anyone else who attended the inquiry and asked to be notified. The inspector's decision is deemed in law to be the decision of the Secretary of State and the inspector has the same powers as the Secretary of State over the whole appeal (Schedule 9). In the rest of this chapter we shall use the term 'Secretary of State' to refer to the decision-maker whoever he may be.

The appeal process is not particularly speedy. There may be several months' delay before the inquiry is held and the decision may be anything from one month to about a year after that. The inquiry itself normally lasts one day but can extend indefinitely. A large number of appeals — about 35% — are successful, and most enforcement notices are appealed against. Arguably, the right of appeal is too generous.

Written representation procedure is quicker and cheaper than the inquiry procedure but, because enforcement appeals often involve detailed disputes about the facts, written representation procedure is used less often than is the case with planning permission appeals. In enforcement cases delay is sometimes in the appellant's interest.

The notice of appeal should be accompanied by a copy of the enforcement notice. For this purpose, copies of the notice should be served in duplicate. The appellant should also include a statement of the grounds of appeal with supporting facts. It is for the appellant to prove on balance of probabilities the existence of facts contradicting the allegations in the notice. This is another result of a deliberate judicial policy in favour of the smooth operation of the planning system. (See *Nelsovil Ltd* v. *Minister of Housing* (1962).)

Delays in the processing of enforcement appeals have been caused by applicants who did not submit details of their grounds of appeal and supporting evidence until the last minute — sometimes at the inquiry itself. This problem is met by section 88(4)(5) and by the Town and Country Planning (Enforcement Notices and Appeals) Regulations 1981 (SI 1981 No 1742). These were the government's response to the Court of Appeal's decision in *Howard* v. *Secretary of State* (1974), which appears to have caused considerable irritation in Whitehall. It was held in *Howard* that, although an appeal must be lodged within the statutory time limit, the supporting facts and even the grounds of appeal can be supplied later, thus making it difficult for the DoE to process the appeal.

The regulations deal with this by empowering the Secretary of State to require the appellant to deliver an outline statement of facts and grounds of appeal within 28 days. The local authority is under an automatic duty to provide a summary of its response to each ground of appeal and a statement as to whether it would be prepared to grant planning permission. Failure to comply with these requirements entitles the Secretary of State to dismiss or allow the appeal, as the case may be and without a hearing (see section 88(6)(8)). Furthermore, if the appellant's statement is incomplete the Secretary of State may decide the appeal without it (section 88(9)).

Once the date of the inquiry is fixed, both parties are obliged to disclose the evidence on which they propose to rely, but in the case of the appellant only if so requested by the Secretary of State (Town and Country Planning (Enforcement) (Inquiries Procedure) Rules 1981, SI No 1743 R6).

The procedure at the inquiry is broadly similar to that applicable to planning permission appeals. Each party may make statements, call witnesses and cross examine. However, *planning permission* appeals are now governed by different regulations which permit the Secretary of State to impose a tight timetable on the proceedings. They also allow the Inspector to take a more active role than is perhaps appropriate in enforcement cases where the parties are likely to be more hostile to each other. The law governing inquiry procedure is outside the scope of this book and is the subject of a companion volume in this series.

THE GROUNDS OF APPEAL

Eight grounds of appeal to the Secretary of State are set out in section 88(2). As we have seen, the general principle is that these grounds cannot be raised in any other proceedings (section 243(1)). There are, however, three exceptional but very limited cases where some of the grounds may be admissible elsewhere. They can be summarised as follows, and are discussed more fully later.

(i) Persons not served with a copy of the notice have certain defences to a prosecution (section 243(2) (see below)).
(ii) Where a use is discontinued in obedience to a notice but later resumed, the resumption must *in fact* be a breach of planning control (section 93(2)).
(iii) Where the authority exercises its power to enter the land to carry out works, it must arguably give a hearing on the merits to persons who had no opportunity to appeal to the Secretary of State (see below).

The grounds of appeal are as follows. It must be remembered that it is for the *appellant* to establish these grounds.

(a) That planning permission ought to be granted for the development to which the notice relates or, as the case may be, that a condition or limitation alleged in the enforcement notice not to have been complied with ought to be discharged.

This gives the Secretary of State a wide power to consider the planning merits. He cannot grant permission for any development other than that alleged in the notice although he can grant permission for part of it (section 88B(1)). He is not bound by the views of the inspector at any previous appeal about matters of planning policy. Thus there can be a re-run of a previous appeal against a refusal of planning permission. The Secretary of State can also discharge any conditions or limitation and substitute another for it whether more or less onerous (section 88B(2)). When granting planning permission he may also attach conditions in the same way as the local planning authority. However, if he is merely asked to discharge a condition he cannot attach additional conditions.

Every appeal is automatically deemed to be an application for planning permission, whether or not the appellant raises this as one of his grounds. For the purposes of the register of planning applications, a planning permission granted on appeal is treated as if it were granted on an application for planning permission made to the local planning authority and 'called in' for decision by the Secretary of State. It therefore features in the register in the normal way (section 88B(3)).

(b) '...that the matters alleged in the notice do not constitute a breach of planning control.'

Here, the appellant can argue (i) that his activities are not development at all, or (ii) that they do not need planning permission, or (iii) that as a matter of interpretation they do not breach the terms of a planning permission. The appellant is not precluded from raising these arguments even if he has previously applied for and received planning permission for the activities in question.

In *Newbury District Council* v. *Secretary of State* (1981), temporary planning permission was given to a company for the storage of certain goods in an old aircraft hangar. A condition was attached requiring that the hangar be demolished when the permission expired. The company continued to occupy the hangar after the expiry date and an enforcement notice was issued. The House of Lords were faced with a rich profusion of legal issues. It was held, firstly, that the condition was invalid because it was not related to the storage use which was the subject of the permission. It was also held that the company was not bound by the permission even if the condition had been valid. The use in question counted as a 'repository' within the Use Classes Order and had therefore never been development requiring planning permission. It was irrelevant that the company had chosen to apply for and apparently accept the planning permission. An unnecessary planning permission is, as far as the law is concerned, so much waste paper.

In relation to this ground (and also presumably to the next two grounds), a decision in a previous appeal will bind the Secretary of State where the appeal was between the same parties on the same issue. This is because the issues are issues of *fact* and not issues of planning policy. In *Thrasyvoulou* v. *Secretary of State* (1988), an inspector at a previous appeal decided that the planning use of the plaintiff's properties, which was to provide temporary accommodation for the homeless, was that of a hotel as opposed to a 'hostel'. This was within the existing rights of the plaintiff. An enforcement notice was later issued alleging use as a 'hostel'. The inspector upheld the notice. The Court of Appeal held that the concept of 'issue estoppel' applied so that the Inspector in the second appeal was bound by the findings in the earlier appeal.

Issue estoppel is a doctrine normally associated with the decisions of courts of law. It means that where substantially the same issues are raised between the same parties in two proceedings, findings of law or fact in the earlier proceedings are binding in the later proceedings. The Secretary of State had argued without success that in the public interest planning law should not be subject to the restrictions of issue estoppel and that previous decisions should be given weight but should not tie the hands of inspectors. On this view, a citizen could only challenge the second decision in the courts if it was arbitrary or unfair but could also claim costs against a local planning authority who renews an enforcement notice without good cause.

The implications of *Thrasyvoulou* for the inspectorate and local planning authorities are obvious. The court based its reasoning on the need to protect occupiers against 'the unfair but well intentioned repetition of proceedings'. The limits of the *Thrasyvoulou* decision should be emphasised. Firstly, the onus is on the person seeking the protection of issue estoppel to prove that the issues are the same. For example, the use of the land would have to be materially the same at all relevant times, and there must be no fraud or false evidence affecting the earlier case. Secondly, the doctrine has no application to policy decisions such as whether planning permission should be granted. It concerns findings of fact, e.g. whether development has taken place, or whether the development took place before the relevant time limits for issuing an enforcement notice.

(c) '... that the breach of planning control alleged in the notice has not taken place'.

This is, of course, completely different from (b). Here the appellant can argue either (i) that the events described in the notice have not happened at all, or (ii) that the authority has described what has happened incorrectly. This is the ground under which to argue that the wrong kind of development or other breach has been specified in the notice (see above). The second kind of argument is less profitable because, as we shall see, the Secretary of State has wide powers to amend the notice.

This ground does not allow the appellant to argue that he has in fact obeyed the notice. Indeed, there is no ground of appeal covering this. However, such an argument can be raised as a defence to any later proceedings.

(d) In the case of (i) operational development, and (ii) change of use to use as a single dwelling house, that the development took place at least four years before the date on which the notice was issued (see above).

(e) In other cases, that the breach of planning control occurred before the beginning of 1964 (see above). For the purpose of this ground, an 'established use certificate' is conclusive evidence of the facts stated in it (see above).

Whether or not the appellant actually alleges these grounds, the Secretary of State has power to determine what is the lawful use of the land (section 88B1). He can therefore decide that the appellant's activities do not need planning permission, or that they are covered by a planning permission. This power does not relate to operations (section 290(1)).

(f) That copies of the enforcement notice were not served as required by section 87(5) (see above). This ground of appeal covers failure to serve upon the right persons, and also defective service, for example disregard of time limits. In the case of failure to serve a copy of the notice upon a person required to be served, the Secretary of State can disregard the failure 'if neither the appellant nor that person has been substantially prejudiced by the failure to serve' (section 88A3).

This does not seem to cover a case where someone has been served but not within the time limit of 28 days before the notice took effect. In *Porritt* v. *Secretary of State* (1988), a copy of an enforcement notice was served 27 days before the date specified in the notice. The Inspector refused to quash the notice because no one had actually suffered any injustice. There was no specific statutory provision entitling him to do this. Nevertheless, the court held that his decision was valid. It took the view that the Secretary of State has a general discretion to disregard minor procedural errors if no injustice has been suffered. Furthermore, a person who actually appealed to the Secretary of State cannot argue in any *other* proceedings that he was not duly served with a copy of the notice (section 110(2)). The judge thought that it was at least arguable that 'other proceedings' include an appeal to the court against the Secretary of State's decision. With respect, this seems unconvincing. The appeal to the court is based upon the Secretary of State's decision being erroneous in law. This must surely include errors in relation to the service requirements.

(g) 'That the steps required by the notice to be taken exceed what is necessary to remedy any breach of planning control or to achieve a purpose specified in section 87(10)' (the 'cosmetic' steps see above). This ground allows the *Mansi* rule to be raised (see above), as well as including general questions of fact and planning policy.

(h) 'That the period specified in the notice as the period within which any step is to be taken falls short of what should reasonably be allowed.'

This ground of appeal depends entirely on the facts of the particular case, including the question of whether there were previous warnings to or discussions with the developer. Personal factors such as hardship should also be considered.

The appellant can raise any or all of these grounds even if they are inconsistent. Additional grounds and evidence can be added at a later stage, but subject to the timetable powers of the Secretary of State which have already been discussed (see above) and also to the discretion of the Inspector who presides over the inquiry (see Town and Country Planning (Enforcement) (Inquiries Procedure) Rules 1981 (S1 1981 No 1743, R.11)). Current government practise is to emphasise the importance of processing appeals reasonably swiftly.

There is no specific ground of appeal based on inadequate reasons for issuing the notice. This can therefore be pursued in the ordinary courts.

FEES

A fee is charged for making an appeal. This is for the deemed application for planning permission. (See Town and Country Planning (Fees for Applications and Deemed Applications) Regulations 1983 (S1 No 1674 as amended).) No fee is payable in certain special cases. These include (i) the loss of rights conferred by the General Development Order or Use Classes Order, (ii) certain operations for the benefit of the disabled, (iii) The renewal of earlier grants of planning permission or earlier applications, and (iv) where the development is subject to another appeal.

The fee is refunded in cases where the appeal succeeds on grounds (b) to (f), or where the enforcement notice is legally defective. In these cases, the local planning authority is at fault and there is no need to grant planning permission. An exception to this concerns caravans stationed for human habitation. Here, planning permission is necessary as a formality in order to obtain a caravan site licence under the Caravan Sites and Control of Development Act 1960 – so that the Secretary of State will always consider whether to grant permission.

The fee is also refunded if the local authority withdraws the enforcement notice or if the appellant withdraws his appeal before the inquiry or, in the case of written representations, before the site visit.

The amount of the fee is regularly reviewed and depends on the nature of the development. The amounts range from £33 for small building operations, through to £66 per building for other building operations, up to a maximum of £3 300. Change of use development is normally £66 but continuing a use in breach of condition is £33. There is a special scale for advertisements. (See generally DoE circular 1/87.)

COSTS

The general principle is that the parties bear their own costs. However, under section 282 and Schedule 9 as modified by the Housing and Planning Act 1986, the Secretary of State or the Inspector may award costs to any party. If costs are awarded against the appellant, he may have to pay not only the local planning authority's costs but also the DoE's expenses. In the case of enforcement appeals, costs can be awarded whether or not an inquiry is held (Town and Country Planning Act 1971 section 110(1)).

The application for costs should normally be made at the inquiry or as part of the written representations process.

In practice, costs are awarded only against a party whom the Secretary of State or Inspector considers to have behaved unreasonably, for example by causing unnecessary delay or lodging a hopeless appeal. Examples of this might be cases where there are no special circumstances justifying an exception to normal 'green belt' policy. In the case of the local planning authority failing to make adequate investigations or to give adequate reasons for its decision, or making serious errors, or failing to negotiate with the appellant, all might attract costs (see Circular 2/87, para 14). The power to award costs can therefore be used as an instrument of central government policy, for example as a means of discouraging local planning authorities from enforcing planning controls strictly. Insisting on an inquiry is not a reason for awarding costs.

THE POWERS OF THE SECRETARY OF STATE

In addition to the power to grant planning permission, the Secretary of State may quash the enforcement notice (section 88A(1)). He may also

> '... correct any informality, defect or error in the enforcement notice or give directions for varying its terms, if he is satisfied that the correction or variation can be made without injustice to the appellant or to the local planning authority' (section 88A(2)).

The Secretary of State can probably quash the notice only on the grounds specified in the Act. He cannot quash it simply on the basis that no proper reasons exist for issuing it. In such a case, he could grant planning permission. In an extreme case he could refuse to hear the appeal on the ground that the notice is a nullity.

Until the introduction of this provision in 1981, defects in an enforcement notice were divided into those which were 'material' and those which were not material. An example of a material defect would be an incorrect description of the nature of the alleged breach of planning control. Although the cases were not wholly in agreement, the dominant view was that if a defect was 'material' the enforcement notice *must* be quashed on appeal (see e.g. *Copeland District Council* v. *Secretary of State* (1976)).

As a result of the introduction of the more widely drawn power to quash, it is arguable that the Secretary of State may be able to amend the notice in all cases unless injustice is caused in the particular circumstances (see *Harrogate Borough Council* v. *Secretary of State* (1987) – van bodies placed on the site; mistake as to whether operation or change of use).

However, in *Hughes* v. *Secretary of State* (1985) Mr Justice Hodgson seemed to apply the old distinction. The enforcement notice had alleged that a breach of planning control had taken place 'after the end of 1963', although this was a case where the four year time limit applied. The inspector corrected the notice. Mr Justice Hodgson held that the error went to the 'substance' of the allegation and could not therefore be corrected. However, he also thought that the notice could not be corrected without injustice in the particular case because by specifying the wrong time limit the landowner may have been misled as to his chances of success on appeal. This second line of reasoning seems preferable. Indeed, Mr Justice Hodgson's approach was criticised by Mr Justice Webster in the *Harrogate* case (above).

Perhaps we must distinguish three separate cases:

(i) cases where the notice wrongly pigeonholes the kind of development (as in *Harrogate* (above));
(ii) cases where the notice fails to describe the nature of the breach at all; and
(iii) cases where the notice wrongly describes the nature of the breach, i.e. development or breach of condition.

Case (i) is clear and the notice can be amended on appeal. In case (ii), the notice is probably a nullity (see above). It therefore cannot be

Challenging an enforcement notice

amended and the Secretary of State has no power over it at all. Case (iii) is the difficult one. The cases conflict. The weight of authority suggests that the notice should be quashed but these cases were decided before the present broad power of amendment was introduced, and even then strong reservations have been expressed. (See *Copeland Borough Council* v. *Secretary of State* (above); *Garland* v. *Minister of Housing* (1969); *Pilkington* v. *Secretary of State* (1980); *West Oxfordshire District Council* v. *Secretary of State* (1988).)

It is suggested that the Secretary of State should be able to exercise a discretion as to whether to amend the notice on appeal. The distinction between breach of condition and development without permission is often highly technical. It goes against the grain of the modern law to insist on striking out enforcement notices on purely technical grounds. The most recent decision supports this view and emphasises the desirability of a common sense non-technical approach. (*R* v. *Secretary of State ex parte Ahern* (1989).)

Lesser defects such as ambiguous descriptions or wrong descriptions of the land or of the breach of planning control can, of course, be amended on appeal (see *Hammersmith London Borough Council* v. *Secretary of State* (1975)). It is not clear what the distinction between correcting and varying a notice means. The Secretary of State's power is the same in either case. Indeed, in *Harrogate Borough Council* v. *Secretary of State* Mr Justice Webster thought that it was

'...neither necessary nor desirable to attempt to define either a correction or a variation for the purposes of this Act nor to draw any fine line of distinction between the two words'.

This is probably just as well! However, his Lordship thought that the term 'variation' was wider than 'correction' and that

'...no alteration could be made which was wider or more fundamental than what could properly be described as a variation'.

An alteration that would be too fundamental to count as either a correction or a variation would be where the notice is changed to refer to a different area of land or different activities altogether. In such a case, then unless the alteration is trivial, the notice must probably be quashed. In general, the notice cannot be corrected or varied so as to impose a more onerous burden on the recipient than it did originally. The court seems to lean in favour of amending a notice. For example, in *Hammersmith London Borough Council* v. *Secretary of State* (1975) Lord Widgery CJ said (at 21-22): '... it is, I think, the Secretary of State's duty to try to get the enforcement notice in order'. This was followed in *Bath City Council* v. *Secretary of State* (1985) where Mr Justice Woolf said that the Secretary of State must give clear reasons for a decision not to amend a notice.

Challenging the Secretary of State's decision

There is a right of appeal against the decision of the Secretary of State to the High Court (section 246). This can be exercised by the appellant, the local planning authority or any other person with an interest in the land. Appeal lies on a point of law only. The appeal must be lodged within 28 days, which probably runs from the date on which the decision is notified to the appellant (SC Ord 5SR 4(4)). However, there is authority at Divisional Court level, which is not a binding precedent, that time runs from the date on which the decision letter was posted (*Ringroad Investments Ltd* v. *Secretary of State* (1979)).

The court's powers under section 246 are limited. Firstly, if it allows the appeal its only remedy is to send the matter back to the Secretary of State with the opinion of the court (RSC Ord. 94 R.12(5)). The enforcement notice remains suspended and the Secretary of State must consider the whole matter again. In practice, 'remitted' cases are decided in Whitehall and not by an Inspector.

Secondly, the court has no power to decide issues of fact or to go beyond the material that forms the basis of the decision, i.e. the decision letter and the Inspector's report (*London Parachuting Ltd* v. *Secretary of State* (1986)). This means that even legal issues may sometimes be excluded, e.g. disputes as to what evidence was put forward at the inquiry, and complaints about unfair procedure. However, the *London Parachuting* case is hard to reconcile with RSC Ord 55R7(2) which allows the court to receive further factual evidence. In other contexts, the courts are certainly reluctant to examine questions of fact and cannot usually investigate whether the facts found at the inquiry are true, but they do occasionally look at factual issues, e.g. if there are allegations of fraud or procedural defects, or if it is argued that a government decision was made without taking into account relevant material. In *Kingswood Investments* v. *Secretary of State* (1988), Mr Graham Eyre QC thought that even in section 246 proceedings outside evidence could be used to decide what material was actually before the inspector. (See also *Forkhurst* v. *Secretary of State* (1982); *Gwillim* v. *Secretary of State* (1988).)

The courts are rightly cautious about examining factual evidence because of their fear of exceeding the bounds of judicial propriety by taking on a task that inspectors can do better. On the other hand, it is part of the judicial function to decide whether a decision was fair and reasonable. This requires the court at least to investigate whether the Inspector's report is an accurate reflection of the issues raised at the inquiry.

There are two other methods of challenging the Secretary of State's decision in the courts, both of which entitle the court to hear factual evidence to the limited extent that has just been outlined. Firstly, if the appeal is rejected on the ground that planning permission should not be granted, any 'person aggrieved' can challenge this in the High Court under section 245 which covers ministerial decisions of many kinds. The grounds of challenge under section 245 are that the decision is outside the powers of the Act or that a requirement of the Act or of any other law has not been complied with. These grounds are at least as wide as the 'point of law' basis of the section 246 appeal. It is doubtful whether Parliament intended this overlap. The main function of section 245 is to deal with appeals to the Secretary of State against refusals of planning permission by local planning authorities. Nevertheless, because every appeal against an enforcement notice is deemed to be an application for the planning permission (see above), it follows that section 245 also applies in enforcement cases. Factual evidence is admissible under section 245 in cases where it is alleged that the decision does not fairly deal with the evidence that was available at the inquiry (*East Hampshire District Council* v. *Secretary of State* (1978); compare *Glover* v. *Secretary of State* (1981) – evidence not admissible which was not available at the time of the inquiry).

Alternatively, any citizen affected by the Secretary of State's decision could apply to the High Court for judicial review. A three month time limit applies, compared with the 28 days available under section 246. However, unlike a section 246 appeal, judicial review requires leave to apply from a High Court judge, thus filtering out hopeless cases. Section 246 does not exclude judicial review, but in cases where the section 246 procedure is adequate to do justice the court is likely to insist that section 246 be used. Judicial review is always discretionary and the court can, in its discretion, consider factual evidence.

The most obvious case for judicial review is where the enforcement notice itself is alleged to be a nullity (see below). Here, the Secretary of State should not have been dealing with the matter at all. Judicial review might also be appropriate for the purpose of considering complaints which raise procedural questions. In *Rhymney Valley District Council* v. *Secretary of State* (1985), the court treated an improper appeal under section 246 as if it had been properly instituted by way of judicial review although the basis for doing this is unclear. There is no reason why a Section 246 appeal and a judicial review application should not be heard together by the same judge.

Judicial review is also appropriate in a case where the Secretary of State improperly refuses to hear an appeal. Suppose, for example, he wrongly believes that an appeal is out of time or improperly refuses to consider late submissions. In such a case a successful challenge means that the appeal remains alive and the enforcement notice remains suspended. If the application for judicial review fails, the notice is treated as effective from the date of the Secretary of State's decision to refuse jurisdiction (see *Lenlyn Ltd* v. *Secretary of State* (1985)). However, there is conflicting authority. In *Button* v. *Jenkins* (1975) the Secretary of State refused to hear an appeal, wrongly alleging that it was out of time. It was held that this counted as a decision on the appeal and that the proper remedy was to appeal to the court under section 246 (above). The notice therefore became active once the 28 days time limit for section 246 had expired. The *Lenlyn* reasoning seems preferable.

The law governing challenge to the Secretary of State's appeal decision badly needs an overhaul. It is complicated, confused and offers traps for the unwary. It is suggested that the ordinary judicial review procedure suffices in all cases. The court has a range of remedies available, including quashing the enforcement notice or referring the matter back to the Secretary of State to decide again.

Challenging an enforcement notice in the courts

There remains the option of not appealing to the Secretary of State but of challenging the enforcement notice directly in the courts. Because of section 243(1), this option is not available on any of the grounds provided for appealing to the Secretary of State. Other complaints cannot be taken to the Secretary of State but can either be raised in court or not at all.

There are two routes through which the validity of an enforcement notice can be challenged in the courts. The first is to do nothing and raise a defence to any proceedings taken by the authority. The second is to take the initiative and apply for judicial review, either of the notice itself or the decision to issue it. In both cases the central argument is that the enforcement notice is a complete nullity and therefore does not have to be obeyed. The challenger's victory may, of course, be shortlived because the local planning authority can often issue another enforcement notice without the defect that the court condemned.

An enforcement notice is a nullity in three kinds of case.

(1) If the decision to issue it is invalid because, for example, it was issued by the wrong person or the decision to issue it was made for improper reasons (see *Davy* v. *Spelthorne Borough Council* (1983)).
(2) If the notice is incomplete on its face, i.e. if any of the matters which it is required to state are missing as opposed to wrong. This probably includes a failure to state which of the two kinds of breach of planning control is alleged and an inadequate statement of reasons for issuing the notice. These points are discussed in Chapter 4.
(3) If any part of the notice is so badly expressed as to have no ascertainable meaning. This is also discussed in Chapter 4.

In *Scarborough Borough Council* v. *Adams & Adams*, Lord Justice Watkins suggested that a notice might be void if the persons named in it were neither owners nor occupiers. It is submitted that this is wrong. The identity of owners and occupiers relates to the question of service, not the jurisdiction to issue the notice. Questions of service can be challenged only by appealing to the Secretary of State. The Act does not require the notice to state anything about the owners or occupiers, only that it be served on these persons. As we have seen, defective service is a ground of appeal and therefore cannot make the notice void.

If a notice is a nullity there cannot be an appeal to the Secretary of State, so that even if any of the statutory grounds of appeal could also be alleged they are irrelevant.

The judicial review procedure is governed by section 31 of the Supreme Court Act 1981 and by the Rules of the Supreme Court (see RSC Ord 53). The applicant has no right to a full trial but must first seek leave to apply for judicial review from a High Court judge. This preliminary filter is designed to exclude frivolous or hopeless applications and is a safeguard for the government which has no parallel in the statutory appeal procedures. These can be brought as a matter of right. Application for judicial review must be made within three months of the date the notice was issued or, in the case of a person served with a copy of the notice, within three months of service. The court may extend this time limit in exceptional cases, but in any event there must be no 'undue delay'. The applicant must also have 'sufficient interest' in the matter. In the case of an enforcement notice, any person affected by the notice would satisfy this (see *IRC v. National Federation for the Self-Employed* (1982)). The court may suspend the *implementation* of the enforcement notice while the case is being heard, but not the notice itself.

The court's powers include the power to quash the notice or more strictly declare it void, and the power to remit the notice to the local planning authority with directions.

Judicial review is the only method of challenging government action in certain types of case. Judicial review is specifically designed for public law disputes involving the validity of government action. It is believed to be against the public interest for litigants to seek to evade the judicial review procedure by taking other kinds of legal action where the procedure is more favourable to the individual. The judicial review procedure is designed to protect the interests of government, notably the short time limit, the need for leave to apply and the court's discretion in relation to factual evidence (see *O'Reilly v. Mackman* (1982)).

However, judicial review is probably not exclusive in enforcement notice cases. It has been held that where a person is threatened with civil or criminal proceedings he can normally allege the invalidity of government action as a defence to such proceedings. This is because

Challenging an enforcement notice

Table 1 Methods of challenging enforcement notices.

GROUND OF CHALLENGE	Appeal to Secretary of State	Appeal to High Court under section 246	Defence to prosecution	Application for judicial review	Civil action if LPA enter land	OUTCOME
1 No breach of planning control	✓	✓				Notice quashed
2 Established use right	✓	✓				Notice quashed
3 Service defect	✓	✓	✓ certain cases (see Chapter 7)		✓ certain cases (see Chapter 7)	Secretary of State has discretion
4 Notice excessive	✓	✓				Secretary of State may quash or correct
5 Breach wrongly described	✓	✓				Secretary of State may quash or correct
6 Notice uncertain			✓	✓	✓	Notice a nullity
7 Notice incomplete			✓	✓	✓	Notice a nullity
8 Notice not disobeyed			✓		✓	Acquittal
9 Allegations untrue	✓		certain cases (see Chapter 7)			Notice quashed Acquittal
10 Notice issued by wrong person			✓	✓	✓	Acquittal; damages; injunction
11 Abuse of power or unfairness in decision to issue			✓	✓	✓	Acquittal; damages; injunction
12 Other errors in the notice	✓					Secretary of State has discretion to quash or correct
13 Developer in ignorance of relevant facts			✓ certain cases (see Chapter 7)			Acquittal

a person can assert his 'private rights' in any legal proceedings. The threat of criminal penalties always involves private rights (see *Wandsworth Borough Council* v. *Winder* (1984); *R* v. *Reading Crown Court* (1988), but cf. *Plymouth City Council* v. *Quietlynn* (1987)). To deny an individual this basic right would be unjust. In *R* v. *Jenner* (1983), it was held that a landowner could challenge a 'stop notice' (see below) by way of a defence that his development was outside the relevant time limits. However, *Jenner* can be explained narrowly on the basis that the accused was not challenging the validity of the notice as such but merely saying that it did not apply to his development. This seems artificial. In *Davy* v. *Spelthorne Borough Council* (1983), the House of Lords held that a local planning authority could be sued for negligence in the ordinary courts for improperly misleading the plaintiff to think that an enforcement notice would not be implemented. The validity of the enforcement notice was not directly in issue in that case.

The law therefore remains unclear. It is suggested that, although judicial review can be used, a citizen threatened with an invalid enforcement notice may alternatively await prosecution and raise the invalidity of the notice as a defence. Similarly, if the local planning authority enter his land in reliance on an invalid notice, he may sue the authority for trespass (see below). The law relating to these matters depends upon the precise method chosen by the local planning authority to implement the notice. This will be discussed in the next chapter.

Table 1 outlines the most common grounds of complaint against an enforcement notice and sets out the normal methods of challenge appropriate to each ground. The table should be read with Chapter 7 as well as with this chapter.

Chapter 7

Implementing an enforcement notice

The effect of an enforcement notice

Once an enforcement notice has taken effect, disobedience to it becomes a criminal offence (section 89). In addition, the local planning authority may enter the land and carry out remedial work themselves, recovering the cost of doing so from the landowner (section 91).

The local planning authority can withdraw an enforcement notice before it takes effect (section 87(14)). Otherwise an enforcement notice remains in force until the activities in it are given planning permission. It binds all persons concerned with the land in question. An enforcement notice is not discharged by being obeyed (section 93(1)). If a building is removed or altered and later reinstated, this is a breach of the original notice 'notwithstanding that its terms are not apt for the purpose'. The new building need not be similar to the previous building. The resumption of a use after it has been discontinued is also treated as a breach of the notice (section 93(3)) but only if the resumption is at the time a breach of planning control (section 93(2)). To this limited extent the language of the notice is not conclusive, and matters such as whether or not development has taken place can be raised.

Apart from this, the language of an enforcement notice is conclusive. As we have seen, because of section 243(1), questions which could have been raised by appealing to the Secretary of State such as whether a breach of planning control has taken place or time limits or service cannot be raised in any other proceedings (see above). Other possible defences depend upon the ingredients of the particular offence. A developer can always argue that the enforcement notice is a complete nullity or that he has in fact obeyed the notice. There is authority that an enforcement notice may be construed more strictly against the interests of the local planning authority in criminal proceedings than in other cases (see *Ivory* v. *Secretary of State* (1985)).

It seems to be too late for the developer to argue that the notice has not accurately described the activities on his site. This kind of argument falls within one of the grounds of appeal to the Secretary of State, namely 'that the alleged breach of planning control has not taken place'. In *R* v. *Keeys* (1989), the appellant had stationed a residence on his land comprising two mobile homes and a caravan bolted together. Separate enforcement notices were served, one referring to a 'mobile home' and the other to a 'residential caravan'. The appellant argued that there was no case to answer because neither notice addressed itself to the structure as it was at the time of the prosecution. Therefore he said that the prosecution had not proved its case. He claimed that the facts must be examined only at the time of prosecution and not as they were when the notice was issued, although in this case 'by a striking coincidence' the facts were identical at both times.

The Court of Appeal was unconvinced by this sophistry. Section 243(1) clearly prohibited the validity of the notice from being challenged on the ground that its allegations were false. The purpose of the section was to do away with technical objections to enforcement notices and to settle disputes by means of the Secretary of State's powers.

On the other hand, could not the accused in appropriate circumstances argue that he is not challenging the *validity* of the notice at all and therefore does not fall foul of section 243(1)? He is merely arguing that the notice does not apply to him because what it alleges has not in fact happened on his land.

By virtue of section 92, if planning permission is granted at any time after a copy of the notice is served for the retention of buildings or works or the continuation of a use covered by an enforcement notice, the notice ceases to have effect but only to the extent of the planning permission. The notice remains fully in force for all other purposes, e.g. conditions relating to other land and 'cosmetic' conditions. Therefore section 92 offers the Secretary of State an alternative device to quashing or varying a notice. He may use section 92 to grant permission for that part of a development which he thinks should remain, leaving the notice otherwise intact. This simple device has been recommended by the High Court (see *Dudley Borough Council* v. *Secretary of State* (1980)).

Section 92 applies even if the new planning permission does not match exactly the allegations in the notice. In *Havering Borough Council* v. *Secretary of State* (1983), an enforcement notice prohibited the storage and distribution of building materials. Planning permission was later granted subject to a large number of conditions. These were not complied with. Mr Justice Hodgson held that the inspector was correct in regarding the enforcement notice as ineffective. Provided that the same planning unit is involved and that the uses were the same, section 92 applied. The practical result is that another enforcement notice must be issued alleging breach of condition.

There are two provisions to deal with technical problems that may arise when an enforcement notice is obeyed:

(1) This applies to cases involving the erection of a building or the carrying out of works without planning permission. Where the notice requires the 'cosmetic' measures authorised by section 87(10)b to be taken (see above) compliance means that planning permission is deemed to be granted for the development as modified (section 87(16)).

(2) Of more general significance is section 23(9). This deals with the discontinuance of a use. It will be recalled that once a change of use from use A to use B has taken place, planning permission is normally required to resume use A. Section 23(9) provides that, where a use is discontinued in obedience to an enforcement notice, no planning permission is required for a use which would have been lawful had the offending development not been carried out. The key word here is *lawful*. A lawful use must either have planning permission or be exempted from requiring planning permission. A use which is immune from enforcement because of lapse of time is not lawful (*LTSS Print and Supply Services* v. *Hackney Borough Council* (1976)). So if a developer changes from a use that has existed since before 1963 to a use which is the subject of an enforcement notice, he loses all protection and there is no use to which he can lawfully return. Furthermore, the lawful use must have existed immediately before the offending use or must be part of a continuous chain of uses none of which was unlawful. Thus a developer cannot retrace the history of the site so as to find a safe haven in some previous lawful use (*Young* v. *Secretary of State* (1983)).

Suppose, for example, the site has the following history: (1) 1948-1960, flats with planning permission; (2) 1960-1980, offices without planning permission; (3) 1980 to the present, flats without planning permission. An enforcement notice now prohibits the flats use. The developer cannot reinstate the office use which was immune but not lawful. The previous flats use was lawful but that is now irrelevant. The flats use did not exist immediately before the notice was issued and its benefit was lost in 1960 because of the change of use to offices. There is therefore no use, other than agricultural, to which the developer can revert under section 23(9). Had the 1960 change of use to offices been at any time given planning permission, the developer could, of course, revert to office use.

Suppose the use which preceded the offending use has been abandoned so that the land was disused immediately before the offending use. A strict application of section 23(9) means that the abandoned use cannot be resumed because it did not exist at the relevant time. However, in *Fairchild* v. *Secretary of State* (1988) Judge Marder QC thought that a developer could revert to an abandoned use. There had been a previous use for sawing logs. The site was currently used unlawfully for storing and distributing soft fruit. An enforcement notice was aimed at this activity. It was doubtful on the facts whether the log sawing use had been abandoned, but it was held that section 23(9) permitted a return to the *latest* use of the land even if that use did not exist immediately before the offending use took place. This reasoning seems inconsistent with the *Young* case (above) and also with the language of section 23(9) which focuses on the state of affairs immediately before the offending use took place. Section 23(9) can be contrasted with other provisions which authorise landowners to revert to earlier uses. These refer to the 'normal' use of the land and are not therefore analogous (see sections 23(5), 23(8)).

When does an enforcement notice take effect?

An enforcement notice cannot be implemented until the notice has taken effect and the time limit specified in the notice for compliance has expired. This time limit does not begin to run until the date on which the notice takes effect. The notice specifies the date on which it is to take effect (section 87(13)). In practice, this is governed by the provisions for service of the notice. As we have seen, copies of the enforcement notice must be served on all persons entitled to be served not later than 28 days before the date specified in the notice as the date on which it is to take effect.

The taking effect of the notice is suspended once an appeal to the Secretary of State has been launched until all appeal proceedings are concluded (section 88(10)). After a period of uncertainty, the Court of Appeal has held that the notice remains suspended until any appeal from the Secretary of State to the Court has also been concluded (*R* v. *Kuxhaus* (1988)). At the earliest, therefore, an enforcement notice cannot take effect until the end of 28 days after the Secretary of State's decision (treating the day following the decision as day one) because this is the time provided for an appeal to the High Court (see above). If an appeal to the High Court is launched, the operation of the notice may be postponed for many months until all further rights of appeal up to the House of Lords are exhausted. Thus a determined developer can take advantage of a barrage of delaying tactics, perhaps for years.

Suppose an appeal to the High Court is successful. The court's only power is to remit the enforcement notice to the Secretary of State to reconsider the matter. The notice still remains dormant. The Secretary of State must then reconsider the whole case in the light of any change in circumstances since his original decision (*Newbury District Council* v. *Secretary of State* (1988)). His second decision can also be appealed to the court, and all the time the notice remains suspended. There is a danger of an appeal being lodged purely to buy time, perhaps solely upon the ground that inadequate reasons have been given. The courts dislike such tactics but cannot do much about them. In *London Residuary Body* v. *Secretary of State* (1988), Mr Justice Simon Brown, said that a challenge on the grounds of inadequate reasons 'should be advanced sparingly, scrutinised critically and not readily acceded to'. We have already seen that the courts have taken some steps to resist the same questions being repeatedly reopened in a series of appeal decisions and are reluctant to allow purely technical challenges to the drafting of an enforcement notice.

There are further possibilities of delay. Suppose the Secretary of State refuses to consider an appeal against an enforcement notice, regarding it as out of time or outside his powers (see above). His refusal could be challenged by means of an application for judicial review. If this is successful, the appeal will be considered as active so that the notice remains suspended. Therefore the authority should not implement the notice pending the litigation. Indeed, the court has a discretion to suspend the *operation* of the notice. However, this is not the same as suspending the notice itself. If the judicial review proceedings are not successful, the notice will be treated as active from the date on which the time for appealing to the Secretary of State expired.

The authority remains at risk even after the time limits for appeal to the Secretary of State are safely past. If it prosecutes the landowner, he could then apply for planning permission for the development forbidden by the notice. He can appeal to the Secretary of State against any refusal and challenge the Secretary of State's decision in the courts. The criminal court could then adjourn the proceedings pending the outcome of the appeal (see *R* v. *Polly Newland* (1987)). Lord Hailsham, the then Lord Chancellor, disapproved of this course of action unless the application and appeal had 'real merit' (speech to the Magistrates Association, 1984). However, given the uncertainties of the planning appeal process such advice may not be particularly helpful, quite apart from the constitutional impropriety of the executive attempting to interfere with the judicial process.

Criminal proceedings

It is important to remember that the gist of the criminal offences is disobedience to an enforcement notice and not breach of planning control as such.

In theory, anyone can prosecute a person alleged to have disobeyed an enforcement notice. In practice, proceedings are normally taken by the local planning authority. The offences are triable either summarily (i.e. in the magistrates court) or on indictment (in the Crown Court before a jury). The penalty in summary proceedings is currently £2 000 for a first offence and £200 per day for subsequent convictions. The Crown Court can impose an unlimited fine. On the other hand, Crown Court proceedings are slower and more expensive, and the outcome of a jury trial is unpredictable.

All proceedings are begun in the magistrates court by lodging an 'information' alleging the basic ingredients of the offence. If either party requests a trial on indictment, the magistrates must decide whether they feel able to decide the case themselves. They take account of the seriousness of the case and the level of punishment they can impose (Magistrates Courts Act 1980, section 19(3)(4)). They are not concerned at this stage with matters personal to the accused, such as defences or mitigating circumstances. If they decide that they are able to hear the case, the accused has the right to opt for jury trial. Even if summary trial takes place, the accused can be committed to the Crown Court for sentence.

The criminal proceedings may be protracted and even if successful may end in a trivial penalty. Meanwhile, the accused may repeatedly apply for planning permission and be successful on appeal. In *R v. Polly Newland* (1987), enforcement notices were served in January 1984 in respect of the appellant's mobile home. Appeals against the notices were dismissed in April 1985. In October 1986 the appellant pleaded guilty in the Crown Court and was fined £3000. Meanwhile, she was applying for planning permission and appealing to the Secretary of State against its refusal. The planning issue was whether the appellant had a gypsy nomadic lifestyle deserving of special concessions. In March 1987 the Court of Appeal reduced the fine to £300, partly because of the appellant's limited resources and partly because the trial judge should have adjourned the case until the planning appeal was concluded. The appellant was also successful in the planning appeal.

The offences

An information is invalid if it is 'duplicitous', that is, if it alleges a single offence in the guise of two or more offences. It is therefore invalid if it fails to distinguish between the different offences which can be committed by developing an enforcement notice. These are as follows:

(1) Failing to take steps required by the notice other than the discontinuance of a use (section 89(1)).
(2) Failing to secure compliance with the notice following a first conviction under (1) above (section 89(4)).

These two offences have been described as involving 'do' notices, and mainly concern operational development (see *Chiltern District Council* v. *Hodgetts* (1983)). They could also embrace failure to comply with a condition requiring the taking of positive steps, e.g. provision of amenities.

(3) Using the land or 'causing or permitting' the land to be used in breach of a requirement that a use be discontinued, or failing to comply with conditions or limitations in respect of uses or operations (section 89(5)). This has been described as involving 'desist' notices (*Chiltern District Council* v. *Hodgetts* (loc cit above). This offence also applies to the resumption of a use that has been discontinued (section 93(2)).
(4) Continuing a use following conviction (section 89(5)).
(5) Reinstatement or restoration of buildings or works following conviction (section 93(5)). Unlike the other offences, this is triable only summarily.

There are important distinctions between offences involving 'do' notices and those involving 'desist' notices. These relate to who commits the offence and the defences available (below). The main defence that applies in all cases is that the notice is so seriously defective, either in itself or in relation to the decision to issue it, that it is a complete nullity which can be ignored (see above).

It is usually said that enforcement notice offences require *mens rea* - a guilty mind. This means that the accused must be aware of facts that, if true, make his behaviour unlawful, i.e. that an effective enforcement notice exists, and that he is carrying out the relevant activities. He need not believe that as a matter of law his activities are prohibited by the notice. The landowner's understanding of the notice or of the law is irrelevant.

It has been held that a landowner must take reasonable steps to check whether an enforcement notice affects him (*South Cambridge District Council* v. *Stokes* (1981) - whether an appeal had been concluded). In this respect it is worth remembering that, as well as being registered in their own public register (see above), enforcement notices are registerable as local land charges under the Local Land Charges Act 1975. Registration under this Act gives notice of the enforcement notice to 'all persons and for all purposes connected with the land' (Law of Property Act 1985, section 198). However, it should not be assumed that 'notice' under section 198 is the same as

Implementing an enforcement notice 101

knowledge for the purposes of the criminal law. Not only is this important for the question of *mens rea*, but it also matters for the purposes of a statutory defence of 'ignorance of the notice' which is sometimes available to persons who were not served with copies of the notice.

Delays experienced in searching the local land charges register have in the past been a serious problem, and it would be extremely unjust if a landowner's criminal liability depended upon the mechanics of the register. Section 198 is primarily concerned with technical issues involving purchasers of land as against interests binding on the land. In *Rignal Developments* v. *Halil* (1987), it was held that any attempt to equate notice with knowledge was highly suspect: 'Notice, even actual notice, has nothing to do with a person's state of mind.' The case itself involved a dispute between vendor and purchaser which turned on whether the purchaser can be taken to have knowledge of a registered local land charge. It is arguable that this reasoning applies even more strongly in the criminal law where the state of mind of the accused is usually a crucial factor.

On the other hand, *mens rea* may not be an ingredient of enforcement notice offences at all. The case of *R* v. *Wells Street Magistrates Court* (1986) concerned the offence of demolishing or altering a listed building in breach of another provision of the Act (see below). It was held that *mens rea* was not required. The offence was one of strict liability because the statute is concerned to bring about a socially desirable objective and strict liability promotes this by demanding greater vigilance from landowners and developers. This was not an enforcement notice case but it is arguable that the same reasoning applies with even greater force. Firstly, enforcement notice offences are not punishable with imprisonment, imprisonment being a factor pointing towards *mens rea*. Secondly, enforcement notice law contains certain safeguards for innocent third parties (below). In *Maidstone Borough Council* v. *Mortimer* (1980), it was held that disobedience to a tree preservation order (see below) is an offence of strict liability. The court emphasised that the existence of the order could easily be discovered, a fact that applies equally to ordinary enforcement notices.

We have seen that an information must not be duplicatious (see above). Until the case of *Chiltern District Council* v. *Hodgetts* (above), it was arguable that failure to comply with an enforcement notice was a 'continuing offence'. This would mean that the offence was committed afresh every day in which the notice was not implemented. In the *Chiltern* case, the House of Lords held that the offences were single offences capable of being committed over a period of time and that only one offence could be alleged. They accepted that the formula which planning authorities normally used ('on or since' a given date) was lawful but thought that where a first offence was alleged it would be preferable to describe the offence as taking place between two dates. The first date is the earliest date when there was evidence of a breach of the notice. Presumably, this is the expiry of the time limit for obeying the notice. The second date should be not later than the date of the information.

It would seem to follow that the offence of continuing to disobey an enforcement notice following conviction can only be prosecuted once since no one can be tried twice for the same offence. There seems therefore to be no criminal penalties for a 'third' offence where the unlawful activity has continued throughout. In this kind of case an injunction may be appropriate (see below). However, there are special offences applicable where the unlawful acts are stopped and later resumed (see below). It has also been suggested that an information might allege different periods of time during which the notice was disobeyed (Brand, *Enforcement of Planning Control* (1988)).

THE INDIVIDUAL OFFENCES

(1) FAILING TO TAKE STEPS REQUIRED BY A 'DO' NOTICE (section 89(1))

This offence is committed by the person who was the owner of the land on the date when a copy of the notice was served on him. As we have seen (see above) there can be more than one owner. If the identity of the owner has changed since the date in question, the accused can require the subsequent owner to appear before the court (section 89(2)). The subsequent owner can be convicted if it is proved that he was in default. The registration machinery to which all prospective purchasers have access means that the subsequent owner is unlikely to have the excuse that he was unaware of the notice. If the subsequent owner is convicted and if the original defendant can prove that he took all reasonable steps to comply with the notice, he must be acquitted (section 89(3)b).

Service of a copy of the notice on the accused is an essential ingredient of this offence. The prosecution must therefore prove that it has served a copy of the notice. However, the defence cannot allege that service was not valid or effective except by way of an appeal to the Secretary of State (section 243(1) see above). Therefore as long as the prosecution shows *prima facie* evidence of valid service, no challenge is possible. Furthermore, by virtue of section 110(2) it cannot be argued in any other proceedings that a person who in fact appealed to the Secretary of State was not duly served.

The prosecution must also prove that the steps required by the notice have not been taken within the prescribed time.

Few defences are available. As we have seen, arguments about whether the alleged breach of planning control has taken place are irrelevant, as are arguments about the time limit for issuing an enforcement notice (see above). The accused may raise the following arguments:

 (i) that the notice is a nullity;
 (ii) he was not the 'owner' at the relevant time;
 (iii) as a matter of fact or of interpretation of the notice he has complied with the notice;
 (iv) appeal proceedings are still pending so that the notice has not taken effect (see above);
 (v) that a subsequent owner was responsible (above).

An occupier cannot be prosecuted as such for this offence. Therefore if the owner is not served there can be no prosecution. (See *R v. Greenwich Borough Council ex parte Patel* (1985) (see above).)

(2) FOLLOWING CONVICTION, FAILURE TO SECURE COMPLIANCE (section 89(4))

The validity of the previous conviction cannot be questioned except by alleging that the justices or Crown Court had no jurisdiction to convict. The prosecution must prove that the accused had the power to secure compliance with the notice but failed to take all practicable (not just 'reasonable') steps to do so. For this offence there is no special power to bring in subsequent owners, but the accused will usually be acquitted if the blame lies with the subsequent owner because he will have no power to secure compliance.

It is arguable that once an owner has been convicted then on any subsequent sale or lease he should enter into a contract with the purchaser or lessee requiring the necessary work to be carried out. Otherwise he may not have taken all 'practicable' steps. However, the new owner might be liable in his own right if he reinstates the offending development (see below). It is also arguable that if the offending development has been continuously in place then the new owner could be served with a copy of the enforcement notice and prosecuted for the main offence under section 89(1). Service is out of time (see above) but failure to comply with the statutory requirements as to service does not invalidate an enforcement notice. Failure to serve properly can be challenged by way of appeal to the Secretary of State (above) but the new owner cannot do this because the time limit for appealing expired when the notice first took effect.

(3) USING OR CAUSING OR PERMITTING USE OF THE LAND IN BREACH OF AN ENFORCEMENT NOTICE ('DESIST' NOTICES) (section 89(5))

This offence is wide and quite draconian. It can be broken down into four categories.

(a) Using the land in breach of a requirement in an enforcement notice that a use be discontinued;
(b) causing or permitting the land to be so used;
(c) the continuation of the use after conviction;
(d) using the land or carrying out operations or causing or permitting the use or the carrying out of operations in breach of a condition or limitation.

Category (d) includes a breach of condition relating to operational development as well as to change of use development. The conditions involved are likely to be negative, e.g. not to use proscribed building materials. They therefore fall naturally within this group of 'desist' offences. Conditions could also be positive, e.g. to provide landscaping. In the case of a positive condition, the owner of the land could be charged under section 89(1) above, whereas anyone carrying out the operation could be charged under section 89(5). There is therefore an overlap. However, the 'second offence', provision (c), refers only to the continuation of a use. There is therefore no special penalty for a second offence in respect of failure to comply with a condition or limitation except in the case of positive conditions falling within section 89(1).

Any person carrying out the offending use or breaking the offending condition can be charged, whether or not the accused has an interest in the land and whether or not the accused was served with a copy of the notice. Thus co-habitees, licensees, contractors and even casual visitors and trespassers may be at risk. Furthermore, persons without interests in the land cannot appeal to the Secretary of State even if they have been served with copies of the notice, so that they are particularly at risk. On the other hand, a person *with* an interest in the land who was not served with a copy of the notice has certain additional rights by way of defence (below).

The prosecution must prove that the accused carried out an act in breach of the notice. It is in this context that questions of interpretation of the notice are likely to arise. The accused may be given the benefit of any ambiguity in the drafting of the notice even though the notice may not be drafted badly enough to be void for uncertainty. For example, in *Warrington Borough Council* v. *Garvey* (1988) the enforcement notice did not adequately specify the nature of the condition alleged to have been broken. In *Duffy* v. *Pilling* (1977), an enforcement notice prohibited 'multiple paying occupation' of a building. It was held that this required the flats in the building to be separately occupied and controlled so that the accused was not guilty where parts of the premises were shared by all the occupants. However, *Duffy* was decided before the ground of appeal to the Secretary of State was introduced that the breach alleged in the notice 'has not taken place' (see above).

Matters covered by the appeal grounds cannot be raised as a defence to a prosecution. Therefore if the facts of *Duffy* were to be repeated today it would probably not be a defence that the notice's description was inaccurate. (See *R* v. *Keeys* (above).) On the other hand, if the notice requires the land to be restored to its previous condition then the prosecution would have to prove what that actually was.

PERSONS NOT SERVED WITH A COPY OF THE NOTICE

For the offence under section 89(5), the accused need not have any interest in the land, nor need a copy of the enforcement notice be served on the accused. The injustice faced by a person who was not served is partly alleviated by section 243(2). It will be recalled that section 243(1) prevents the validity of an enforcement notice being questioned in any other proceedings on any of the grounds of appeal to the Secretary of State. This includes failure to serve a copy of the notice. However, section 243(2) provides that section 243(1) does not apply to proceedings brought under section 89(5) against a person who:

(a) has held an interest in the land since before the enforcement notice was issued; and
(b) did not have a copy of the notice served on him; and
(c) satisfies the court:
   (i) that he did not know and could not reasonably have been expected to know that the enforcement notice had been issued; and
   (ii) that his interests have been substantially prejudiced by the failure to serve him with a copy of it.

This is a limited exemption. Firstly, it does not apply to everyone liable to be charged under section 89(5) such as contractors, or licencees. However, it could be argued that a squatter has an interest in the land by virtue of a possessory title.

More importantly, the common assumption that section 243(2) permits *all* the grounds of appeal to be raised as a defence seems to be without foundation. The subsection merely removes the exemption created by section 243(1). It does not create any defences in itself, so that the matter depends on the ingredients of the particular offence. These are using or causing or permitting the use of the land in contravention of the notice.

Many of the grounds of appeal are therefore irrelevant. These grounds include (a) that planning permission should be granted or a condition discharged; (b) that the allegations do not constitute a breach of planning control (see above); (d) and (e) time limits for enforcement; (g) excessive steps required; (h) unreasonable period for compliance. Furthermore, none of the appeal grounds make the notice void (see above).

This leaves only two grounds. One is ground (c) — that the breach of planning control alleged has not taken place. This would seem to be a good defence. The accused could argue that he has not disobeyed the enforcement notice because the facts have been wrongly described in the notice. The other ground is failure to serve a copy of the notice properly. The problem here is that service is not an ingredient of the offence, nor does failure to serve invalidate the notice. This was accepted in *Scarborough Borough Council* v. *Adams & Adams* (1983), where the accused were in fact served. However, the court said that a person who was not served might have a defence if he was unaware of the notice. This can be justified on the basis of elementary principles of natural justice. A difficulty here is the possibility that section 198 of the Law of Property Act 1925 applies, so that registration of the enforcement notice gives notice of it to the whole world. We have already discussed this (see above).

CAUSING OR PERMITTING

A landowner may be convicted under section 89(5) if he fails to prevent tenants, licensees or visitors from disobeying the notice. A person 'causes or permits' any act which he has the power to prevent and fails to prevent. However, a test of reasonableness applies. For example, in *Ragsdale* v. *Creswick* (1984) it was held that a failure to institute legal proceedings against a squatter does not in itself mean that the landowner causes or permits the squatter's activities. All the circumstances of the case are relevant, including the landowner's resources and his willingness to explore other possible avenues. The court will also take into account whether it is reasonable for the local planning authority to take action directly against the user of the land. On the other hand, a landowner can 'cause or permit' by doing nothing. Encouragement or connivance is not required.

Where a landlord cannot evict a tenant, he will not usually cause or permit the tenant's activities (*Johnstone* v. *Secretary of State* (1974)). In the case of residential tenants who are protected tenants under the Rent Act 1977, special provisions enable the landlord to take steps required by an enforcement notice (section 91(3) and(4)).

CONTINUING THE USE AFTER CONVICTION

This is a separate offence but does not apply to conditions relating to operational development. The owner may be convicted under section

89(4) for breaching such conditions if they require the taking of positive steps (see above).

REINSTATEMENT OFFENCES

Section 93(5) makes it a summary offence for any person to reinstate or restore buildings or works which have been demolished or altered in compliance with an enforcement notice, but also states that the owner cannot be charged under section 89(1) to (4) in relation to reinstatement offences. Thus only summary proceedings are possible. As regards uses which are reintroduced, the basic offence in section 89(5) is wide enough to include any resumption of a prohibited use by anyone. This is because section 93(2) states that a requirement that a use be discontinued means discontinued permanently. However, the prosecution must prove that the resumed use is *in fact* a breach of planning control. This is an ingredient of the offence separate from the question of the validity of the notice itself, so that section 243(1) does not prevent the accused from arguing that the use is not development.

Power of entry

In addition to the criminal sanctions, the local planning authority may enter the land and take the steps required by the enforcement notice other than the discontinuance of a use (section 91). This is in addition to the power conferred by section 280(8) to enter in order to ascertain whether an offence has been committed. The section 91 power is not limited to entry at a 'reasonable time', but where the offending act is the reinstatement of buildings or works at least 28 days' notice must be given to the owner and occupier.

Having entered the land, the authority may take the steps required by section 87(7)(a) to remedy the breach other than the discontinuance of a use. This does *not* include the additional steps that may be required by a notice to make the development comply with a planning permission or remove injury to amenity.

It can recover its reasonable costs including a reasonable amount of 'establishment charges' (Local Government (Miscellaneous Provisions) Act 1976, section 36). It must do this by means of a civil action against the person who was owner of the land at the time of entry (section 91(1)). This owner may not be to blame, in which case he can recover the whole amount from the person by whom the breach of control was committed (section 91(2)). The costs can be charged on the land (section 91(5)).

Several other statutory provisions are incorporated into section 91 to supplement the power of entry (section 91(3)). The Town and Country Planning General Regulations 1976 SI No. 1419 governs this. The main provisions are:

(1) The local planning authority may sell materials removed from the land in executing works but must account to the owner for the proceeds minus their expenses. The owner must first be given three days to take the material away himself.
(2) The occupier of the premises (e.g. a tenant) must permit the owner to carry out works for implementing the notice, thus avoiding the local authority having to enter the land.
(3) If the owner holds the land as an agent or a trustee for someone else and has not been provided with sufficient funds, his personal liability is limited to the funds in his possession for the purpose.

The power of entry can be defeated by showing that the enforcement notice is a nullity. If this is so then the owner may either seek judicial review of the notice or simply bring an action for trespass against the local planning authority. Apart from this, section 243(1) applies as usual so that the notice cannot be challenged on any of the grounds of appeal to the Secretary of State. It is irrelevant whether or not the owner or occupier was able to appeal (see above). However, the power of entry, although dependent on a valid notice, is a separate discretionary power. As with all statutory powers, it must be exercised fairly and reasonably. In *R* v. *Greenwich London Borough Council ex parte Patel* (1985) (see above) the Court of Appeal suggested that fairness requires that a person who was not in a position to appeal to the Secretary of State should be given a chance to show, for example, that no breach of planning control had taken place. Section 243(1) is not an obstacle because the validity of the enforcement notice is not being challenged as such. However, it is possible that, should the issue arise, a court might take a broad view of section 243(1) and reject this argument.

Conclusion

The law governing the sanctions for implementing an enforcement notice is far from ideal. It is overcomplex and in places irrational. It could profitably be replaced by a single offence of disobedience to an enforcement notice with prescribed defences for the benefit of persons who could not reasonably have been expected to appeal.

Section 3(2) of the Statutory Instruments Act 1946 provides an analogy. It is a defence to a prosecution for disobedience to a statutory instrument (i.e. a central government regulation) to show that the statutory instrument has not been properly published unless the prosecution can show that reasonable steps have been taken to bring the purport of the instrument to the notice of the public or persons affected by it or of the person charged.

Chapter 8

Supplementary methods of enforcement

We have seen that the ordinary enforcement process is beset by delay and uncertainty. However, there are two mechanisms that can be used in exceptional cases as more powerful weapons and to counter delaying tactics. They provide relatively speedy and draconian methods of restraining unlawful development but they are hedged around with restrictions and should only be used as a last resort. One method, that of stop notices, is provided by the Act. The other, the injunction, is a creature of the ordinary law. In addition to these specific methods, a local authority could supplement its enforcement powers by making agreements with landowners.

Stop notices

Under section 90, once a copy of an enforcement notice has been served the authority can serve a 'stop notice' on any person who appears to them to have an interest in the land or to be engaged in any activity prohibited by the enforcement notice. It is then an offence to carry out any activity prohibited by the stop notice. A stop notice can prohibit any activity specified in the enforcement notice other than:

(a) the use of any building as a dwelling house;
(b) the use of land as a caravan site occupied by any person as his only or main residence;
(c) the taking of any steps required by the enforcement notice;
(d) the carrying out of any 'activities', whether continuous or not, which began more than 12 months previously unless they are incidental to building, engineering, mining or other operations. It is irrelevant whether or not the activities had planning permission for some of the time (*Scott Markets Ltd* v. *Waltham Forest District Council* (1979)).

It should be noted that the word employed in relation to stop notices is 'activity' and not 'use'. Activity is a broader term than use. For example, a breach of condition can be an activity if the condition is one which requires the landowner to refrain from doing something, e.g. not to open a restaurant except at stipulated times, or not to deposit specified materials.

A stop notice applies equally to activities commenced after it was served (*Runnymede Borough Council* v. *Smith* (1986)). Thus a fluctuating community of caravan occupiers can be made subject to a stop notice subject to the 'main residence' exception.

A stop notice cannot require operations that have already been carried out to be undone, but it could require objects associated with a use, e.g. caravans, stores, vehicles, etc. to be removed. A stop notice is flexible in that it does not have to prohibit the whole of the alleged breach of control but can direct itself to any activities within the scope of its parent enforcement notice.

PROCEDURE

A stop notice can only be served once its parent enforcement notice has been served on the person concerned. However, the authority can simultaneously resolve to issue both. A stop notice cannot be served once the enforcement notice has taken effect so that it cannot be used as a method of duplicating prosecutions. The main advantage of a stop notice is that it can prevent development continuing during the appeal process.

The stop notice must either spell out the activities it wishes to prohibit or refer to the enforcement notice (*Westminster City Council* v. *Jones* (1981)). A copy of the enforcement notice must be annexed to the stop notice.

A stop notice takes effect on a day specified in it. This must not be earlier than three days after service and not later than 28 days. Once it has taken effect *any person* who disobeys it or who causes or permits it to be disobeyed (see above) is guilty of an offence. The penalties are the same as for disobeying an enforcement notice (see above).

In addition to the stop notice itself, the authority can display a 'site notice' on the land (section 90(5)). This draws attention to the stop notice and warns of prosecution. Any person who disobeys the site

Supplementary methods of enforcement

notice is guilty of an offence. Where a site notice is displayed, a prosecution can be launched at once. If there is no site notice there must be a breathing space of two days after the stop notice takes effect.

A stop notice remains effective until either:

(i) the enforcement notice is withdrawn or quashed; or
(ii) the period allowed for compliance with the enforcement notice expires; or
(iii) the stop notice is withdrawn — this can be done by the same service and site notice procedure as applied to the stop notice itself.

The decision to issue a stop notice should take into account the costs incurred by the person or firm whose activities are prohibited. Such matters as the deterioration of equipment and materials and possible loss of markets are very important. As usual, the DoE recommends negotiation with the persons concerned (see Circular 4/87).

CHALLENGE

There is no right of appeal against a stop notice but challenge by judicial review is possible. This can be a very speedy procedure but is available only on limited grounds. These have been discussed earlier. In the context of stop notices, a citizen could argue:

(i) that the *enforcement notice* is a nullity so that its creature, the stop notice is, itself void;
(ii) that the stop notice is void because it is incomplete or uncertain;
(iii) that the stop notice was not served properly;
(iv) that the decision to serve the stop notice was irrational, unfair or taken by the wrong person.

However, a stop notice is not invalid merely because its parent enforcement notice was not properly served provided that the authority took all practicable steps to do so (section 90(9)).

The accused may also defend a prosecution on the same grounds, except perhaps ground (iv). This arises also in relation to *injunctions* and will be discussed later. There are two other defences:

(i) that the acts in question were outside the scope of the stop notice, e.g. because of the 12 month's rule (above) – see *R* v. *Jenner* (1983);
(ii) that the accused was not served with a stop notice and that he neither knew nor could reasonably have been expected to know of its existence. A stop notice is registerable in the register of enforcement notices and also as a local land charge.

COMPENSATION

Stop notices are not widely used. One reason for this may be that the authority is liable to pay compensation if the parent enforcement notice comes to grief (section 177). This applies:

(i) where an enforcement notice is quashed by the Secretary of State on appeal on any ground other than by granting planning permission (ground (a));
(ii) where the enforcement notice is varied to exclude the activities prohibited in the stop notice;
(iii) where the enforcement notice is withdrawn except in consequence of granting planning permission or removing a condition; or
(iv) if the stop notice is withdrawn (section 177(2)).

Compensation is payable in respect of loss or damage *directly* attributable to obeying the stop notice. This is wider than the ordinary legal notion of reasonable foreseeability. It would include legal costs, interest charges, loss of profits and good will, laying off workers, the cost of materials, and the cost of any breach of contract caused by obeying the notice (section 177(5)). This could include not only building contracts but also providing temporary accommodation for purchasers of dwellings (see, e.g. *J Sample (Warkworth) Ltd* v. *Alnwick District Council* (1984); *Robert Barnes & Co Ltd* v. *Malvern Hills District Council* (1985)).

The compensation bill can be reduced if the claimant failed to comply with an information notice served under section 284 (see above) or made any misstatement in response to such a notice.

Disputes about compensation are referred to the Lands Tribunal. The DoE has attempted to minimise fears about compensation, pointing out the various limits on the right to compensation and also stating that on the available evidence compensation is infrequent and payable by relatively few LPAs (see Circular 4/87, Annex 3). However, statistical evidence can tell us nothing about individual cases. Given that the enforcement process is fraught with uncertainty and that potential liability is open-ended, this advice is not especially reassuring.

Injunctions

An injunction is an order from the court which can immediately prohibit an unlawful act from taking place. A breach of planning control is an unlawful act even if no enforcement notice has been served. However, injunctions are most effective as 'last resort' remedies after the normal enforcement machinery has been tried and proved inadequate.

A private individual cannot obtain an injunction in respect of a breach of planning control because such breaches are public and not private matters. A local planning authority, other than an urban development corporation, can obtain an injunction. This is due to section 222 of the Local Government Act 1972 which empowers a 'local authority' to institute legal proceedings of any kind in order to protect the inhabitants of its area (see below). There is no doubt that enforcing planning control is within this power.

THE POWER TO GRANT AN INJUNCTION

Injunctions are in theory very effective. They can prohibit unlawful acts and a *mandatory* injunction could require the land to be restored to its original condition. They can be granted very quickly – in a matter of hours in an emergency. An *interim* injunction can temporarily restrain the development pending a full trial. For this, the authority has to show only that it has an arguable case and that the court should exercise its discretion in its favour in view of the harm caused by the development and the ineffectiveness of other remedies.

The sanction behind an injunction is imprisonment for contempt of court. Moreover, unlike a private litigant a local planning authority does not have to undertake to pay compensation if an interim injunction is later discharged, because it is attempting to enforce the law.

The court has a discretion as to whether or not to grant an injunction. A crucial factor here is that the planning legislation does, after all, provide a comprehensive code with its own penalties for enforcing the law. Would it not be improper for a local planning authority to use an injunction to short circuit this, impose more draconian penalties, and even deny the citizen his right of appeal to the Secretary of State? Moreover, the courts are reluctant to decide questions of fact and policy that should be decided by the Secretary of State, since that is an abuse of the judicial role.

Hence there is no hope of obtaining an injunction unless (i) the defendant has clearly acted unlawfully, and (ii) the authority can show that the ordinary enforcement mechanism, including stop notices, is likely to be ineffective.

In *Waverley District Council* v. *Hilden* (1988), Mr Justice Scott said (at 822):

'...if it is clear that the sanctions of criminal prosecutions are unlikely to deter the defendants and if there is no other means of securing obedience to the law then in my view an injunction should in principle be granted.'

The simplest case is where convictions have already been obtained and where fines have not persuaded the defendant to cease his offences (e.g. *Westminster City Council* v. *Jones* (1981)). An injunction could also be granted where enforcement notices have been issued but no prosecutions have yet taken place. For example, in *Runnymede District Council* v. *Ball* (1986) injunctions were granted because the breach of control, a gypsy caravan site, was 'deliberate and flagrant', there was evidence of permanent injury to green belt land and the prosecution process was likely to be too slow and ultimately ineffective. The court held that the purpose of the injunction was to enable the authority to perform its duty to protect the local environment. By contrast, in *Runnymede District Council* v. *Smith* (1986), an injunction was refused. The defendants had appealed against the enforcement notice which was therefore suspended. There was no guarantee that they would lose the appeal and there was neither permanent damage nor an intention to defy the law. (See also *Attorney General* v. *Morris* (1973).) The court saw no reason why developers should not exploit their legal rights.

In principle, an injunction could also be sought even without issuing an enforcement notice (*Attorney General* v. *Smith* (1958)). However, this would be very exceptional. (In *Smith*, a series of previous notices had been circumvented.) In *Bedfordshire County Council* v. *Central Electricity Generating Board* (1985), an injunction was sought to prevent preliminary bore holes being sunk by public bodies responsible for radioactive waste disposal. Enforcement notices would have been pointless because the operations took only three days. Nevertheless, the court refused to grant an injunction because it was not clear that such minor operations were development at all. Nor was there any significant harm to the local environment.

The local authority must apply to the High Court for an injunction. The High Court could transfer the case to the County Court.

CHALLENGING AN INJUNCTION

From the point of view of the defendant there are two separate issues. First of all, is the decision of the local authority to seek an injunction under section 222 a valid one? This involves the question of whether they are genuinely acting in the interests of the inhabitants of their area and whether they have genuinely considered using the ordinary enforcement powers. For example, administrative cost and inconvenience is not in itself enough to justify an injunction. These issues can be challenged only by means of an application for judicial review and not as a defence to the injunction itself. This is because the decision to seek an injunction is a matter of *public law* and does not directly affect anyone's private rights (See *Waverley Borough Council* v. *Hilden* (above).)

The distinction between public and private law causes considerable problems. It is open to criticism, because of its artificiality and because it may deny the developer access to his local county court. On the other hand, judicial review procedure is very speedy and contains several safeguards designed to protect the government (see above).

The second issue is whether an injunction should be granted. The defendant can raise arguments about this as a defence to the injunction itself. Once an enforcement notice has been served on him he cannot challenge it by arguing that he has not committed a breach of planning control, or that the notice is out of time or not properly served, since these matters are exclusively for the Secretary of State on appeal (section 243(1) (see above)). He could, however, argue that the enforcement notice and any related stop notices were void or that he had in fact obeyed the notice. If no enforcement notice had been served he could argue that his activities were not a breach of planning control. As we have seen, the court requires strong evidence of guilt.

THE COURT'S DISCRETION

Injunctions are discretionary remedies. Even if the allegations are proved the court is not bound to grant an injunction but can balance all the relevant considerations including personal hardship. However, it seems that if the defendant has 'deliberately and flagrantly' broken the law the court will not be softened by sympathy to his motives. In the *Waverley* case (above), the defendants refused to move their gypsy encampment despite a series of convictions. They had nowhere else in the area to go and were seeking judicial review against the decision of another local authority who was alleged to have unlawfully failed to provide them with a camping site. Nevertheless, an injunction was granted.

The court will look harshly on deliberate and flagrant breaches of planning control, particularly where the developer profits from them (*Stoke on Trent City Council* v. *B & Q (Retail) Ltd* (1984)), but will also consider other factors including the impact of the development on the locality. On the other hand, the local planning authority is unlikely to obtain an injunction merely because there are practical difficulties in serving an enforcement notice unless the normal procedures are likely to be completely ineffective.

Because injunctions are remedies of last resort, the scope of an injunction will be the minimum necessary to prevent permanent damage. For example, in the *Waverley* case (above) the court refused to order the developers to remove the hard standing and other infrastructure of their caravan site because the local authority had the power to do that themselves. The injunction merely restrained the developers from using the land as a caravan site. On the other hand, an injunction can restrain *future* breaches of planning control anywhere within the local planning authority's territory (*Attorney General* v. *Morris* (1973)). An enforcement notice, by contrast, can apply only to the planning unit in which a breach has already taken place.

An injunction issues only against named individuals whereas an enforcement notice binds all persons who breach its terms and all subsequent owners of the land. However, if a third party does some act, e.g. he chops down a tree that destroys the purpose of the injunction, then if he knows of the injunction (which can be registered as a court order) he too may be guilty of contempt of court.

INJUNCTIONS AND THE ATTORNEY GENERAL

We have said that a private individual cannot apply for an injunction. However, any person can request the Attorney General to seek an injunction in his capacity as the guardian of the public interest. This is called a 'relator' action. The Attorney can also institute proceedings on his own initiative. If the local planning authority is an urban development corporation, this is the only way to obtain an injunction. Urban development corporations are not local authorities and cannot therefore use section 222 (*London Docklands Development Corporation* v. *Rank Hovis McDougal Ltd* (1986)).

If the Attorney General agrees to take up the case then the 'relator' (the person making the request) conducts the case on a day-to-day basis and pays the costs. Nevertheless, the Attorney General retains full powers of control over the litigation.

Unlike a local authority decision, the decision of the Attorney General as to whether or not to take on the case cannot be challenged in the courts at all (*Gouriet* v. *Union of Post Office Workers* (1977)). The Attorney has a completely free discretion. However, the court can still decide in its discretion whether or not to grant the injunction. Even here the court will assume that the Attorney General has adequately considered whether other possible remedies are more appropriate and is unlikely to refuse an injunction on those grounds (*Attorney General* v. *Bastow* (1957)).

The scope of the Attorney General's power to seek an injunction has been said to be narrower than the power of a local authority under section 222. In section 222 cases, the basis of the action is the local authority's duty to safeguard the interests of the inhabitants of its area. In the planning context this means primarily the preservation of local amenities (see *Kent County Council* v. *Batchelor* (1978) - tree preservation order). The powers of the Attorney General, on the other hand, may be confined to emergencies or to cases where the criminal penalties are *in general* wholly inadequate to act as a deterrent (see *Gouriet* v. *Union of Post Office Workers* (above)). Therefore the Attorney General will interfere only in the most extreme and blatant cases.

'Section 52 agreements'

An alternative or supplement to an enforcement notice is an agreement made between a local planning authority and a landowner requiring the landowner to refrain from specified activities or to carry out works on his land. By virtue of section 52 of the Town and Country Planning Act 1971, 'negative' agreements made between landowners and local planning authorities for planning purposes can bind successors in title to the land. A negative agreement is an agreement that, however it is worded, requires the landowner to refrain from doing something.

For example, an agreement to use premises only for the purpose of a private residence is a negative agreement. *Positive* agreements, e.g. an agreement to provide and maintain roads, drains, landscaping, etc. also bind successors in title by virtue of the Local Government (Miscellaneous Provisions) Act 1982, section 33, provided that the agreement is made under seal.

Planning agreements raise very controversial issues concerning the legality of 'bargaining' for 'planning gain' and also the extent to which a particular agreement must relate to the development which is the subject of a planning permission. For example, can planning permission be given for site A on condition that site B at the other side of town be used to house people who are currently homeless? Or could permission to develop site A be granted on condition that some of the resulting profits be used to subsidise necessary public facilities or historic conservation elsewhere? In *R* v. *Westminster City Council ex parte Monahan* (1989), a legal attack by the Covent Garden Community Association against a grant of planning permission for office development failed. The Court of Appeal held that the authority could lawfully grant permission, subject to the development

Supplementary methods of enforcement

profits being used to restore and improve the Royal Opera House. However, the development and the Opera House were part of an interdependent scheme and the Court made it clear that planning gain, whether obtained by agreement or under ordinary development control powers, must be related to the particular development. It was also emphasised that an agreement cannot be used for purposes which could not lawfully be achieved under the ordinary development control powers. (See also *Bradford Metropolitan Borough Council* v. *Secretary of State* (1986).)

It is settled that an agreement cannot be used to *restrict* the exercise of statutory enforcement powers by the LPA in any way (*Windsor & Maidenhead Royal Borough Council* v. *Brandrose Investments Ltd* (1983)).

From the enforcement perspective, a planning agreement is therefore a supplementary weapon. A local planning authority could sue a landowner directly for breach of contract, thereby by-passing the enforcement notice procedure and the system of appeals and judicial review. There is no right of appeal to the Secretary of State in respect of planning agreements. As long as the landowner's behaviour is a breach of the agreement, it is irrelevant whether or not it is also a breach of planning control in the ordinary sense. In *Avon County Council* v. *Millard* (1985), the developer was granted a temporary planning permission for working a mine and also entered into a section 52 agreement that all operations should cease after the specified date and that a new access road should be constructed. The Court of Appeal granted an injunction on the basis of a breach of the agreement. It made it clear that the grant of an injunction in this kind of case is quite different from the grant of an injunction in support of the ordinary enforcement powers. This was a separate matter of breach of contract so that the questions relating to the statutory enforcement machinery are irrelevant. Moreover, the LPA could obtain damages and the costs of a breach of contract action are normally born by the losing party. Thus a successful section 52 action is cheaper than ordinary enforcement proceedings (see also *Beaconsfield District Council* v. *Gams* (1974) – occupation of bungalow in breach of agreement to demolish neighbouring farmhouse – injunction granted).

Chapter 9

Crown land, Scotland and Northern Ireland

Introduction

In this chapter we shall discuss three topics linked only by the fact that in each case the enforcement regime applicable to private land in England is modified in certain respects. The Crown, meaning for this purpose the Queen and the central government, has always enjoyed special privileges and immunities in the law, and development control is no exception. Scotland and Northern Ireland have separate legal systems, that of Scotland in particular diverging from English law in several respects. Moreover, the intellectual climate of Scottish law is noticeably different from that of England, being less pragmatic, more vigorously analytical and more concerned to discover basic general principles. By contrast, English law is sloppy and disjointed.

The differences in enforcement law between England, Scotland and Northern Ireland are in themselves relatively minor. Although each country has its own planning legislation, those of Scotland and Northern Ireland mainly follow the English Act of 1971. Scottish land law is different in many respects from English land law but, as we have seen, Town and Country Planning Law makes little use of private land law principles.

Crown land – special enforcement notices

Enforcement proceedings cannot be taken against the Crown (section 266(3)). In the case of development carried out by other people on land owned by the Crown, for example by tenants, enforcement proceedings can be taken but only with the consent of the 'appropriate authority' (section 266). The 'appropriate authority' means the government department responsible for the land in question (section 266(7)).

Crown land, Scotland and Northern Ireland

Land is Crown land if the Queen, the Duchy of Cornwall or Lancaster or any government department has an interest in it. The Crown need not own the freehold but might have a lease or mortgage or even some lesser interest such as a right of way or a restrictive covenant. The term 'government department' is defined to include any Minister of the Crown (section 290(1)). Bodies which are not directly controlled by Ministers such as many 'quangos' and nationalised industries are not part of the Crown. The question as to whether a particular public agency is part of the Crown is fraught with difficulty. In the absence of guidance in the particular legislation creating the agency, the test involves looking closely at the degree of *legal* control exercisable by a minister (*Tamlin* v. *Hannaford* (1950)). The *political* question of how much control is in fact exercised is not relevant. Fortunately, modern statutes which create government agencies usually state expressly whether the agency is part of the Crown.

In a recent case the argument was advanced that a person who owned the right to hold a market, derived from a royal grant by Charles I, was immune from planning control (*Spook Erection Ltd* v. *Secretary of State* (1988)). The Court of Appeal decisively rejected the argument. There is a clear distinction between the legal source of a right over land and control over the actual use of the land. Planning law is concerned with the latter. Such bodies as universities derive their rights from Royal Charter but do not act on behalf of the Crown.

The existence of Crown land has caused problems in relation to roadside verges and similar areas of unoccupied land. Motorways and trunk roads are owned by the Crown and are susceptible to unauthorised development by squatters and itinerant traders. The problem here is that the developer may be difficult to identify but the Crown itself would be immune. The Town and Country Planning Act 1984, section 3, authorises the local planning authority to issue a 'special enforcement notice' where development has taken place on Crown land 'otherwise than by or on behalf of the Crown at a time when no person is entitled to occupy it by virtue of a private interest'. The consent of the 'appropriate authority' is required.

This procedure therefore applies only where a trespasser has carried out the development. The law is generally similar to that governing ordinary enforcement notices. There are certain important differences. They include the following (see also Town and Country

Planning (Special Enforcement Notice) Regulations 1984 SI No 1016):

(i) The notice must be served on the person carrying out the development and the occupier, unless the authority cannot trace them after reasonable inquiry.
(ii) The notice must also be served on the 'appropriate authority'.
(iii) The developer or the occupier can appeal to the Secretary of State but only on the ground that no development has taken place (section 3(7)). Rights of challenge in the courts are similar to those under the general law.
(iv) The occupier is subject to the section 89(1) offence of disobedience to the notice. The use offence in section 89(5) is committed by the person carrying out the use as under the ordinary law.

A stop notice can also be issued where a special enforcement notice has been served (see below).

Scotland

As is perhaps to be expected, the law relating to the enforcement of planning control in Scotland is in most respects similar to and in many respects identical to that which operates in England and Wales. The primary and delegated legislation are similar, though there are some differences in the nature and content of policy guidance issued to planning authorities by the respective government departments. Though there are far fewer court decisions on enforcement in Scotland than there are in England and Wales, there are several significant differences in law and practice. It is with these differences that this section is primarily concerned. These differences are discussed after brief consideration of Scotland's distinctive administrative framework.

Crown land, Scotland and Northern Ireland

THE ADMINISTRATIVE FRAMEWORK

(a) THE SECRETARY OF STATE FOR SCOTLAND

Overall responsibility for the administration of town and country planning in Scotland rests with the Secretary of State for Scotland. The Secretary of State's responsibilities for town and country planning are mainly discharged through the Scottish Development Department (SDD). The Secretary of State for Scotland is also responsible for other governmental functions such as roads, housing and agriculture; this may be of assistance in the co-ordination of land use policies in Scotland. As is the case in England and Wales, the Secretary of State's role is primarily of a supervisory, advisory and appellate character. Effective supervision requires good liaison and Scotland's small population may perhaps allow the SDD to establish a closer working relationship with planning authorites than is possible in England and Wales.

(b) LOCAL PLANNING AUTHORITIES

Administration of the town and country planning system at a local level is in the hands of regional, general and district planning authorities. The distribution of planning functions between regional and district councils effected by the Local Government (Scotland) Act 1973 ('the 1973 Act') is not uniform over the whole of Scotland. Planning powers and duties are conferred on only 49 of the 65 Scottish local authorities, and the 49 authorities with planning powers are of three different types: regional, general and district planning authorities (1973 Act, section 172).

Over the most heavily populated parts of Scotland – in the Central, Fife, Grampian, Lothian, Strathclyde and Tayside regions – planning functions are divided between the two tiers of local government. In these six regions the regional councils – termed for this purpose 'regional planning authorities' – are responsible for 'regional planning functions' (see 1973 Act, Schedule 22, part I). The main regional planning functions relate to the making and safeguarding of the structure plan. District councils within these six regions – 'district planning authorites' – are responsible for 'district planning functions'. District planning functions consist of all those powers and duties that are not regional planning functions and therefore include local plan functions, development control powers and the enforcement of planning control (1973 Act, Schedule 22, part II).

In the three most sparsely populated regions – Borders, Dumfries and Galloway, and Highland – responsibility for both regional and district planning functions lies with the regional council. District councils within these regions have no planning functions. These three regional planning authorities are termed 'general planning authorities' (1973 Act, section 172). The three 'all purpose' island councils – Orkney, Shetland and the Western Isles – are also general planning authorities responsible for all planning functions in their areas (1973 Act, section 172).

Wherever the term 'planning authority' appears in any statute it is, unless otherwise provided, to be construed as a reference to a general planning authority and to a district planning authority (1973 Act, section 172(3)). In the pages on Scotland which follow, the term 'planning authority' is used in the same sense.

ENFORCEMENT OF PLANNING CONTROL

The law of Scotland on the enforcement of planning control differs in a number of respects from that in England and Wales. Some of these differences result from different legislation, some result from diverging decisions of the courts, while others are a consequence of differences in the two legal systems. Individually the differences are relatively minor but cumulatively they make effective enforcement even more difficult for Scottish planning authorities.

CRIMINAL LAW

Scotland has its own distinctive system of criminal justice and procedure. This affects enforcement in two main ways. First, in the Sheriff Court (in which a planning prosecution will invariably take place) decisions on prosecution are in all cases made by a public prosecutor, the procurator-fiscal. Even though the planning authority may consider that a particular case merits prosecution, it is for the procurator-fiscal not only to decide whether there is evidence sufficient to justify prosecution but also to determine, in the light of his very wide discretion whether, taking account of factors such as pressure on prosecuting resources, his view of the seriousness of the offence and his estimation of how seriously the Sheriff will view the offence, criminal proceedings should be instituted. Some planning authorities have suggested that procurators-fiscal are reluctant to prosecute in planning cases. However, a research report *The Enforcement of Planning Control in Scotland* (Rowan-Robinson, Young and McLarty, SDD 1984) found that there was, in general, little evidence to substantiate this claim.

Secondly, obtaining the evidence necessary to justify a prosecution in Scotland is likely to be much more expensive in planning authority staff time than in England and Wales. This is because in Scotland no one can be convicted of an offence unless there is corroboration, i.e. the evidence of at least two witnesses implicating him or her in the commission of the offence with which he or she is charged. Often, therefore, an enforcement officer will have to be accompanied by a colleague to provide the necessary corroboration.

Section 86 of the Town and Country Planning (Scotland) Act 1972 ('the 1972 Act') provides that where an enforcement notice requires the discontinuance of a use of land or compliance with conditions or limitations relating to a use of land or to the carrying out of operations thereon then any person who, without a grant of planning permission, uses the land or causes or permits it to be used, or carries out those operations or causes or permits them to be carried out, in contravention of the notice is guilty of an offence. It seems that *mens rea* (guilty intention) may be necessary for the commission of an offence under section 86. As we have seen, the position in England is unclear.

In *Pirie* v. *Bauld* (1975), the Sheriff held that the accused lacked the *mens rea* necessary for the commission of the offence of non-compliance with an enforcement notice in that they believed that they had appealed to the minister against the enforcement notices in question. The Sheriff did not, however, find it necessary to decide the case solely on that ground; he was satisfied that a letter sent by one of the accused to the Secretary of State had to be construed as an appeal against the notice under section 85 and that as the effect of such an appeal is to suspend the operation of an enforcement notice until the final determination of the appeal, the prosecution necessarily failed.

INFORMATION

Under section 270 of the 1972 Act a planning authority can, as a preliminary to enforcement action, require the provision of information as to interests in land. Although it is an offence not to provide the required information, such notices are widely disregarded, thus increasing the risk that an enforcement notice may fail as a result of some inaccuracy. However, because of the attitude of some sheriffs to what they may regard as simply 'bureaucratic' prosecutions, some Scottish planning authorities see little point in reporting such offences.

Scottish planning authorities are at something of a disadvantage compared with their English counterparts in obtaining information as to the planning history of a site, in that section 270 of the Scottish Act does not allow, as does the English legislation, for inquiry as to the time when activities on a site began (see above).

DIRECT ACTION

In contrast to the position in England and Wales, failure to comply with an effective enforcement notice requiring the taking of steps other than the discontinuance of a use is not an offence in Scotland, and the only remedy available is for the planning authority themselves to take direct action – for example, to remove an unauthorised building. Few authorities have made use of these powers of direct action: private contractors may be reluctant to undertake such work and there is the risk that it may turn out to be impossible to recover the cost of direct action from the landowner.

The Scottish courts have not shown a sympathetic attitude to planning authorities in cases in which the validity of enforcement notices has been at issue (see, for example, *McDaid* and *McNaughton* (below)). The general level of fines imposed on conviction for failure to comply with an enforcement notice – a level described by the Convention of Scottish Local Authorities as 'derisory' (and lower than the level in England and Wales) – may also be indicative of a lack of judicial sympathy towards enforcement.

Even where direct action is the only remedy for a breach of planning control, the recipient of the enforcement notice is responsible for complying with the notice. In *Mcdonald* v. *Glasgow Corporation* (1960), the Sheriff-Principal said:

'It appears to me that there cannot be the slightest dubiety that ... the person upon whom the enforcement notice is properly served is responsible for the removal of not only what he has done without planning permission but what had been done by his predecessors, and that he has only the doubtful remedy of a civil claim for the appropriate proportional repayment due in respect of the operations of each successive predecessor.'

That 'doubtful remedy' is contained in subsection (2) of section 88 which provides that any expenses incurred by the owner, lessee or occupier of any land for the purpose of complying with an enforcement notice and any sums paid by the owner or lessee under section 88(1) in respect of expenses incurred by the planning authority in taking steps required by the notice are recoverable from the person by whom the breach of planning control was committed.

PRECLUSIVE CLAUSE

In an important case on a clause seeking to exclude the courts' jurisdiction, the Scottish Court of Session reached a conclusion different from that of the English courts. This was the case of *McDaid* v. *Clydebank District Council* (1984). The right to challenge an enforcement notice in the courts on ordinary administrative law principles or on other legal grounds is restricted by the provisions of section 85(10) of the 1972 Act. That subsection provides that 'the validity of an enforcement notice shall not, except by way of appeal [to the Secretary of State] under this section be questioned in any legal proceedings whatsoever on any of the grounds specified in paragraphs (b) to (e)' of section 85(1). The purpose of the preclusive clause in section 85(10) would appear to be that if it is considered that the planning authority are in error in alleging that the activities in question constitute a breach of control, or in alleging that a breach of control has taken place, or are in error in describing the breach of control, have erred regarding questions of immunity from enforcement action or have erred in the service of the notice, the only way in which the mistake may be challenged is by way of appeal to the Secretary of State.

In England, the equivalent clause, section 243(1), has been given a broad effect. In *Miller-Mead* v. *Minister of Housing*, Lord Denning explained the legislation's effect in the following terms:

'You used previously to be able to raise any of these matters before the courts. But by reason of section 33(8) of the Act of 1960 [the terms of which were very similar to those of section 85(10) of the 1972 Act] you can no longer do so. You cannot raise it by an action for a declaration. You cannot raise it by appeal to the justices. Nor by waiting until there is an attempt to enforce it by criminal proceedings. You can only raise it by an appeal to the Minister. And even if you succeed in your appeal, the Minister can at the most quash it. He cannot declare it to be a nullity or hold it to be void from the beginning. In this way the legislature has disposed of the suggestion that an enforcement notice is a "nullity" on any such ground.'

However, Lord Denning's exposition of the law and a number of other English and Scottish decisions on the effect of the preclusive clause in section 85(10) must, so far as Scotland is concerned, now be read in the light of the decision in *McDaid* v. *Clydebank District Council* (1984). That decision indicates that section 85(10) is not effective as a bar to all challenges of the validity of an enforcement notice on grounds which might be thought to come within the ambit of paragraphs (b) to (e) of section 85. In *McDaid*, enforcement notices were served on the occupier of land but not on the owners. Although section 85(1)(e) provides that it is a ground of appeal to the Secretary of State that an enforcement notice has not been served as required by the 1972 Act, the First Division of the Court of Session held:

(i) that the court's jurisdiction was not excluded by section 85(10) in a case where, for reasons beyond the control of a person seeking to challenge the enforcement notice, the appeal procedure provided by the legislation could not be used; and
(ii) in respect that the enforcement notices had not been properly served, that they were nullities.

It could scarcely have been the intention of Parliament, said Lord Cameron:

'... that a failure in duty by the planning authority in the matter of service of notice should have the bizarre consequence of depriving a person with an interest as owner, lessee or occupier of any right to challenge the validity of such a notice, which because of the failure in duty he never received, and of which he had no knowledge during the period provided for lodging an appeal, and the effect of which may be to cause him as owner material and serious loss.'

In the court's view, section 85(10) only applied to enforcement notices in the terms and form prescribed by the Act. Here there were no such notices and the preclusive clause could not apply.

This was not, the court considered, a mere error in the manner or requirements of service; so far as the owners were concerned, there was no service on them at all. Since the notice was lacking 'an essential element', it was 'not such a notice as the statute required and thus a nullity'. The owners had lost their right of appeal as a result of failure in precise obligations laid on the planning authority and the authority ought not to be entitled, the court thought, to take advantage of their failure to comply with the legislation. While it is easy to appreciate the potential injustice to the owners which led the court to this decision, justice may have been bought at the price of certainty.

The decision in *McDaid* leaves considerable uncertainty as to the scope of section 85(10). The broader of the grounds of the court's decision can be read as implying that the preclusive clause is not to apply to an enforcement notice which is *ultra vires* because of a failure to satisfy the requirements of section 84. In that event an enforcement notice might be vulnerable to challenge years after it had purportedly taken effect. The decision in *McDaid* appears to run counter to the decision of the English Court of Appeal in *R* v. *Greenwich London Borough Council ex parte Patel* (1985) (see above).

In the context of section 85(10), it may be mentioned that in *Pirie* v. *Bauld* (1975), the Sheriff considered unsound the suggestion that the word 'proceedings' employed in the phrase 'any proceedings whatsoever' in section 85(10) was not intended to include criminal proceedings under section 86 of the 1972 Act. He declared that:

'... if the legislature had intended to exclude criminal proceedings from the provision of the subsection they would have said so clearly and would not have used the phrase "any proceedings whatsoever"'.

He considered that the matter was:

'... put beyond any possible doubt by section 85(11) which provides an exception to the preceding subsection in relation to criminal proceedings brought under section 86 against a particular class of offender.'

REQUIREMENTS OF ENFORCEMENT NOTICE

It may be that the Scottish courts will take a stricter view of enforcement notices than will the courts in England and Wales. One might, for example, contrast the decision in *Ormston* v. *Horsham Rural District Council* (1965) with that in *McNaughton* v. *Peter McIntyre (Clyde) Ltd* (1978). In *Ormston*, the Court of Appeal held that a notice which required the restoration of land to its condition before unauthorised development took place, but did not specify the land's condition prior to the development, was sufficiently certain. The owner knew what the site was like before he began the development and could therefore restore it accordingly. A similar decision was reached in *Bath City Council* v. *Secretary of State for the Environment* (1983).

However, it seems that a stricter test will apply in Scotland. In *McNaughton*, the High Court of Justiciary stated that 'a notice should be precise so that a person on whom a notice is served knows exactly what he should do'. The court held that a notice which required the removal of 'stone, rubble, timber and metal objects and other material on land namely the foreshore *ex adverso* the boatyard occupied by you ...' was bad for lack of specification. The land in question had been used since 1938 as part of the boatyard and quantities of stone and rubble had from time to time been deposited for the maintenance of slipways and the provision of an area of hardstanding, and for their protection against the sea. Against that physical background it was difficult to know what had to be removed. Furthermore, the court refused to accept that the notice could be saved by the state of knowledge of the recipients, saying that:

'... this suggestion fails to meet the criticism that the complaint [similar to an English summons] and the enforcement notice themselves should state clearly and in precise terms what is to be done and what should have been done in terms of the enforcement notice. Section 86 [of the 1972 Act] is a penal section which prescribes penalties for non-compliance with enforcement notices. Persons and companies, like the respondents, who are exposed to penal consequences are entitled to know, precisely and unambiguously, from the notice and complaint what they are required to do and why they are required to do it if they are to avoid penal consequences.'

(It appears to have escaped everyone's notice that a failure to comply with an enforcement notice relating to operations on land is not a criminal offence (above).)

The judgment in *McNaughton* makes no mention of the test propounded in *Miller-Mead* v. *Minister of Housing* (1963) — that an inaccuracy or misrecital will not of itself make an enforcement notice bad, provided that the notice tells the recipient fairly 'what he has done wrong and what he must do to remedy it'. But it would seem that *McNaughton* should be read as requiring a greater measure of formality in the way in which the prescribed matters are to be dealt with in Scotland.

STOP NOTICES

An enforcement notice does not take effect until any appeal against the notice has been finally determined or withdrawn (1972 Act, section 85(3)). As in the legislation for England and Wales, the Scottish legislation provides that where a planning authority have served an enforcement notice in respect of any land, they may at any time before the enforcement notice takes effect serve a stop notice for the purpose of prohibiting the carrying out or continuing of *any* activity which either is alleged in the enforcement notice to constitute or involve a breach of planning control, or is so closely associated therewith as to constitute substantially the same activity (1972 Act, section 87(1)). In England and Wales, where an activity has been carried on for 12 months or more it cannot generally be the subject of a stop notice. There is no such restriction in Scotland.

Although there is no right of appeal against a stop notice, there is nothing to prevent a person seeking judicial review of the planning authority's actions in deciding to serve a stop notice on the ground that the authority would be acting *ultra vires* or outside their powers. In *Central Regional Council* v. *Clackmannan District Council* (1983), the Court of Session refused to continue an interdict (equivalent to an injunction) preventing service of a stop notice on the ground that there was no allegation that the planning authority would be acting *ultra vires*. A similar decision was reached in *Earl Car Sales Ltd* v. *City of Edinburgh District Council* (1984). In that case, the only argument in support of the contention that the stop notice was *ultra vires* was a statement that the use of the land in question for the storage of cars was not an 'activity' in the sense of section 87(1) of the 1972 Act (above).

These decisions suggest that the approach adopted in *Marine Associates Ltd* v. *City of Aberdeen District Council* (1978), in which interim interdict against the enforcement of a stop notice was granted on the balance of convenience (loss of employment and interruption of business), was misconceived.

INTERDICT AND ENFORCEMENT

There is very considerable uncertainty about whether a planning authority may resort to a civil action for interdict (injunction) to supplement the statutory procedures and penalties available for the enforcement of planning control. The principal objection to the use of interdict in such cases was summarised by the Lord Chancellor in *Institute of Patent Agents* v. *Lockwood* (1894) in this way:

> 'The mode of procedure and the amount of the penalty are often regarded by the legislature as of the utmost importance where they are creating a new offence, and the law would, I believe, contrary to their intention, be most seriously modified if it were held that the party committing a breach of that which for the first time is made an offence were to subject himself by so doing to proceedings of this kind which might result in a committal to prison.'

The Scottish courts have therefore been reluctant to sanction resort to the common law process of interdict for the purpose of enforcing regulations where statute makes clear provision for penalties for a breach of control.

In *City of Dundee District Council* v. *Peddie* (1983), a planning authority sought to interdict the defenders from erecting a dwelling house because the required planning permission had not been obtained. The Sheriff held that the planning authority, as a statutory body exercising statutory powers, could only exercise their powers in accordance with the statute. The Sheriff said:

> 'The planning Acts provide their own system of enforcement and, in my judgment, the pursuers [the planning authority] are restricted to the use of that system. I was informed on behalf of the pursuers that there were certain difficulties in proceeding under the planning Acts but this reinforces the defenders' argument as it does not seem to me to be right to seek to avoid difficulties in the statutory procedure by resorting to a common law remedy.'

It should be said that in this case not only had the statutory procedures not been exhausted – they had not even been started.

On the other hand, in *Hamilton District Council* v. *Alexander Moffat & Son (Demolition) Ltd* (1984) the Sheriff was prepared to grant interim interdict to prevent demolition operations which were *ex facie* in breach of planning control. It is perhaps significant that the Sheriff found that there was no suitable alternative statutory procedure available to the planning authority and he therefore considered interdict appropriate.

REGISTER

Section 87A of the 1972 Act places a duty on all district and general planning authorities to maintain a register of wasteland, enforcement and stop notices served in relation to land in their district. Regulation 7 of the Town and Country Planning (Enforcement of Control) (Scotland) Regulations 1984 prescribes the information to be kept on this register. The prescribed information is to be placed on the register within nine days of the event to which it relates.

IMMUNITY FROM ENFORCEMENT ACTION

It has been considered desirable in certain circumstances to impose what might be described as 'limitation periods' on the power to take enforcement action. In Scotland an unauthorised material change of use other than a change to a single dwelling house is immune from enforcement action if the breach occurred before 1965 (1972 Act, section 85(1)(d)). In England and Wales the relevant date is 1964.

Northern Ireland

INTRODUCTION

Effective planning control was only introduced into Northern Ireland comparatively recently. British housing and planning legislation did not extend to Ireland and it was not until 1931 that the Northern Ireland Parliament first enacted a form of planning legislation (Planning and Housing Act (NI) 1931). This was only permissive, empowering authorities to prepare development control schemes. By the outbreak of war, none of the 40 odd planning authorities had prepared schemes. As part of the plans for post-war reconstruction, a Planning Commission and an Advisory Board were established in 1942. Two years later, the Planning (Interim Development) Act (NI) 1944 deemed that each planning authority had resolved to prepare a scheme under the 1931 Act and provided for a system of interim development control pending the adoption of such a scheme. Immediately after the war, the Northern Ireland government encouraged the preparation of Outline Advisory Plans and the Planning Commission itself produced some plans. Sir Robert Matthew, in his report, the *Belfast Regional Survey and Plan* (1962), which proved to be the turning point in the introduction of planning, observed (at para 882–3) that these plans, which lacked statutory force, were prepared with inadequate knowledge and were unrelated to any particular programmes of development. No attempt was made to relate them to an overall plan for the country as a whole and they were only intended as a framework within which development proposals could be judged, pending the completion of schemes.

In fact, no schemes were prepared. There seem to be two reasons for this failure. First, the authorities, with a couple of exceptions, were too small to afford the expertise necessary for the preparation of plans. Secondly, there were certain compensation difficulties.

Northern Ireland legislation was made under the Government of Ireland Act 1920, section 5, that contained a prohibition on the taking of property without compensation. Consequently, planning authorities were reluctant to impose restrictions that might result in the legislation being held to be unconstitutional, which would then place a considerable financial burden on the authority.

From a development control viewpoint, the system created by the 1944 Act was defective. There were two major flaws. There was no need for planning permission; neither the 1931 nor the 1944 Act had declared development without permission unlawful. The practical effect of this omission can be seen in the *Matthew Report*, which estimates that half the houses built in the post-war period were built without planning permission. The second problem related to the weakness of the enforcement powers. Section 4 of the 1944 Act did provide for certain enforcement action, but it was only exercisable if the authority was satisfied that it was 'necessary or expedient to do so having regard to the provisions then proposed to be included in the planning scheme'. As the authorities had little intention to make a scheme, this was a clear disincentive to action.

Matters began to improve in the post-Matthew period. The creation of a central planning authority was proposed, and a Ministry of Development was created in 1965. It began to produce some plans, called area plans, which were similar to the detailed 'old style' development plans which were used in Britain until the 1970s. The compensation problem having been solved by the repeal in the Northern Ireland Act 1962 of the constitutional limitation on the powers of the Northern Ireland Parliament, the Land Development Values (Compensation) Act (NI) 1965 transferred responsibility for the payment of compensation from the local planning authorities to the Ministry and gave the Ministry the power, on an application for compensation for refusal of planning permission, to reopen the planning decision. The Planning and Land Compensation Act (NI) 1971 extended enforcement powers by enabling a notice to be served if a planning authority considered it 'necessary or expedient to do so having regard ... to any ... material consideration'. Finally, in the Planning (NI) Order 1972, comprehensive planning legislation arrived at last, having been delayed by the political controversies connected with the reform of local government.

THE 1972 ORDER

The 1972 Order is an Order in Council made under the Northern Ireland (Temporary Provisions) Act 1972. As such Orders, by virtue of section 2(3), have the same validity and effect as an Act of the Northern Ireland Parliament, they are subject to the vires limitations in the 1920 Act. Later Orders in Council have been made under the Northern Ireland Act 1974 and are a form of delegated legislation. They are subject to the vires limitations in the Northern Ireland Constitution Act 1973, but unlike those in the 1920 Act the former do not contain any protection for property rights.

The 1972 Order is based on the English Town and Country Planning Act 1971. The former, however, is a greatly simplified version of the latter for, in Northern Ireland, planning control is centralised in a single planning authority, now the Department of the Environment. There is therefore no need for the many provisions in the 1971 Act setting out the relationship between local planning authorities and the Secretary of State for the Environment.

While the Department is the sole authority, its planning service has its own internal structure. A centrally based strategic planning team is responsible for the preparation of development plans.

Articles 3 to 10 of the 1972 Order and the Planning Development Plans Regulations (NI) 1973 govern the adoption of development plans. The regulations classify plans into area, local and subject plans. While there have been some local studies, the only plans that have been formally adopted are area plans which are similar to local plans under the 1971 Act. Some, but not all, of the non-statutory pre-1972 area plans were adopted as statutory plans after 1972 and there is now an area plan in force for nearly all of Northern Ireland. There is no statutory provision for a structure plan for Northern Ireland and the closest approximation to one is the *Regional Physical Development Strategy 1975–1995* published by the Department in 1977. As we have seen, it is prepared to abolish structure plans in England.

The planning service handles development control work through eight local offices, each of which determines applications for planning permission and undertakes enforcement action for an area which comprises that of three or four of the 26 district councils into which Northern Ireland is divided. The role of the district councils, in both the preparation of development plans and the determination of planning applications, is purely consultative. The service maintains a district development office in each district council area, to provide a channel for such consultation and to provide information to the public. A centrally based three-man planning directorate also exists, to which difficult or controversial development control decisions can be referred. It is a regular practice for cases where the local office and the district council disagree to be referred to the directorate.

Special provision had to be made for planning appeals and the 1972 Order created a Planning Appeals Commission. The Commission consists of a number of full-time and part-time members, appointed by the Secretary of State for Northern Ireland. Some members are chartered town planners; others have a general public administration background and three have legal qualifications. The Commission hears and decides appeals from the Department's determinations on planning applications and enforcement notices. On these matters the Commission's decision is final. It also conducts inquiries and makes recommendations relating to objections to development plans and representations relating to major planning applications and on hearings into a number of minor matters. On these matters the Commission reports to the Department, whose decision is final. In all cases the Commission appoints one of its members to conduct the appeal, inquiry or hearing, who then reports with a recommendation to the commission which collectively makes a decision or recommendation, as the case may be. Provision exists for the making of rules governing procedure, but it has not been exercised. In practice, procedure is modelled on the equivalent proceedings in Great Britain.

DEVELOPMENT CONTROL GENERALLY

The Order defined development in the same terms as the 1971 Act and introduced, for the first time, a requirement that permission be obtained for the carrying out of any development of land. As the 1972 Order came into operation on 1 October 1973, development without permission after that date became, for the first time, unlawful. Procedures for planning applications are similar to, although not exactly the same as, those in Great Britain. The Planning (Use

Classes) Order (NI) 1973 (amended in 1974) is similar to the Town and Country Planning (Use Classes) Order 1972. There has yet been no equivalent to the new use classes order made in 1987 and there is some doubt if an equivalent for Northern Ireland will be made. The Planning (General Development) Order (NI) 1973 (amended twice in 1981 and also amended in 1984 and 1985) on the other hand, differs significantly from the Town and Country Planning General Development Order 1988.

ENFORCEMENT POWERS

The Department's enforcement powers are contained in articles 42 to 51 of the 1972 Order and were broadly similar to the original provisions in English Law. The 'four-year rule' in the 1972 Order, requiring that an enforcement notice be served within four years of the breach of control was originally of general application, applying to all breaches. Also appeals from enforcement notices went originally to courts of summary jurisdiction. The Planning (Amendment) (NI) Order 1978 among other relatively minor amendments, brought Northern Ireland broadly into line with changes made in Great Britain in 1960 and 1968, by transferring appeals from the courts to the Planning Appeals Commission and limiting the scope of the four-year rule, as in Great Britain, to operational development and changes of use to use as a single dwelling house. The 1978 Order came into operation on 25 August 1978, thus making 25 August 1974 a crucial date for changes of use. An unpermitted change of use before that date is still immune from enforcement, while such a change after that date will always be liable to enforcement.

The enforcement provisions were extensively amended by the Planning (Amendment) (NI) Order 1982, which inserted into the 1972 Order new articles 42, 43, 43A, 43B, 49, 50, 50A, and 50B. These largely brought Northern Ireland into line with the changes made in Great Britain in 1981. In view of the close similarity of the legislation it is proposed just to indicate the correspondence between the Northern Ireland provisions and those for Great Britain, and then to draw attention to the differences between the two.

ENFORCEMENT NOTICES

The provisions in article 42 on issuing enforcement notices and their contents are the same as in section 87 of the 1971 Act, omitting the latter's power for the Secretary of State to make regulations requiring additional matters to be specified in the notice and the giving of information by way of an explanatory note. Article 42(4) adds to the four-year rule a qualification that where there is a failure to comply with a condition relating to mining operations, time runs from the date when the failure came to the knowledge of the Department; and in article 42(12) a court of summary jurisdiction is given a power to order an occupier of land to permit the owner to execute works required by an enforcement notice. This power also applies to action in respect of listed buildings and trees.

The grounds on which an appeal may be brought and the powers of the Commission (Art 43) are the same as in section 88 of the English Act, except that the 1972 Order omits the power in section 88B(1)(c) to determine the previous lawful use. The procedures, however, differ slightly in that all appeals must be advertised and the relevant district council consulted (Art 43 (4)(6).

The provisions relating to penalties for non-compliance with an enforcement notice (Art 44), the execution and cost of works required by an enforcement notice (Art 46), the effect of planning permission on an enforcement notice (Art 47) and the effect of an enforcement notice on subsequent development (Art 48), are the same. With regard to stop notices, the protection for dwellings only applies to the use of a building, caravan or other structure as a person's 'permanent residence' and there is no protection for activities begun more than 12 months prior to the notice (Art 45).

It is difficult to make any general observations about practice in Northern Ireland, as it is generally acknowledged that enforcement is the 'Cinderella' of the planning service. This can be seen from the fact that, in the six and a half years since the 1982 Order transferred appeals to the Planning Appeals Commission, only 30-odd such appeals have been digested by the Bulletin of Northern Ireland Law. In these, the Commission takes the view that it is improper for the Department to serve a notice merely to obtain the fee that would be payable on an application for planning permission, 5 (1984) BNIL 86 (EA2/1984). The Commission has quashed a notice alleging a material change of use where it should have stated that the breach was a material change by intensification of an existing use (1985) 7 BNIL 88 (EA 14/1983) and expressed the view that the same notice should not be used for both operational development and a material change of use (1984) 4 BNIL 114 (EA27/1983). These cases may show a stricter approach than is currently the case in England, and quashed a notice because of the unfairness of earlier administrative procedures (1985) 3 BNIL 139 (EA18/1984). On the other hand the Commission has declined to consider that a notice alleging breach of planning control involving renovation work to the ruins of a former dwelling and requiring that 'the work already carried out' be removed was a nullity (1988) 4BNIL 145 (EA9/1987) and upheld a notice alleging breach of an implied condition (1986) 7 BNIL 99 (EA12/1985). The Commission appears to take a generous approach to the period for compliance with a notice; the time for removal of vehicles from a site was extended from 28 days to 90 and the time for the relocation of an unauthorised motor sale and repair business was extended from 90 days to 6 months (1983) 8 BNIL 96 (EA12/1983) 7 BNIL (EA3 and 4/1983).

Finally, there are three possible gaps in the Northern Ireland legislation with regard to enforcement and stop notices.

First, there is no equivalent to section 23(9) in the English Act, which provides that there may be a reversion to the immediately preceding lawful use where an enforcement notice has been issued. This could create a serious problem, for if an earlier lawful use is held to be abandoned as a result of the occupier changing from that use to an unpermitted use, then in the event of an enforcement notice requiring the discontinuance of the unpermitted development, the occupier could find that strictly speaking he requires permission to resume the use.

LISTED BUILDING ENFORCEMENT NOTICES

The power to issue a listed building enforcement is the same as in Great Britain with the exception that under Art 49(3) such an enforcement notice cannot be issued in respect of a breach before 9 December 1978, being four years before the 1982 Order came into operation. There is then an additional ground for appeal relating to this exception, but there cannot in Northern Ireland be an appeal on the grounds that the building is not of special architectural or historic interest. The provisions relating to non-compliance with an enforcement notice, and for the execution and cost of works required by an enforcement notice, are extended to listed building enforcement notices. No provision is made for the effect of listed building consent on a listed building enforcement notice, nor for urgent works for the preservation of unoccupied buildings.

ENFORCEMENT OF DUTIES AS TO THE REPLACEMENT OF TREES

The position with regard to the enforcement of duties as to the replacement of trees is generally the same as in Great Britain, the only significant difference being that there is no limitation on the grounds of appeal (Art 50B). The provisions for penalties are also similar (Art 40).

ADVERTISEMENTS

The provision on the enforcement of advertisement control is the same as in Great Britain (Art 51).

WASTE LAND

There being no equivalent in the 1972 Order to the notice under section 65 of the 1971 Act (see below), there are no related enforcement provisions.

INJUNCTIONS IN AID OF ENFORCEMENT

There is no reason to suppose that the practice of the courts in Northern Ireland would differ from those in England. If anything, there will be fewer procedural problems as the planning authority is not a local authority but part of central government.

JUDICIAL REVIEW

The 1972 Order contains no equivalent of section 246 of the 1971 Act, which provides for an appeal to the High Court from the Secretary of State's decision in an enforcement appeal. Consequently, any legal proceedings after, or perhaps even before, appeal to the Planning Appeals Commission must be by way of an application for judicial review. In some respects, judicial review procedure is advantageous and, of course, avoids the confusing problem of procedural choice that exists in English Law. The courts have taken a fairly generous approach as to who is a person aggrieved for such applications.

For example, in *R (Bryson)* v. *Ministry of Development* (1967), a nearby landowner whose amenities were affected by proposed development was held to have sufficient locus standi for application for certiorari. In *R (Thallon)* v. *Department of the Environment* (1982) which was an application for judicial review by a leading member of the local community association, the Department did not even raise the issue of standing. Instead of a 28-day period for commencing actions, there is a three-month period for a judicial review application, and a judicial discretion to grant leave to apply after that time if no hardship will be caused. The Northern Ireland courts have taken a generous approach to applications out of time, particularly where a public body is the respondent. See, for example, *In re Hughes's application* (1986), where it was held that no hardship was caused by a prisoner challenging a governor's ajudications five years after the events. (See Hadfield, *Delay in applications for judicial review – a Northern Ireland perspective* (1988).)

On the other hand the need to obtain leave for an application acts as a filter which could stop the case at an early stage and the applicant will probably be deprived of the benefit of the recent English appeal court decision in *R* v *Kuxhaus* (see above) as an application for judicial review is unlikely to be regarded as part of the determination of an appeal by the Planning Appeals Commission. If that is the case, then the suspension of an enforcement notice during an appeal to the Commission will end with the Commission's decision.

Chapter 10

Enforcement in special cases – (I) Conservation

In this chapter and the next some special methods of enforcement which apply in cases where the ordinary development control machinery is thought either to be too weak or not applicable will be discussed. In some cases the development control machinery can be used in conjunction with the special controls.

The special controls are as follows:
 (i) buildings of special architectural or historic interest;
 (ii) trees;
 (iii) derelict land;
 (iv) 'hazardous substances';
 (v) advertisements.

Except in the case of derelict land, it is *automatically* an offence to carry out acts on land which fall within the special controls. Therefore unlike the case with development control, the ordinary citizen could enforce the law without resort to the local planning authority by bringing a private prosecution.

Because this book is about enforcement, the substantive law cannot be discussed in detail. However, the law will be described sufficiently to make sense of the enforcement machinery. This chapter will discuss conservation powers relating to buildings and trees. The following chapter will discuss amenity controls.

Listed buildings

The Secretary of State may place any building which he considers to be of 'special architectural or historic interest' on a list. Copies of the list must be available for public inspection and must be entered on the local land charges register against the land concerned (section 54). In practice the list is divided into grades of building, ranked according to age and importance. This has no direct legal significance but affects the way in which the discretionary powers are exercised.

For the purpose of the list, a building includes:

(a) any object or structure fixed to the building; and
(b) any object or structure within the curtilage of a building which, although not fixed to the building forms part of the land and has done so since before 1 July 1948 (section 54(9)).

The 'curtilage' of a building is the area of land occupied along with the building as a single unit. Thus outhouses, statues, etc., are subject to listing. To fall within this requirement the structure or object must be subordinate or incidental to a main building which is itself listed. In *Debenhams plc* v. *Westminster City Council* (1987), two buildings linked by a footbridge and a tunnel were used as a single commercial unit. One of the buildings was listed and the House of Lords held that the other was not entitled to be treated as part of the listed building but had to qualify for listing in its own right.

A building can be listed not only if it is intrinsically of architectural or historic value but also if 'its exterior contributes to the architectural or historic interest of any group of buildings of which it forms a part' (section 54(2)a). A building can also be listed on the basis of:

'...the desirability of preserving, on the ground of its architectural or historic interest, any feature of the building consisting of a man-made object or structure fixed to the building or forming part of the land and comprised within the curtilage of the building' (section 54(2)b).

The owner of a building, fearing that the building might be listed, might be tempted to demolish or alter it before it could be listed. The local planning authority is empowered by section 58 to serve a 'building preservation notice' on the owner and occupier of a building, stating that the building appears to them to be of special architectural or historic interest and that they have requested the Secretary of State to consider listing it (section 58). A notice has effect, for most purposes, as if the building were listed. It expires after six months, or if the building is actually listed.

If the Secretary of State notifies the authority that he does not propose to list the building, they in turn must notify the owner and occupier of this and cannot serve another notice in respect of the same building within 12 months (section 58(5)).

In urgent cases the authority can serve a building preservation notice by fixing it conspicuously on some object on the building (section 58(b)).

There are certain exemptions from listed building control (section 56(1)). These are as follows:

(a) An ecclesiastical building actually in use as such. This controversial exemption can be restricted or withdrawn by the Secretary of State in particular cases. In doing so he can discriminate between different religions or denominations or different areas as well as between types of building, parts of building or types of work (section 58AA). The exemption does not apply to complete demolition of any building because a building cannot be in actual use once demolition has started (*Attorney General* v. *Trustees of the Howard United Reform Church Bedford* (1976)). The exemption is not confined to Christian churches although it is arguable that to fall within the exemption a building must fulfil broadly the same function as a Christian church. A clergyman's residence is not included in the exemption (section 56(1)).

(b) An ancient monument scheduled as such under the Ancient Monuments and Archeological Areas Act 1979. This has its own system of control.

THE CONTROLS

The special régime applying to listed buildings can be summarised as follows:

(i) It is an offence to alter, extend or demolish a listed building in a way that affects its architectural or historic character without a special 'listed building consent' from the local planning authority or the Secretary of State.
(ii) Intentional damage to a listed building is an offence.
(iii) Notice of a proposal to demolish a listed building must be given to the Royal Commission on Historical Monuments (England) or to the equivalent body for Wales and Monmouth. Having

given notice, members of the Commissioners must be given reasonable access to the building for one month in order to record it, unless they state in writing that they do not intend to record (section 55(2)).
  (iv) A special 'listed building enforcement notice' can be issued.
  (v) There are special powers to enter the land and carry out repairs and of compulsory purchase.

Listed building control is more stringent than ordinary development control in five respects:
  (i) Development is not in itself an offence.
  (ii) Internal alterations are not normally subject to development control.
  (iii) Demolition as such is not development (see above).
  (iv) There can be imprisonment for a listed building offence (section 55(5)).
  (v) Listed building offences are strict liability offences and can therefore be committed in ignorance of the existence of the listing. This is because of the special social importance which Parliament places upon historic conservation. In *R* v. *Wells Street Magistrates Court* (1986), a firm called 'Amazing Grates' was engaged in removing fixtures and fittings from an unoccupied listed building in London. They acted under the owner's instructions apparently in order to prevent some valuable items from being stolen. They did not know that the building was listed, but it was held that this was irrelevant to the liability of individual members of the firm (but see below).

CRIMINAL LIABILITY

'Any person who executes or causes to be executed any works for the demolition of a listed building or for its alteration or extension in any matter which affects its character as a building of special architectural or historic interest' is guilty of an offence unless he has a special 'listed building consent' from the local planning authority (section 55(1)). This offence does not strike at the owner or occupier as such but they are subject to the listed building enforcement notice procedure and could therefore also be charged with failing to remedy the damage (below). As we have seen, the offence is one of strict liability. However, under section 55(6) it is a defence to show:

(a) that works to the building were urgently necessary in the interests of safety or health or for the preservation of the building; *and*
(b) that it was not practicable to secure safety or health or the preservation of the building by works of repair or works for securing temporary support or shelter; *and*
(c) that the works carried out were limited to the minimum measures immediately necessary; *and*
(d) that notice in writing justifying in detail the carrying out of the works was given to the local planning authority as soon as reasonably practicable.

It is also an offence to do or permit the doing of any act which causes or is likely to cause damage to a listed building unless the act has either planning permission or listed building consent.

Certain offences apply also to unlisted buildings in a conservation area. It is an offence to *demolish* such a building without a special conservation area consent from the local planning authority or the Secretary of State (section 277A). There are certain exemptions. They include:

(a) the ecclesiastical and ancient monument exemption which we mentioned earlier;
(b) certain small buildings (11.5 cubic metres or less);
(c) certain small gates, walls, fences or railings (less than 1 metre if abutting a road or public path, otherwise 2 metres);
(d) any building existing since 1 January 1914 and used or last used for agriculture or forestry;
(e) any part of a building last used for an industrial process up to 10% of cubic content or 500 square metres of floor space, whichever is greater;
(f) a building to be demolished under various statutory powers including an ordinary enforcement notice.

LISTED BUILDING ENFORCEMENT NOTICES **(section 96)**

A listed building enforcement notice can be issued and served upon the owner-occupier and anyone else with an interest in the land, thus requiring the damage to be put right and extending the range of criminal liability. An owner and occupier could thus be prosecuted for causing the original damage and again for failing to put it right in accordance with the notice. A listed building notice must, of course, relate only to the special architectural or historic features of the building and cannot do more than require restoration of the building to its state immediately before the offending works were committed. It cannot therefore be used to require improvement to be carried out (*Bath City Council* v. *Secretary of State* (1983)).

A notice can issue even where the whole building has been demolished provided that sufficient of its components remain to enable restoration to take place. A notice cannot require a replica to be constructed. The owner of the dismantled parts is the owner of the building provided that he owns sufficient of the parts to be reasonably so described. The matter is one of common sense. In *R* v. *Leominster District Council* (1988), a barn had been dismantled and its timber frame and roof tiles were sold to the applicant for export to the USA. It was held that a listed building enforcement notice could be directed to the applicants requiring them to return the components to the site and to restore the building as far as reasonably practicable. It was irrelevant that this might involve some incidental improvements.

The law relating to procedure, service, content and appeals is modelled on ordinary enforcement notice law. There are the following differences:

(a) There is no time limit for issuing a listed building enforcement notice. Thus the four year rule familiar in the case of ordinary operational development is irrelevant.
(b) There are two special grounds of appeal to the Secretary of State:
  (i) that the building is not of special architectural or historic interest; and
  (ii) that works to the building were urgently necessary in the interests of safety, etc. (see above).

Where the authority consider that it would not be reasonably practicable or desirable to require the building to be restored to its original state, the notice can require further work to be carried out which they consider necessary to alleviate the effect of the work which was carried out without consent (section 96(1)(b)(ii)).

This power cannot be used to require steps to be taken that are more burdensome than restoring the building to the state it was in at the date of listing. For example, in *Bath City Council* v. *Secretary of State* (1984) a listed building was roofed partly with natural slate and partly with asbestos tiles. The owners re-roofed the whole building with asbestos tiles. Mr Justice Woolf held that a listed building enforcement notice could not require the whole building to be roofed with natural tiles. However, the authority could require, for example, that gaps be plugged in a perimeter wall as an alternative to insisting that outbuildings be restored which previously formed part of the wall and which were demolished without consent.

The provisions for challenge, criminal liability (section 98) and for the local planning authority to enter the land and do the work itself (section 99) are similar to those for ordinary enforcement notices.

URGENT REPAIRS

Irrespective of any enforcement notice, the authority has power to enter the land to carry out works which are *urgently* necessary for preserving a listed building (section 101). This also applies to conservation areas designated by the Secretary of State. The cost is recoverable from the owner (section 101A). At least seven days' notice must be given to the owner detailing the work to be done (section 101(4)) and work cannot be done to parts of the building that are in use (section 101(3)). The work can include long term shoring up with scaffolding or supports.

The owner can make representations to the Secretary of State within 28 days on the ground that some or all of the work is unnecessary or that the cost is unreasonable or that its recovery would cause him hardship. The Secretary of State has a complete discretion in the matter (section 101A(5)).

COMPULSORY ACQUISITION

The Secretary of State can authorise a local authority compulsorily to acquire a listed building (other than the excepted kinds) if it appears to him that reasonable steps are not being taken for properly preserving it (section 114). He can also compulsorily acquire it himself, and in Greater London can authorise the Historic Buildings and Monuments Commission to acquire it. Any person with an interest in the building has 28 days after the start of the compulsory purchase process to apply to a magistrate to stop the proceedings. The only ground on which the magistrate can do so is that he is satisfied that reasonable steps have been taken for properly preserving the building (section 114(6)). There is a right of appeal to the Crown Court.

Before the Secretary of State takes the drastic step of compulsory purchase, the local planning authority or the Secretary of State must have served a 'repairs notice' on the owner of a building at least two months previously (section 115). This must specify the works they consider reasonably necessary for the proper preservation of the building and must explain the relevant law. The owner cannot evade his responsibilities by demolishing the building because the compulsory purchase order can be made anyway (section 115(2)).

The question of what works are reasonably necessary is one of fact. A broad view can be taken. For example, mending a hole in a roof to stave off future deterioration would count. The owner's means are not relevant (see *Rolf* v. *North Shropshire District Council* (1988)). The building's historic character is an important factor so that restoration work might be required. However, it is probably going too far to require items to be restored which had disappeared before the date of listing. The standard of presentation relates to the date of *listing* and not to the date on which the notice is served. However, the notice is not wholly invalid if some items are excessive (*Robbins* v. *Secretary of State* (1989)). The Secretary of State has a broad discretion which is subject to the usual legal requirements of fairness and reasonableness (see *Robbins* v. *Secretary of State* (1989)). There is a right of appeal to a magistrate's court (section 117).

The compulsory purchase order can be challenged in the courts within six weeks of the date it is made on legal grounds (Acquisition of Land Act 1981, section 23).

Compensation is payable for the compulsory purchase. Normally, any adverse effects on the value of the land caused by the listing are ignored for this purpose (section 116). However, if the building has been deliberately left derelict 'minimum compensation' can be paid. This means the value of the site on the assumption that it would get no permission for anything.

Once it has acquired the building, the authority need not undertake the work of repair itself but can dispose of the premises, for example to a private sector conservation organisation (section 126(1)).

These powers relating to disrepair must be considered before the local authority contemplates making a 'dangerous structures order' under other legislation (section 56C).

Trees

TREE PRESERVATION ORDERS

Trees are a prominent and much-loved feature of the British landscape. The felling or mutilation of trees is not development but can be brought within planning controls by means of a condition attached to a planning permission. Indeed, by virtue of section 59 local planning authorities must:

> '...ensure whenever it is appropriate that in granting planning permission for any development adequate provision is made, by the imposition of conditions for the preservation or planting of trees.'

There is also a special system of control over trees. A local planning authority can make a tree preservation order (TPO). This prohibits the mutilation or destruction of a tree or of a group of trees without the consent of the authority (section 60). Consent can be subject to conditions, for example requiring replanting or a management scheme. (See Town and Country Planning (Tree Preservation Order) Regulations 1969 SI 1969 No 17.) Individual trees or groups of trees can be designated by TPO. The regulations also permit an order to cover all trees within a designated area (Schedule 1). A TPO must be accompanied by a map or plan.

The Act does not define 'tree'. According to Lord Denning a tree, at least in woodland, must be 'something over seven or eight inches in diameter' (*Kent County Council* v. *Batchelor* (1977)). If this is correct, then coppices and also the thinning of saplings escape control. However, this approach was rejected in *Bullock* v. *Secretary of State* (1980) in favour of relying on the ordinary meaning of 'tree'. It seems to be accepted that a tree must have an identifiable main woody stem and must be relatively large or potentially so. Beyond that a court is unlikely to interfere with the local planning authority's opinion unless it is entirely unreasonable. The *Bullock* approach means that the cutting of saplings can be dealt with under a TPO by appropriate consents.

A tree preservation order does not become effective until it is confirmed by the local planning authority after publicity and opportunity to object. However, a provisional order can take effect immediately if it so provides. In such a case it becomes enforceable for up to six months pending confirmation (section 61).

There is no right of appeal against a TPO but there is a right of appeal to the Secretary of State against a refusal of consent or a condition (Regulations, Schedule 3). The validity of a TPO can be challenged in the High Court within six weeks of its confirmation (section 245(1)(3)).

Tree preservation order powers relate only to trees as 'amenity', that is, for 'pleasure, protection and shade' (*Barnet Borough Council v. Eastern Electricity Board* (1973)). They cannot therefore be exercised for economic or agricultural purposes. The Forestry Act 1967 provides separate controls over commercial operations and these are linked in various ways with the tree preservation system (below).

CRIMINAL PENALTIES

There are two main offences:
  (i) It is an offence to cut down, uproot or wilfully destroy a tree in contravention of a tree preservation order or to wilfully damage, top or lop it in such a way as to be likely to destroy it. The penalty on summary conviction is £2 000 or twice the value of the tree, whichever is the greater. There is also provision on indictment for an unlimited fine. In this case the court must take account of the profit which has accrued or appears likely to accrue to the accused as a result of the offence (section 110(1)).
  (ii) Other contraventions of a TPO are triable summarily, the maximum penalty being £1 000.

In both cases there is a penalty of £50 per day on summary conviction for a continuing offence after conviction.

Both offences are strict liability offences. Therefore the accused need not know of the existence of the TPO or of the absence of

Enforcement − conservation

consent. In *Maidstone Borough Council* v. *Mortimer* (1981), a contractor was convicted for felling a tree even though he was told by his employer that the local planning authority had given its consent. Furthermore, wilful destruction of a tree can be committed even though the tree may survive for several years. In *Barnet Borough Council* v. *Eastern Electricity Board* (1973), the Board was convicted because its workman severed the roots of a tree, sentencing the tree to a lingering death.

In any event, there is ample provision for people to be aware of the existence of a TPO. Thus:

(i) Certified copies of all TPOs, including a map, must be deposited for inspection 'at a place or places convenient to the locality and lodged with the Conservator of Forests and the District Valuer' (1969 Regulations, Reg 5).
(ii) A tree preservation order is registerable as a local land charge, thus giving all persons notice of it 'for all purposes connected with the land affected' (Law of Property Act 1925 section 198(1)); but see above.
(iii) The local planning authority must keep a public register of applications for consent made under tree preservation orders (1969 Regs, Schedule Art 2).

In certain cases, innocent behaviour is a defence. An accused may argue that his ignorance of the order was the local planning authority's fault, as in *Vale of Glamorgan Borough Council* v. *Palmer* (1984) − failure to place a copy on deposit. Nor is the landowner responsible if an intruder or an independent contractor acting without instructions commits the wrongful act (*Groveside Homes Ltd* v. *Elmbridge Borough Council* (1987)). An employer is, however, liable for the wrongs of his employee.

REPLANTING

(i) The authority can impose a condition of a TPO consent requiring the replacement of any tree by one or more trees on the site or in its immediate vicinity (1969 Regs, Schedule Art 4). Trees planted under this power are not automatically subject to the original TPO unless, of course, the TPO designates an area rather than individual trees.

(ii) Where consent is given for felling any part of a woodland, the authority must make replanting directions (1969 Regs, Schedule Art 6; see section 60(1)b). It can dispense with these only in three cases:
  (i) with the approval of the Secretary of State;
  (ii) where consent is given for the purpose of a planning permission;
  (iii) where the consent is given for the purpose of silviculture thinning.

(iii) By virtue of section 62, if a protected tree is removed, uprooted or destroyed then the current owner must replace it as soon as he reasonably can. Except in cases to which the TPO applies as part of a woodland, the same duty applies if the tree dies or if it is removed, uprooted or destroyed under the provision which allows dying, dead or dangerous trees to be removed (below). The LPA can dispense with these replanting requirements in the TPO.

In the case of a woodland, replanting need not be exact but the same number of trees must be replanted on or near the site or elsewhere, with the agreement of the authority. In all cases, the authority can designate the place of replanting. In *Bush* v. *Secretary of State* (1988), it was held that even in non-woodland areas, where the TPO designates a group of trees by reference to an area on a map, replanting can still be required even if the individual trees and their locations are not identifiable. Section 62 refers to 'the same place', but this can apparently mean the area designated by the order. The court took the view that section 62 contemplates negotiations between the landowner and the authority.

Unlike other replanted trees, trees planted under section 62 are automatically subject to the original TPO.

There is no right of appeal under section 62. There is a right of appeal to the Secretary of State against other replanting requirements because these form conditions of the TPO consent.

Another special feature of section 62 is that breach of its replanting requirements is not an offence. Enforcement takes the form only of a special tree preservation notice under section 103 (below). In other cases, breach of replanting requirements will be a breach of the TPO itself and will therefore be an offence.

REPLANTING NOTICES

A special variety of enforcement notice is provided by section 103 to deal with a failure to replace trees destroyed or removed contrary to a tree preservation order or contrary to section 62. This must be served on the owner of the land within four years and can specify the size and species of trees to be replanted. The duty imposed by section 62 can be enforced *only* by this means. In other cases, the authority may either serve a replanting notice or prosecute or both.

There is a right of appeal against a replanting notice to the Secretary of State (section 103(3)) and from him to the High Court (section 246(1A)). The grounds of appeal are:

(a) that the replanting duties do not apply or have been complied with;
(b) that the requirements of the notice are unreasonable in respect of the period or the size or species of trees specified;
(c) that the replanting is not required in the interests of amenity or would be contrary to good forestry;
(d) that the prescribed place for replanting is unsuitable.

The powers of the Secretary of State and the procedure are similar to those applying to ordinary enforcement notices.

There is no counterpart in tree preservation law to section 243(1) which, it will be recalled, prevents the grounds of appeal against ordinary enforcement notices and listed building enforcement notices from being raised in other proceedings. Ground (a) therefore seems to be available as a defence to a charge of failing to replant. The other grounds for appeal appear to be irrelevant to any prosecution.

There is no specific offence of disobedience to a replanting notice but the authority can enter the land and carry out the replanting itself in accordance with section 91, which has already been discussed (section 103(5); see above).

CONSERVATION AREAS

The various offences applicable to tree preservation orders apply to trees in conservation areas which are not subject to tree preservation orders (section 61A). There are various exceptions to this. These are similar to the exemptions in tree preservation notice cases. However, they also include the cutting down, uprooting, topping or lopping of trees to encourage the growth of other trees. In the case of cutting down or uprooting, the diameter of the tree must not exceed 1000 millimetres. In other cases the diameter must not exceed 75 millimetres (See Town and Country Planning (Tree Preservation Order) (Amendment), etc. Regulations 1975 (No 148).)

If advance notice of intention to do the act in question was served on the local authority, it is a defence to prove either that the accused had consent from the authority or that the act was done after the expiry of six weeks but before two years from the date of the notice (section 61A(3)). This gives the authority a chance to make a TPO.

There is a public register of notices and consents (section 61A(7)).

COMPENSATION

As a general principle, there is no compensation for planning restrictions. However, the tree preservation regulations do provide for compensation in certain cases where consent is refused or granted subject to conditions (section 174). The right to compensation is not limited to direct loss, e.g. the value of the tree, but includes the 'opportunity costs', i.e. the loss to the landowner of lucrative alternative uses that could have been carried out. The amount is fixed by the Land Tribunal based upon the value of the land at the date of the decision to refuse consent or to impose a condition. It is a question of fact for the tribunal as to what alternative uses are compensatable (see *Bell* v. *Canterbury City Council* (1986)). This very generous measure of compensation has caused considerable doubt about the effectiveness of TPOs in woodland areas.

However, no compensation is payable where the local planning authority certifies that the trees concerned are of outstanding or special amenity value. This applies to woodland and non-woodland trees. (Town and Country Planning (Tree Preservation Order) (Amendment) Regulations 1988 SI No 963.) There is a right of appeal to the Secretary of State.

RELATIONSHIP WITH FORESTRY COMMISSION POWERS

Under the Forestry Act 1967, the Forestry Commission has a range of powers relating to commercial forestry activities. They include the award of grants, the approval of various management schemes and plans, and the making of forestry dedication covenants. These powers include amenity considerations. There is therefore some overlap with TPO law but arrangements have been made to minimise conflict.

In general terms, tree preservation orders can be made over land subject to Forestry Commission grants or loans or forestry dedication covenants only with the consent of the Commission (section 60(7)), and in any event cannot prohibit work carried out in accordance with Forestry Commission schemes (section 60(8) 1969 Regs, Second Schedule Art 1). Except in Inner London, a Forestry Commission licence is usually required to fell a tree in addition to any TPO consent (section 60(10); Forestry Act 1967, section 9).

Where the purpose of the felling does not affect the status of a woodland, the Forestry Commission in practice refers applications for felling consent to the local planning authority. The matter will therefore be decided on amenity grounds and replanting can be required. However, where the purpose of a woodland felling is to convert the land to agriculture or where the owner does not intend to use it as woodland, the Commission decides the application itself. If it proposes to refuse consent, the amount of compensation payable under forestry legislation is less than is the case under TPO law (above). If it proposes to give consent and the local planning authority object, the application is referred to the Secretary of State who decides according to TPO law.

EXEMPTIONS

In various special cases, the 1969 Regulations allow a TPO to be disregarded (Art 3). Not surprisingly, these include the activities of many public bodies and public utilities such as British Telecom, the Ministry of Defence, gas and water undertakings. However, these public bodies must usually have shown that injuring or removing the tree is necessary for the performance of their official functions.

Private individuals also have certain exemptions:

(i) trees which are dangerous, dead or dying (section 60);
(ii) cultivated fruit trees in an orchard or garden (1969 Regs Art 3);
(iii) acts 'immediately required' for the purpose of implementing a planning permission (1969 Regs, Schedule 2, para 2(c)).

Trees can also be mutilated or removed to comply with any statutory obligations or to prevent or reduce a nuisance (section 60(6)). This would include various kinds of obstruction, including obstruction of the highway and also interference with rights of way or rights of light.

It can be noticed in passing that English law does not recognise any private right to a pleasant view nor any automatic right to light. Rights to light can be granted expressly or arise by long use. Apart from that, there is no obligation to cut down trees which interfere with the amenities of neighbours. At common law, a neighbour has a right to lop off branches that overhang his land, a right which is of course taken away by a TPO.

ENFORCEMENT PROBLEMS

Except where Forestry Commission schemes are involved, tree preservation law is relatively straightforward. The courts have made the main offences strict liability offences and have in other ways eased the path of enforcement officers, for example by permitting replanting directions even where the precise site cannot be identified (see above). Nevertheless, there have been few reported breaches of tree preservation law (e.g. 59 in 1986). The liability to pay compensation may, however, be a deterrent to the use of tree preservation powers and tree preservation may have become a victim of recent local government spending cuts. There are certainly difficulties of proof which mean that careful monitoring may be required to secure a conviction. For example, evidence from neighbours that the particular tree was in fact within the designated site may not be enough to secure a conviction without a careful plan and photographic evidence.

As with planning control, local planning authorities have been advised to exercise their TPO powers flexibly, and in particular to avoid exercising controls over woodlands which might encourage owners to let them run wild. Forestry Commission grants and schemes may be more appropriate as general tools of control, leaving TPOs as a last resort (see Circular 36/78).

The government is currently undertaking a general review of tree preservation law.

Chapter 11

Enforcement in special cases – (II) Amenity and safety

Derelict land

'If it appears to the local planning authority that the amenity of part of their area or of an adjoining area is adversely affected by the condition of land in their area they may serve on the owner and occupier a notice under this section' (section 65(1)).

This is a useful power which complements ordinary planning controls by dealing with problems which arise from neglect rather than development. It can also be used to *supplement* ordinary controls where acts of unlawful development have affected amenity, and as an additional remedy to preserve historic or amenity buildings, even unlisted ones. In the case of listed buildings, it will be recalled that only *urgent* repairs can be required unless the authority compulsorily acquires the building (see above). 'Amenity' is wide enough to embrace all aspects of land use which give people enjoyment or convenience so that physical danger is irrelevant. The predecessors of section 65 applied only to open spaces but now any land can be the subject of a section 65 notice. A local authority can also resolve to apply the section to an internal waterway which is not used for commercial or cruising purposes (Transport Act 1968, section 108).

A section 65 notice operates in the same way as an ordinary enforcement notice. It requires specified steps to be taken to put matters right and is backed by criminal penalties and a power to enter the land to carry out the work (section 107). The offence is summary, with a maximum penalty of £1 000 (section 104).

The accused has a similar right to have successor owners and occupiers brought before the court as applies to the owner in ordinary enforcement cases (section 104(3)(4)). If the land is currently unoccupied, the previous owner can have the current owner brought before the court (section 104(5)).

There are provisions for a further prosecution if, following conviction, the accused fails to do all he can to put matters right (section 104(7)).

There is a right of appeal against a section 65 notice to a magistrates court (section 105). This can be exercised by a person served with a notice and by any other person with an interest in the land. There are four grounds of appeal:

(a) That there is no adverse effect on amenity.
(b) The condition of the land is the ordinary result of development which is not a breach of planning control. Thus section 65 primarily concerns neglect but could also be used in cases of unlawful development. There is no time limit for serving a section 65 notice so that operations which are outside the reach of ordinary enforcement notices could be pursued under section 65.
(d) (sic) That the requirements of the notice exceed what is necessary. Section 65 cannot be used to prevent future injury to amenity, and its requirements must be the minimum required to safeguard local amenity.
(e) (sic) That the time for compliance is too short.

The notice procedure has its drawbacks. The main one is that it is modelled on the ordinary enforcement notice procedure as it was before 1981. The law relating to ordinary enforcement notices has subsequently been reformed, but section 65 retains the original drafting with all its problems. In particular, a section 65 notice must take effect after a period of not less than 28 days after it has been served. It is the notice itself that is served, whereas in the case of an ordinary enforcement notice the Act distinguishes between *issuing* the notice and serving copies of it (see above). In the case of a section 65 notice, it seems that all recipients must be served simultaneously because exactly the same 28 day period must apply in all cases. This may cause practical problems.

Defective service is not a ground of appeal and could therefore be raised as a defence to prosecution.

Furthermore, the magistrates' powers on appeal are narrower than those available to the Secretary of State in ordinary enforcement notice cases. They cannot disregard defects in service and can only correct informality, defects or errors in the notice if they are not 'material' (section 105(4)). They can vary the notice only in favour of the appellant (section 105(5)). However, pre-1981 enforcement notice cases suggest that a defect is 'material' if it cannot be corrected without injustice (see *Miller-Mead* v. *Minister of Housing* (1963)).

Finally, some of the appeal grounds can also be raised elsewhere. Grounds (a) and (b) can be raised only by way of appeal to the magistrates (section 243(3)), but grounds (d) and (e) are not restricted. A person who was not served with a notice and who previously held an interest in the land is not restricted by section 243(3) at all if he did not appeal to the justices. Unlike the case with ordinary enforcement notices, it is irrelevant whether he was aware of the notice or whether he was prejudiced by the failure to serve him.

Hazardous substances

A special system of control over 'hazardous substances' was introduced by the Housing and Planning Act 1986 and is currently to be found in sections 58B to 58M of the 1971 Act. Ordinary planning controls can sometimes deal with problems related to dangerous materials, but the special hazardous substance controls apply whether or not development has taken place, for example if a dangerous chemical is used in connection with an existing process.

Hazardous substance control does not apply to materials in transit unless they are unloaded (section 58B(2)) but otherwise comes into play whenever a hazardous substance is present on land unless there is less than 'the controlled quantity'.

Controls take the familiar form of consents backed by criminal sanctions and enforcement notices. In this case, consent is given by 'the hazardous substance authority' who, as usual, is the local planning authority (section 1A). In cases to be specified by regulations, the Health and Safety Executive must be consulted. In the case of the operational land of statutory undertakers, the hazardous substance authority is the central government (section 1A). Statutory undertakers are an important source of potential danger from hazardous substances. They include bodies carrying out public transport functions and also suppliers of electricity, gas, hydraulic power and water (section 290(1)). A statutory undertaker can therefore be a public or a private body.

A hazardous substance consent operates in the same way as a

planning permission and there are similar arrangements for appeals and public registration. As with a planning permission, a hazardous substance consent does not give immunity against other kinds of legal liability, e.g. for common law nuisance or negligence or under the Health and Safety at Work Act 1974.

A hazardous substance consent is stricter than a planning permission in two main respects. Firstly, it is automatically revoked if there is a change in the identity of the person controlling the land, unless a previous application was made to continue it (section 58J(2)).

Secondly, there is automatic criminal liability if a hazardous substance equal to or in excess of the controlled amount is or has been present on the land, either without consent or in breach of a consent (section 58K).

Liability falls on a person who knowingly causes the substance to be present or a person who allows it to be present or the person in control of the land. In the last two cases, knowledge as such is irrelevant. The penalties are similar to those for ordinary breaches of planning control and offences are summary or indictable.

However, unlike ordinary enforcement offences it is a defence to prove that reasonable care was taken to avoid commission of the offence (section 58K(5)). It is also a defence to show that the accused was unaware of the presence of the offending substance or breach of condition (section 58K(6)(7)).

There is also provision for enforcement notices to be issued, in this case known as 'hazardous substance contravention notices' (section 101B). The law is modelled on ordinary enforcement notice law except that there is no time limit for issuing a hazardous substance notice. Criminal liability can be imposed for disobeying a notice. The authority may also be given the same power to enter the land and put matters right themselves that applies to ordinary enforcement notices (section 101B(10)).

Hazardous substance control is therefore an attempt to focus upon a specific and serious environmental problem. However, the system is not particularly strict. It also has the fundamental flaw that it can be activated only by regulations made by central government. All the key concepts and powers, including the definition of 'hazardous substance', the controlled amounts and the effect of an enforcement notice, have been left to be filled in by the regulations. The Act itself gives no hint as to what a hazardous substance is and the government is left with a virtual free hand. Nothing has so far been brought into effect. When and if the system is activated, transitional provisions contained in section 34 of the Housing and Planning Act 1986 mean that consent must be given for any substance present within the 12 months before the system is activated (Housing and Planning Act 1986, section 34). This is subject to conditions intended to preserve the status quo (ibid, section 36(9)).

Apart from this, the system will operate to outlaw existing hazardous substances as well as future activities. There is a six months transitional period of immunity which takes effect once the system is activated. Immunity and consent under the transitional arrangements also depend upon proper notification being given if required under the Notification of Installations Handling Hazardous Substance Regulations 1986 (ibid, section 34(10)). The Act also empowers the Secretary of State to make transitional arrangements (section 58B(5)). These include what appears to be a meaningless power to apply section 23 of the Housing and Planning Act 1986. Since section 23 concerns the sale of leasehold houses, section 34 was presumably the reference intended. As it is, the Secretary of State cannot modify the transitional arrangements contained in section 34.

Advertisements

In the USA, the regulation of advertisements raises major constitutional issues concerned with freedom of speech. In the UK, where we have no legal guarantee of freedom of speech, or indeed of any other civil liberties, advertisements are dealt with almost entirely by delegated legislation made by ministers. Section 63 of the Act permits the Secretary of State to make regulations 'for restricting or regulating the display of advertisements so far as appears [to him] to be expedient in the interests of amenity or public safety'.

The current regulations are the Town and Country Planning (Control of Advertisement) Regulations 1989 (SI 1989 No 670). They are concerned only with amenity and public safety (Reg 4) including historic and architectural conservation. It is automatically an offence to violate the regulations, and if the offending activity is also a breach of general planning control the appropriate enforcement machinery can also be used. Conversely, an advertisement which satisfies the regulations is deemed to have planning permission (section 64).

We must make the following distinctions:

(i) Advertisements which may not constitute development at all under the general law, for example balloons and advertisements placed on trees. Here the criminal offences created by the regulations are the only sanctions.
(ii) Advertisements which are *in themselves* development, e.g. where the advertisement is part of the structure of a building or is a material change of use (see below). Here, ordinary enforcement powers can be used to back up the special advertisement controls. However, compliance with the advertisement regulations operates as a 'deemed' grant of planning permission (section 64).
(iii) Cases where development takes place separately from the advertisement itself. Here, compliance with the regulations does not confer planning permission and a separate planning permission is required for the development. Ordinary enforcement powers are therefore available irrespective of the regulations. Examples are advertisements fixed to a structure such as a blind or canopy, or displayed from a machine fixed to the land. The structure or machine could constitute development in their own right. This will be discussed later.

A local planning authority can regulate the *content* of an advertisement only if *required* in the interests of amenity or public safety (Reg 4(3)). It can also regulate matters of size, appearance, position and fixing (section 63(2)). This has implications for civil liberties. Thus advertisements which might offend, distract or lead to violence could be banned. Public order is a familiar argument in freedom of speech disputes and usually prevails over freedom of speech values in the courts. Thus advertisements which are politically controversial or blatantly sexy could be at risk.

THE SCOPE OF THE REGULATIONS

The advertisement regulations require consent from the local planning authority for the display of advertisements (Reg 5). They give considerable flexibility. Special areas can be designated where controls may be stricter or more relaxed (section 63(3)). These include conservation areas, 'experimental areas' where particular kinds of advertisement can be tried out, 'areas of special control' within rural areas and other areas of high amenity value, national parks and 'areas of outstanding national beauty' (section 83(3)).

Some kinds of advertisement are exempt from control (Reg 3). These include, subject to various conditions and restrictions (Schedules 1 and 2):

(i) advertisements in enclosed private land;
(ii) most advertisements within a building;
(iii) advertisements on vehicles unless primarily used for displaying advertisements;
(iv) advertisements on balloons not more than 60 metres above ground;
(v) advertisements which are part of the fabric of a building;
(vi) advertisements on packages, containers, or dispensers relating to articles for sale;
(vii) election notices;
(viii) traffic signs;
(ix) national flags;
(x) statutory notices.

The regulations create two kinds of consent to the display of advertisements:

(i) There is automatic (deemed) consent in a wide range of cases (Reg 6; Schedule 3).
(ii) Express consent (Reg 9). This can be conditional and is subject to a regime similar to that applying to planning permissions. There are 'standard conditions' (Schedule 1) which apply in all cases. (See Reg 3 (2); Reg 6 (1) and Reg 13 (1).)

The Secretary of State can exclude the benefit of the deemed consents upon representations made by the local planning authority (Reg 7). This power is exercised as a last resort in cases where deemed consents have been abused and where there is serious environmental harm as a result. The local planning authority can order the discontinuance of an advertisement which has deemed consent subject to an appeal to the Secretary of State. It must be satisfied that there is a substantial injury to amenity or a public danger (Reg 8).

The notion of 'substantial' arises in other contexts under the regulations and gives rise to considerable uncertainty. For example, a site being used for the display of an advertisement on 1 April 1974 can continue to be so used, subject to a condition that it is not used to an extent that is 'substantially' different from the extent or manner of use on that day. It has been held, for example, that replacing a printed advertisement on a wall by a hoarding of similar shape and size is not 'substantial' (*Mills & Allen Ltd* v. *City of Glasgow District Council* (1980)).

On the other hand, in another and unrelated context the House of Lords has held that 'substantial' means only 'not trivial' (*Attorney General* v. *English* (1982)).

A discontinuance order cannot take effect until two months after its service.

A discontinuance order cannot be made in respect of election notices and statutory advertisements.

ENFORCEMENT OF THE REGULATIONS

The Act empowers the Secretary of State to make regulations enabling offending advertisements to be removed and applying the ordinary enforcement notice law to breaches of the regulations. So far no such regulations have been made. This is another reason why we should distinguish between breaches of the regulations as such and cases where development is also involved (above).

Under section 109A, district councils or London Borough Councils may remove or obliterate placards or posters in certain cases. This applies only to 'fly posters', i.e. placards or posters displayed in public places. The authority must give at least two days notice in writing to the person responsible for the offending advertisement, unless the placard or poster does not give his address and the authority are unable to ascertain it after reasonable inquiry.

CRIMINAL PENALTIES

In other cases, the only sanction for breach of the advertisement regulations as such is criminal prosecution under section 109. It is an offence to display an advertisement in contravention of the regulations. The offence is only a summary one. It carries a fine of up to £400 and a penalty of £40 per day for continuing the offence after conviction. If the offence ceases and is resumed, there must be a fresh prosecution.

The owner or occupier of the land is deemed to display any advertisement placed on his land. So is any person to whose 'goods, trade, business or other concerns' the advertisement gives publicity. However, these persons have a defence if they can show that the advertisement was displayed without their knowledge or consent (section 109(3)).

Apart from this, the offence seems to be one of strict liability. However, the House of Lords has construed section 109 generously in favour of the accused, thus enabling him to exploit ambiguities in the law. In *Porter* v. *Honey* (1988), their Lordships rested their decision squarely on the interests of justice to the individual. Two estate agents' boards had been placed on the premises in breach of the regulations which stipulate one board only. The issue was whether the estate agent who displayed the original board was guilty of an offence, if another agent later displayed a board on the same premises.

It was held that provided that the first board was erected with deemed consent under the regulations, it could continue to enjoy that consent even after the erection of a second board. The person responsible for the second board could, of course, be convicted. The 1989 regulations have confirmed this. They provide that, where more than one such advertisement is displayed, the first to be displayed shall be deemed to be the one permitted (Schedule 3, class 3 A (b). Nevertheless, in this and in other contexts it may be difficult to obtain evidence proving a breach of the advertisement regulations.

The enforcement of the advertisement regulations may therefore be weak and complicated. There is no emergency procedure corresponding to ordinary stop notices. The regulations are very detailed and technical, and numerous informations may have to be laid relating to repeated offences. The penalties are low and there is the normal six months time limit for prosecuting a summary offence. This runs from the date the advertisement was first displayed (*Hertsmere Borough Council* v. *Alan Dunn Building Contractors Ltd* (1986)). On the other hand, the mechanics of prosecution are relatively simple because no prior enforcement notice procedure is needed. A witness statement, a photograph and proof of absence of consent forms the basis of the case.

ENFORCEMENT NOTICES

If a display of advertisements complies with the advertisement regulations, planning permission is deemed to be granted (section 64). This does not affect listed building control (see above), so that a listed building enforcement notice can be served even where an advertisement complies with the regulations.

In the case of advertisements which violate the regulations, if development is also involved then the local authority has two sets of sanctions: firstly, the criminal penalties attached to the regulations; and secondly, the ordinary enforcement notice machinery. There is also the advantage of 'stop notice' procedure. Moreover, the local planning authority may be able to enter the land under section 91 and remove the advertisement. There are more generous time limits for service of an enforcement notice compared with the six months permitted for a prosecution under the regulations.

Four cases should be distinguished:

(i) Where the placing of the advertisement is in itself a building operation and therefore development. It will be recalled that the definition of building is very wide and includes structures such as walls, fences, flagpoles and masts. A balloon tethered to the land is probably not a building and will therefore be caught only by the advertisement regulations. In *Wadham Stringer* v. *Fareham Borough Council* (1987), a balloon was tethered to a vehicle on the site which was a garage. It was held to be attached to the site for the purpose of the advertisement regulations but it does not follow that this would suffice for development. Attachment to a mobile vehicle would certainly not qualify as development and it is unlikely that a balloon, even if tethered to the land itself, is sufficiently permanent to count as a building operation (see above).

Painting an advertisement on a building probably counts as a building operation, but not displaying an advertisement by means of a projection of light (see above). Fixing posters or placards to a wall are probably not building operation because there is no structural alteration. In this context the use of the building is irrelevant (see *Cooper* v. *Bailey* (1956) — advertisements on the walls and forecourt of a garage).

(ii) Where the display of the advertisement involves a material change of use. The use of any external part of a building for the display of advertisements is a material change of use provided that the particular site is not normally used for that purpose (section 22(5)). The display of an advertisement may also be a material change of use on general principle. This applies where the advertisement relates to activities on some other piece of land. An advertisement relating exclusively to a business carried out on the same site will probably be regarded as an ancillary use (see above).

The authority cannot enter the land under section 91 solely to discontinue a use. For this reason, it may be desirable to establish that operational development is also involved. However, the authority can require physical objects to be removed from the site even if the result of doing so is to make it impossible for a use to continue. Suppose, for example, there was an unlawful change of use to use as for retail trading. The authority could not ensure that the use itself ceased but could, under section 91, require any other steps specified in the enforcement notice to be taken, including the removal of all advertisements. This could even apply where the placing of the advertisement in itself constitutes a material change of use since it could be argued that the physical object which constitutes the advertisement is distinct from the use itself, even if the net result is to make it impossible to carry out the use (see *Midlothian District Council* v. *Stevenson* (1986) — change of use to caravan site — authority entitled to remove vans). On the same principle, a stop notice (see below) could also be issued.

(iii) Where the advertisement is separate from its fixings and the fixings constitute development in their own right. This could apply where an advertisement is attached to a blind or canopy, or perhaps to a flagpole or electronic machine. Assuming that the fixing is development, then whether or not the regulations are complied with a separate planning permission is needed for the fixings. As we shall see, this does not apply to 'hoardings' or similar structures because these have been made part of the definition of the advertisement itself (see below).

(iv) Cases where no development is involved at all. Here criminal penalties are the only sanctions. Examples include advertisements fixed to trees or balloons, mobile display apparatus, holograph images, and advertisements fixed to parts of buildings which are normally used for that purpose.

THE DEFINITION OF ADVERTISEMENT

We have left this question until last because its importance cannot be appreciated without a general acquaintance with advertisement control and its problems.

Section 290(1) defines advertisement very widely to mean

> '...any word letter model sign placard brand notice device or representation whether illuminated or not, in the nature of and employed wholly or partly for the purpose of advertisement, announcement or direction and...includes any hoarding or similar structure used, or adopted for use for the display of advertisements.'

This definition is not confined to commercial advertising and includes such information as the identity of the occupier, or even a house name or number. It also includes political or religious notices. Most of these non-commercial advertisements have deemed consent under the regulations.

The definition has two aspects. Firstly, it includes any kind of visual message including structures such as placards and notices which cannot sensibly be distinguished from the message itself. It includes other structures to which the message is attached only in the case of a hoarding or 'similar' structure.

It is not clear how liberally a court might be prepared to treat such objects as blinds or canopies as similar to a hoarding. The Secretary of State has treated them as similar but with questionable reasoning since the advertisement and its fixings are distinct. Unlike hoardings, blinds and canopies serve independent purposes of their own (see *Millichip* (1988)). As we have seen, this issue is important in relation to enforcement. If the canopy is not part of the advertisement, then even if the advertisement has consent under the regulations a separate planning permission is needed for the canopy. In dealing with this the local planning authority is not limited to the advertisement

Enforcement – amenity and safety

considerations of amenity and public safety. It is unclear whether blinds or canopies can be regarded as analogous to hoardings for this purpose. Perhaps the best approach is to treat them as separate unless they exist primarily for the purpose of displaying the advertisement (see *Young* (1989)).

The regulations provide a definition of advertisement which differs slightly from that in the Act itself (Reg 2(1)). This definition is irrelevant for the purpose of deciding whether an advertisement constitutes development under the general law but governs the scope of the regulations themselves.

The definition in the regulations excludes memorials and railway signals. These are therefore exempt from advertisement control. However, it includes, in addition to 'hoardings and similar structures', 'any balloon used or adopted for use for the display of advertisements'. It is doubtful whether the regulations can lawfully extend the statutory definition to this extent although in the case of a balloon, which is unlikely to have any other purpose, it makes sense to treat the balloon as part of the advertisement itself.

Chapter 12

Reforms?

The enforcement system is complex and lends itself readily to delays and evasions. It is informal at the early stages, and although this has advantages, for example in creating opportunities for negotiation and compromise, it has the disadvantage that there is little provision for monitoring and investigating problems.

As is so often the case in Britain, a large element of the problem lies in lack of available resources. For example, there are very few specialised enforcement officers operating at local level. At appeal level about 4000 enforcement appeals are received each year, of which about 3000 are actually dealt with at an inquiry. About 45 to 50 Inspectors are allocated to enforcement appeals.

In earlier chapters, attention was drawn to some weaknesses in the present law. The government is currently reviewing the legal aspects of the enforcement process. For this purpose, Mr Robert Carnwath QC reported to the Secretary of State early in 1989 following consultation with persons with practical experience of the enforcement system. Key aspects of his inquiry included:

(i) The possibility of formal procedural arrangements before issue of an enforcement notice, including increased powers to obtain information.
(ii) Reducing the present immunities from enforcement action.
(iii) Restricting the right of appeal and perhaps introducing a requirement of leave to appeal to the High Court.
(iv) Reducing the levels of compensation in stop notice cases.

His report was published in April 1989 by the DoE as a consultation document. It includes the following recommendations, all of which are useful technical and practical measures designed to strengthen enforcement powers. No radical change in the structure of the system is envisaged. The following are the main recommendations:

Reforms?

(1) A general power to enter land at all reasonable hours for the purpose of the authority's enforcement functions. At present, entry can be made only where it is already proposed to issue an enforcement notice and 24 hours' notice must be given (see above).

(2) A new power – *contravention notice* – to obtain information and secure compliance by negotiation. Again, the present power is more limited and applies only for the purpose of seving an enforcement notice (see above).

(3) The immunity from enforcement action be confined to 10 years, and the four-year rule no longer apply to breaches of condition relating to operational development. Immunity should result in an automatic 'deemed' planning permission, thus removing the awkward 'established use' notion.

(4) The drafting and serving of enforcement notices should be made less technical and the Secretary of State's power to correct or vary notices on appeal should be widened. In fact, the courts may have already achieved this (see above).

(5) Appeals to the High Court under section 246 should require leave to apply and the court should be able to give directions as to the operation of the notice.

(6) The 'section 53' procedure and the established use certificate procedure should be considered in a single application.

(7) There should be a summary procedure for enforcement of breaches of condition.

(8) There should be no stop notice compensation in respect of any development in breach of planning control.

(9) The time for serving stop notices should be extended.

(10) There should be a broader statutory power for an authority to apply for an injunction.

(11) The power to enter the land and take steps to remedy the breach (section 91) should be extended to any of the steps required by the enforcement notice.

(12) The penalties should be increased and the range of possible defendants widened.

A frequent suggestion for reform is to make development without planning permission an offence in itself, just as is the case now with breach of listed building, tree preservation and advertisement control. This has obvious advantages and would allow private individuals to reinforce the local authority by instituting private prosecutions. It would also lessen delays. However, in my view the disadvantages of this proposal far outweigh its advantages. In particular, the discretionary nature of enforcement is worth preserving and this requires the local planning authority to play a dominant role. For example the question as to whether development has taken place is often a matter of balancing complex factual and planning issues and is quite unsuitable for a criminal court. Hence the existing law channels this kind of issue to the local planning authority and the Secretary of State.

Also, permitting private individuals to launch prosecutions makes nonsense of any coherent planning policy. Enforcement could depend upon random short-term factors such as private resources and vested interests. If English law had a concept of group or collective rights, exercisable for example by a local community, this risk would be less serious. Under the present law there is the possibility of requesting the Attorney General to intervene. This procedure is a sufficient outlet for the public spirited vigilante who obtains no satisfaction from the local planning authority. It embodies safeguards for long-term and wider interests.

Furthermore, listed building and tree preservation offences are once and for all deliberate acts for which punishment is fitting (e.g. cutting down a tree), whereas unlawful development may be accidental or remediable. Hence the existing enforcement law gives a breathing space which can involve putting the matter right or obtaining planning permission.

What is required are increased powers and resources for the monitoring of the development control system. The possibilities of delay could also be reduced by limiting the right of appeal to the Secretary of State or increasing the ultimate penalties. Commercial firms can all too easily treat planning fines as overheads. Greater use could also be made of injunctions.

Jowell and Millichip (1986) recommend that enforcement appeals be handled by independent local tribunals rather than, as now, by DoE inspectors. These would be chaired by a lawyer with two other members, one nominated by developers interest groups, the other by environmental groups. This would possibly speed up the appeal process but would only be feasible if policy questions could not be raised on appeal. Thus planning permission should no longer be granted in appeal proceedings. The tribunal might also have power to impose a fine or grant an injunction. This suggestion has considerable attraction as a method of increasing efficiency and expertise while at the same time reducing the opportunity for delay.

A research paper published by the DoE — *Planning Control Enforcement Notice Appeals Efficiency Scrutiny and Action Plan* (1988) — canvassed two other suggestions. Either could be combined with the independent tribunal notion or considered separately. They address the problem of combining swift and strong enforcement with the flexibility needed to resolve issues of planning policy.

One involves the service of an 'unlawful development notice' (UDN) before formal enforcement proceedings are started. A UDN would warn the citizen that proceedings were contemplated and invite him to make representations, or to comply, or to apply for planning permission within 28 days. Failure to respond would be an offence and an enforcement notice could then be issued in the usual way. The gist of this proposal is that it invites the parties to resolve the issues before the formal enforcement machinery is set in action.

The other proposal was made by Stuart Brooks (Mid-Suffolk District Council) in a paper presented to the RTPI Summer School (September 1987). This involves scrapping the present enforcement system altogether. Under this scheme the LPA is empowered to issue a 'stop notice' on becoming aware of an apparent breach of control. Disobedience to this is an offence. The developer has 28 days either to apply for planning permission *or* to seek a section 53 determination that no planning permission is required. At present, section 53 does not apply to activities that have already taken place. Under the proposal there is a right of appeal to the Secretary of State within two months against an adverse section 53 decision or an adverse decision on the application for planning permission. There would be no appeal against the stop notice as such. If a favourable section 53 decision is made, the local planning authority must pay compensation. There is, of course, no obligation to pay compensation if planning permission is granted. The developer bears the costs of jumping the gun.

The basic stop notice is later followed up by an enforcement notice which can be issued by the LPA if no appeal is launched, or by the Secretary of State on Appeal. There is no right of appeal against the enforcement notice since the developer has already had an opportunity to appeal.

The stop notice is not suspended while the appeal is being pursued. However, the LPA has the power to impose an 'interim planning permission' instead of a stop notice. This gives temporary permission for the activities that have taken place, subject to conditions. It is valid for one year and is renewable.

These proposals have several advantages. They reduce the risk of delays caused by the present appeal process and the parallel opportunity to apply for planning permission. They also provide for immediate cessation of the development. The obligation to pay compensation is more limited than under present stop notice law and may thus be less of a deterrent to local planning authorities than is presently the case.

On the other hand, these proposals place a heavy burden on the authority to determine whether the activities in question really are a breach of planning control. They should therefore be reinforced by larger powers of investigation than are presently available.

Irrespective of these general proposals, there is much to be said for rationalising the procedure for challenging the validity of enforcement notices in the courts and also the criminal provisions. Is there any substantial justification for the special right of appeal under section 246? As the law stands, a person seeking to challenge an enforcement notice must choose between section 246, section 245, ordinary judicial review, and raising a defence according to the particular ground of challenge, the time scale, and the question of service. Section 243(1) adds a further layer of complication, being neither all embracing nor particularly rational. It might arguably suffice to leave challenge to an enforcement notice entirely to the general law of judicial review and, subject to that, to set out a list of clear statutory defences to a prosecution

The relationship between service of an enforcement notice and the right of appeal could also be reconsidered. Whatever the merits of these particular suggestions, and no doubt readers can think up others, there is plainly a need for reform of enforcement law. UK planning law is often admired, albeit from abroad rather than on home territory, as a flexible and sophisticated response to the problems of a fast-changing and highly mobile society. If this is the case, then the enforcement aspects of the system have perhaps tipped the balance towards flexibility too far.

Select bibliography

Alder, J. (1989) *Development Control* 2nd ed. London: Sweet & Maxwell.
Allen, A.R.J. (1988) 'Established use certificates and illegality'. *JPL* **239**.
Bracken, I., and Kingsby, J. (1987) 'An analysis of "stop notice" use in planning enforcement'. *JPL* **588**.
Bourne, F. (1987) *Enforcement and Stop Notices: A Practical Guide.* London: Sweet & Maxwell.
Brand, C.M. (1989) *Enforcement of Planning Control.* London: Longman.
DoE (1988) *Planning Control Enforcement Notice Appeals: Efficiency, Scrutiny and Action Plan.* London: HMSO.
Gilbert, A. (1985) 'Sub-division and the planning unit'. *JPL,* **81**.
Grant, M. (1983) *Urban Planning Law*; with *Supplement* (1986). London: Sweet & Maxwell.
Jowell, J. and Millichip, D. (1986) The enforcement of planning control'. *JPL* **482**.
Moore, V. (1987) *A Practical Approach to Planning Law.* London: Financial Training Publications Ltd.
Millichip, D. (1988) 'Enforcing advertisement control'. *JPL* **382**.
Morgan, P., and Nott, S. (1988) *Development Control: Policy into Practice.* London: Butterworths.
Myers, C. (1988) 'Property in need of maintenance: section 65 notices'. *JPL* **154**.
Nicholson, K. (1986) 'The submission and determination of established use certificates' *JPL* **340**.
Purdue, H. M. (1989) 'Material considerations: an ever expanding concept'. *JPL,* **156**.
Samuels, A. (1985) 'Enforcement: why is it so weak?' *JPL* **232** (see *JPL,* **780**).
Scrase, A. J. (1988) *Agriculture – 1980 Industry and 1947 Definition. JPL,* **447**
Turrell Clarke, R. (1988) 'Planning control and Dutch blinds'. *JPL,* **151**.
Young, E. (1989) 'Shop canopies and advertisements'. *JPL,* **319**.

Appendix I
The allocation of enforcement functions

		MAGISTRATES COURT	DISTRICT COUNCIL	LONDON BOROUGH	URBAN DEVELOPMENT CORPORATION (5)	COUNTY COUNCIL (1)	NATIONAL PARKS AUTHORITY (2)	SECRETARY OF STATE	HIGH COURT
ISSUE OF NOTICE:	FIRST INSTANCE		✓	✓	✓	✓	✓	✓[3]	
	APPEAL							✓	✓
STOP NOTICE:			✓	✓	✓	✓	✓	✓[3]	*[9]
LISTED BUILDING CONTROL:	FIRST INSTANCE		✓	✓[6]	✓		✓	✓[4]	
	APPEAL	✓						✓	✓
AMENITY NOTICE:	FIRST INSTANCE		✓	✓	✓		✓		
	APPEAL							✓	✓
TREE PRESERVATION NOTICE:	FIRST INSTANCE		✓	✓	✓	✓[8]	✓	✓[3]	
	APPEAL							✓[7]	✓
HAZARDOUS SUBSTANCE CONTROL:	FIRST INSTANCE	✓[12]	✓	✓		✓[10]	✓[11]		
	APPEAL							✓	✓
ADVERTISEMENT CONTROL:	FIRST INSTANCE		✓	✓	✓		✓	✓[14]	
	APPEAL							✓	✓[13]
INJUNCTION:	FIRST INSTANCE								✓
	APPEAL								CA

The allocation of enforcement functions

Notes

(1) County Council *may* issue EN in relation to a 'county matter' LGA 1972 Schedule 16 Para 24, 32.

County Matters include:

(i) Mining or quarrying operations and incidental activities.
(ii) Activities related to the transport by rail or water of aggregates.
(iii) The erection of any building plant or machinery for the coating of roadstone, the production of concrete or concrete products or artificial aggregates, where the building is part of or adjoining a mine or quarry or a site used for purposes mentioned in (ii).
In minerals matters, the county acts as the 'minerals authority'.
(iv) Erection of plant machinery or building for cement manufacturing.
(v) Development on ex-mining or quarrying sites which conflicts with 'restoration' or with 'aftercare' conditions.
(vi) Development on land which is partly inside and partly outside a national park.
(vii) The carrying out of development within a class prescribed by the Secretary of State. He has prescribed development for the deposit of refuse or waste and the erection of any building plant or machinery for treating, storing, processing or disposing of refuse or waste (see SI 1980 No 2010). This does not apply in Wales.

(2) Where a national park straddles or originally straddled more than one county, there may be a *Joint Planning Board* of the *County Council* or a *Special Planning Board*. In other cases, there is a special National Park Committee. A majority of its members must be county councillors (see LGA 1972. Schedule 17). There are two planning boards: peak Park Special and Lake District Joint.

(3) Default powers exercisable after consultation with the LPA (see section 276).

(4) Listing: (section 54) default power re listed building enforcement notice, (section 100(1)) Compulsory Purchase. Urgent Repairs (section 101).

(5) Except Cardiff Bay UDC.

(6) Subject to directions as to grant of listed building consent by Historic Buildings and Monument Commission for England (Schedule 11, para 6).

(7) Refusal of a conditional consent.

(8) Only (a) in connection with the grant of planning permission;
   (b) relating to land not wholly within the area of a single district planning authority;
   (c) relating to land in which the county planning authority holds an interest;
   (d) relating to land in a national park.

(9) Judicial review only.

(10) Where the land is in a national park or used for the mining and working of minerals or (in England) the disposal of waste or refuse.

(11) Where there is a joint or special planning board (see LGA 1972, Schedule 17).

(12) The 'appropriate minister' where the land is operational land of statutory undertakers (section 1B).

(13) Against refusal of consent and discontinuance notice.

(14) Withdrawal of some deemed consents on request of LPA.

Appendix II

Town and Country Planning Act 1971 (as amended) – extracts

Power to issue enforcement notice

87.—(1) Where it appears to the local planning authority that there has been a breach of planning control after the end of 1963, then subject to the following provisions of this section, the authority, if they consider it expedient to do so having regard to the provisions of the development plan and to any other material considerations, may issue a notice requiring the breach to be remedied and serve copies of the notice in accordance with subsection (5) of this section.

(2) A notice under this section is referred to in this Act as an "enforcement notice".

(3) There is a breach of planning control—
  (a) if development has been carried out, whether before or after the commencement of this Act, without the grant of the planning permission required in that behalf in accordance with Part III of the Act of 1962 or Part III of this Act; or
  (b) if any conditions or limitations subject to which planning permission was granted have not been complied with.

(4) An enforcement notice which relates to a breach of planning control consisting in—
  (a) the carrying out without planning permission of building, engineering, mining or other operations in, on, over or under land; or
  (b) the failure to comply with any condition or limitation which relates to the carrying out of such operations and subject to which planning permission was granted for the development of that land; or
  (c) the making without planning permission of a change of use of any building to use as a single dwelling-house; or
  (d) the failure to comply with a condition which prohibits or has the effect of preventing a change of use of a building to use as a single dwelling-house.

May be issued only within the period of four years from the date of the breach.

(5) A copy of an enforcement notice shall be served, not later than 28 days after the date of its issue and not later than 28 days before the date specified in the notice as the date on which it is to take effect—
  (a) on the owner and on the occupier of the land to which it relates; and
  (b) on any other person having an interest in that land, being an interest which in the opinion of the authority is materially affected by the notice.

(6) An enforcement notice shall specify the matters alleged to constitute a breach of planning control.

(7) An enforcement notice shall also specify—
  (a) any steps which are required by the authority to be taken in order to remedy the breach;

(b) any such steps as are referred to in subsection (10) of this section and are required by the authority to be taken.

(8) An enforcement notice shall specify the period within which any such step as is mentioned in subsection (7) of this section is to be taken and may specify different periods for the taking of different steps.

(9) In this section "steps to be taken in order to remedy the breach" means (according to the particular circumstances of the breach) steps for the purpose—
    (a) of restoring the land to its condition before the development took place; or
    (b) of securing compliance with the conditions or limitations subject to which planning permission was granted, including—
        (i) the demolition or alteration of any buildings or works;
        (ii) the discontinuance of any use of land; and
        (iii) the carrying out on land of any building or other operations.

(10) The steps mentioned in subsection (7)(b) of this section are steps for the purpose—
    (a) of making the development comply with the terms of any planning permission which has been granted in respect of the land; or
    (b) of removing or alleviating any injury to amenity which has been caused by the development.

(11) Where the matters which an enforcement notice alleges to constitute a breach of planning control include development which has involved the making of a deposit of refuse or waste materials on land, the notice may require that the contour of the deposit shall be modified by altering the gradient or gradients of its sides in such manner as may be specified in the notice.

(12) The Secretary of State may by regulations direct—
    (a) that enforcement notices shall specify matters addition to those which they are required to specify by this section; and
    (b) that every copy of an enforcement notice served under this section shall be accompanied by an explanatory note giving such information as may be specified in the regulations with regard to the right of appeal conferred by section 88 of this Act.

(13) Subject to section 88 of this Act, an enforcement notice shall take effect on a date specified in it.

(14) The local planning authority may withdraw an enforcement notice (without prejudice to their power to issue another) at any time before it takes effect.

(15) If they do so, they shall forthwith give notice of the withdrawal to every person who was served with a copy of the notice.

(16) Where—
    (a) an enforcement notice has been issued in respect of development consisting of the erection of a building or the carrying out of works without the grant of planning permission; and
    (b) the notice has required the taking of steps for a purpose mentioned in subsection (10)(b) of this section; and
    (c) the steps have been taken,
for the purposes of this Act planning permission for the retention of the building or works as they are as a result of compliance with the notice shall be deemed to have been granted on an application for such permission made to the local planning authority.

Appeal against enforcement notice
88.—(1) A person having an interest in the land to which an enforcement notice relates may, at any time before the date specified in the notice as the date on which

it is to take effect, appeal to the Secretary of State against the notice, whether or not a copy of it has been served on him.

(2) An appeal may be brought on any of the following grounds—
  (a) that planning permission ought to be granted for the development to which the notice relates or, as the case may be, that a condition or limitation alleged in the enforcement notice not to have been complied with ought to be discharged;
  (b) that the matters alleged in the notice do not constitute a breach of planning control;
  (c) that the breach of planning control alleged in the notice has not taken place;
  (d) in the case of a notice which, by virtue of section 87(4) of this Act, may be issued within the period of four years from the date of the breach of planning control to which the notice relates, that that period had elapsed at the date when the notice was issued;
  (e) in the case of a notice not falling within paragraph (d) of this subsection, that the breach of planning control alleged by the notice occurred before the beginning of 1964;
  (f) that copies of the enforcement notice were not served as required by section 87(5) of this Act;
  (g) that the steps required by the notice to be taken exceed what is necessary to remedy any breach of planning control or to achieve a purpose specified in section 87(10) of this Act;
  (h) that the period specified in the notice as the period within which any step is to be taken falls short of what should reasonably be allowed.

(3) An appeal under this section shall be made by notice in writing to the Secretary of State.

(4) A person who gives notice under subsection (3) of this section shall submit to the Secretary of State, either when giving the notice or within such time as may be prescribed by regulations under subsection (5) of this section, a statement in writing—
  (a) specifying the grounds on which he is appealing against the enforcement notice; and
  (b) giving such further information as the regulations may prescribe.

(5) The Secretary of State may by regulations prescribe the procedure which is to be followed on appeals under this section, and in particular, but without prejudice to the generality of this subsection—
  (a) may prescribe the time within which an appellant is to submit a statement under subsection (4) of this section and the matters on which information is to be given in such a statement;
  (b) may require the local planning authority to submit, within such time as may be prescribed, a statement indicating the submissions which they propose to put forward on the appeal;
  (c) may specify the matters to be included in such a statement;
  (d) may require the authority or the appellant to give such notice of appeal under this section as may be prescribed, being notice which in the opinion of the Secretary of State is likely to bring the appeal to the attention of persons in the locality in which the land to which the enforcement notice relates is situated;
  (e) may require the authority to send to the Secretary of State, within such period from the date of the bringing of the appeal as may be prescribed, a copy of the enforcement notice and a list of the persons served with copies of it.

(6) The Secretary of State—
  (a) may dismiss an appeal if the appellant fails to comply with subsection (4)

of this section within the time prescribed by regulations under subsection (5); and

(b) may allow an appeal and quash the enforcement notice if the local planning authority fail to comply with any requirement of regulations made by virtue of paragraph (b), (c) or (e) of subsection (5) of this section within the period prescribed by the regulations.

(7) Subject to subsection (8) below, the Secretary of State shall, if either the appellant or the local planning authority so desire, afford to each of them an opportunity of appearing before, and being heard by, a person appointed by the Secretary of State for the purpose.

(8) The Secretary of State shall not be required to afford such an opportunity if he proposes to dismiss an appeal under paragraph (a) of subsection (6) of this section or to allow an appeal and quash the enforcement notice under paragraph (b) of that subsection.

(9) If—
(a) a statement under subsection (4) of this section specifies more than one ground on which the appellant is appealling against an enforcement notice; but
(b) the appellant does not give information required under paragraph (b) of that subsection to each of the specified grounds within the time prescribed by regulations under subsection (5) of this section,

the Secretary of State may determine the appeal without considering any of the specified grounds as to which the appellant has failed to give such information within that time.

(10) Where an appeal is brought under this section, the enforcement notice shall be of no effect pending the final determination or the withdrawal of the appeal.

(11) Schedule 9 to this Act applies to appeals under this section, including appeals under this section as applied by regulations under any other provision of this Act.

88A.—(1) On the determination of an appeal under section 88 of this Act, the Secretary of State shall give directions for giving effect to the determination, including, where appropriate, directions for quashing the enforcement notice or for varying its terms.

(2) On such an appeal the Secretary of State may correct any informality, defect or error in the enforcement notice, or give directions for varying its terms, if he is satisfied that the correction or variation can be made without injustice to the appellant or to the local planning authority.

(3) Where it would otherwise be a ground for determining such an appeal in favour of the appellant that a person required to be served with a copy of the enforcement notice was not served, the Secretary of State may disregard that fact if neither the appellant nor that person has been substantially prejudiced by the failure to serve him.

88B.—(1) On the determination of an appeal under section 88 of this Act, the Secretary of State may—
(a) grant planning permission for the development to which the enforcement notice relates or for part of that development or for the development of part of the land to which the enforcement notice relates;
(b) discharge any condition or limitation subject to which planning permission was granted;
(c) determine any purpose for which the land may, in the circumstances obtaining at the time of the determination, be lawfully used having regard to any past use of it and to any planning permission relating to it.

(2) In considering whether to grant planning permission under subsection (1) of this section, the Secretary of State shall have regard to the provisions of the development plan, so far as material to the subject matter of the enforcement notice, and to any other material considerations; and any planning permission granted by him under that subsection may—
    (*a*) include permission to retain or complete any buildings or works on the land, or to do so without complying with some condition attached to a previous planning permission;
    (*b*) be granted subject to such conditions as the Secretary of State thinks fit; and where under that subsection he discharges a condition or limitation, he may substitute another condition or limitation for it, whether more or less onerous.

(3) Where an appeal against an enforcement notice is brought under section 88 of this Act, the appellant shall be deemed to have made an application for planning permission for the development to which the notice relates and, in relation to any exercise by the Secretary of State of his powers under subsection (1) of this section—
    (*a*) any planning permission granted under that subsection shall be treated as granted on that application;
    (*b*) in relation to a grant of planning permission or a determination under that subsection, the Secretary of State's decision shall be final; and
    (*c*) for the purposes of section 34 of this Act, the decision shall be treated as having been given by the Secretary of State in dealing with an application for planning permission made to the local planning authority.

(4) On an appeal under section 88 of this Act against an enforcement notice relating to anything done in contravention of a condition to which section 71 of this Act applies, the Secretary of State shall not be required to entertain the appeal in so far as the appellant claims that planning permission free from that condition ought to be granted.

Penalties for non-compliance with enforcement notice
89.—(1) Subject to the provisions of this section, where a copy of an enforcement notice has been served on the person who, at the time when the copy was served on him, was the owner of the land to which the notice relates, then, if any steps required by the notice to be taken (other than the discontinuance of a use of land) have not been taken within the period allowed for compliance with the notice, that person shall be liable on summary conviction to a fine not exceeding £2,000 or on conviction on indictment to a fine.

(2) If a person against whom proceedings are brought under subsection (1) of this section has, at some time before the end of the period allowed for compliance with the notice, ceased to be the owner of the land, he shall, upon information duly laid by him, and on giving to the prosecution not less than three clear days' notice of his intention, be entitled to have the person who then became the owner of the land (in this section referred to as "the subsequent owner") brought before the court in the proceedings.

(3) If, after it has been proved that any steps required by the enforcement notice have not been taken within the period allowed for compliance with the notice, the original defendant proves that the failute to take those steps were attributable, in whole or in part, to the default of the subsequent owner—
    (*a*) the subsequent owner may be convicted of the offence; and
    (*b*) the original defendant, if he further proves that he took all reasonable steps to secure compliance with the enforcement notice, shall be acquitted of the offence.

(4) If, after a person has been convicted under the preceding provisions of this section, he does not as soon as practicable do everything in his power to secure compliance with the enforcement notice, he shall be guilty of a further offence and liable—

Effective enforcement of planning control

  (*a*) on summary conviction to a fine not exceeding £100 for each day following his first conviction on which any of the requirements of the enforcement notice (other than the discontinuance of the use of land) remain unfulfilled; or

  (*b*) on conviction on indictment to a fine.

  (5) Where, by virtue of an enforcement notice, a use of land is required to be discontinued, or any conditions or limitations are required to be complied with in respect of a use of land or in respect of the carrying out of operations thereon, then if any person uses the land or causes or permits it to be used, or carries out those operations or causes or permits them to be carried out, in contravention of the notice, he shall be guilty of an offence, and shall be liable on summary conviction to a fine not exceeding £2,000, or on conviction on indictment to a fine; and if the use is continued after the conviction he shall be guilty of a further offence and liable on summary conviction to a fine not exceeding £100 for each day on which the use is so continued, or on conviction on indictment to a fine.

  (6) Any reference to this section to the period allowed for compliance with an enforcement notice is a reference to the period specified in the notice for compliance therewith of such extended period as the local planning authority may allow for compliance with the notice.

Appendix III

Specimen enforcement notices

(1) Enforcement notice: operational development

IMPORTANT:- THIS COMMUNICATION AFFECTS YOUR PROPERTY

(a) _Cantwin District_ Council

TOWN AND COUNTRY PLANNING ACT 1971
(as amended)

Enforcement Notice
Operational Development

(b) _Land at Graydon Edge, Mumpton_

WHEREAS:

(1) It appears to the (a) Council ("the Council"), being the local planning authority for the purposes of section 87 of the Town and Country Planning Act 1971 ("the Act") in this matter, that there has been a breach of planning control within the period of 4 years before the date of issue of this notice on the land or premises ("the land") described in Schedule 1 below.

(2) The breach of planning control which appears to have taken place consists in the carrying out of the building, engineering, mining or other operations described in Schedule 2 below, without the grant of planning permission required for that development.

(3) The Council consider it expedient, having regard to the provisions of the development plan and to all other material considerations, to issue this enforcement notice, in exercise of their powers contained in the said section 87, for the reasons set out in [the annex to] this notice.(c)

NOTICE IS HEREBY GIVEN that the Council require that the steps specified in Schedule 3 below be taken [in order to remedy the breach][(d)]
within [the period of **Twelve** [days][months] from the date on which this notice takes effect] [the period specified in respect of each step in that Schedule].(e)

THIS NOTICE SHALL TAKE EFFECT, subject to the provisions of section 88(10) of the Act, on **the tenth day of March 1989**.(f)

Issued **23rd January** 19**89**

Council's address   (Signed) ....

                         (Designation) ....
            (The officer appointed for this purpose)

SCHEDULE 1
Land or premises to which this notice relates
(address or description) **Land at Graydon Edge Mumpton which said land (hereinafter refererred to as "the land") is**

shown edged [red] [   ] on the attached plan.(g)

SCHEDULE 2
Alleged breach of planning control
(description of operations carried out on the land (h) **The carrying out of a building operation on the land, namely the erection of a dwellinghouse (hereinafter referred to as "the dwellinghouse")**

SCHEDULE 3
Steps required to be taken(j)
(i) **Demolish the dwellinghouse**
(ii) **Remove all building material and otherwise restore the land to its former condition prior to the breach of planning control referred to in Schedule 2 hereof.**

NOTES TO THE LOCAL PLANNING AUTHORITY

(a) Insert the name of the Council issuing the notice.
(b) Insert the address or a description of the land to which the notice relates.
(c) See paragraph 29 of DOE Circular 38/81 (Welsh Office Circular 57/81).
(d) Or, as the case may be, having regard to section 87(7)(a) and (b) of the Act. Where steps are required to be taken for more than one of the purposes provided for in section 87, the purpose for which each step is required should be specified in Schedule 3. Steps may be required as alternatives.
(e) If a single period is to be specified, by which all the required steps must be taken, insert it here. But if a series of steps is required to be taken, with a different compliance period for each step, the appropriate period for each step, the appropriate period should be clearly stated against each step (in columns if more suitable) in Schedule 3.
(f) The date selected must be not less than 28 clear days after all the copies of the notice will have been served (see section 87(5) of the Act).
(g) See paragraph 31 of DOE Circular 38/81 (Welsh Office Circular 57/81).
(h) Where the works being enforced against are on only part of the land identified in Schedule 1, their position should be shown on the plan.
(j) Specify the actual steps to be taken with, if appropriate, the compliance period for each step. The requirements should be clear and precise. See also notes (d) and (e) overleaf.

NOTICE WHY IT IS EXPEDIENT TO SERVE
AN ENFORCEMENT NOTICE IN RESPECT OF
LAND AT GRAYDON EDGE, MUMPTON

The development complained of:-

(1) represents unwarranted development in the open countryside and is contrary to national and local aims of preserving and enhancing the countryside.

(2) does not allow sufficient visibility for drivers of motor vehicles entering and leaving the land and therefore represents an unacceptable risk to highway safety.

(2) Enforcement notice: material change of use

THE FACTS

Stanley owns an area of land (the site) which he purchased by auction in 1968. the site formerly comprised part of the "Wheel and Hammer" garage, the remainder of which continues to thrive on the opposite side of the County Road. In the 1960's the site had served as an overspill parking area for the garage and where cars had from time to time been repaired and sold. With a change of management in the garage in 1961 trade fell away considerably and use of the site for the above purposes became very spasmodic until its complete decline in 1967. It was this decline which had paved the way for the sale of this surplus land in 1968. Stanley has managed to resuscitate the business gradually and in 1981 he erects on half of the site a building to enclose the activities of his business. Since that time trade has completely taken off and the Local Planning Authority is confronted with complaints from neighbours about the noise arising from the repairs of vehicles and the loss of amenity and safety through the generation of additional traffic to the site.

IMPORTANT - THIS COMMUNICATION AFFECTS YOUR PROPERTY

CANTWIN DISTRICT COUNCIL

TOWN AND COUNTRY PLANNING ACT 1971 (as amended)

ENFORCEMENT NOTICE

WHEREAS it appears to the Cantwin District Council who are the Local Planning Authority for the purpose of Section 87 of the Town and Country Planning Act 1971 as amended that there has been a breach of planning control on land opposite the Wheel and Hammer Garage, Brent Road, Mumpton, which said land is hereinafter referred to as "the land" and is shown edged red on the plan annexed hereto in respect of which you are the owner/occupier by the carrying out without the grant of planning permission required in that behalf in accordance with Part III of the Town and Country Planning Act 1971 as amended of the following development:- The making of a material change in the use of the land to use for the purpose of the sale, storage and repair of motor vehicles.

NOW THEREFORE the Cantwin District Council do hereby require you in pursuance of their powers under Section 87 of the Town and Country Planning Act 1971 as amended for the purposes of restoring the land to its condition before the said development took place, to remedy the said breach of planning control by taking the following steps:-

1) Cease using the land for the sale storage and repair of motor vehicles.

2) Remove from the land all motor vehicles stationed thereon in connection with the sale, storage and repair thereof.

within 2 months from the date on which this Notice takes effect

SUBJECT TO THE PROVISIONS OF SECTION 88(10) OF THE TOWN AND COUNTRY PLANNING ACT 1971 AS AMENDED THIS NOTICE SHALL TAKE EFFECT ON THE thirtieth DAY OF March 1989.

Issued this Twenty third day of January 1989.

Signed   Robert Chittern

Solicitor
Cantwin District Council

YOUR ATTENTION IS DRAWN TO THE NOTES ON THE REVERSE SIDE.

NOTICE WHY IT IS EXPEDIENT TO ISSUE AN
ENFORCEMENT NOTICE IN RESPECT OF LAND
OPPOSITE THE WHEEL AND HAMMER GARAGE,
BRENT ROAD, MUMPTON

The development complained of:-

(1) Causes nuisance and annoyance and loss of residential amenity to owners and occupiers of nearby residential properties.

(2) The roads leading to the site are inadequate in width and alignment to cater for the development complained of. This, together with restricted visibility available to drivers of motor vehicles entering or leaving the site renders the said development an unacceptable risk to driver and pedestrian safety.

(3) Enforcement notice: breach of condition

IMPORTANT – THIS COMMUNICATION AFFECTS YOUR PROPERTY

TOWN AND COUNTRY PLANNING ACT 1971
ENFORCEMENT NOTICE

TO:- 1. Jan Donald Dow,
         23 Magi Road
         Mumpton

WHEREAS:

1. You are the owner and/or occupier of the land situate at and known as 23 Magi Road, Mumpton, in the County of Wessex, which is more particularly delineated on the attached plan and thereon coloured red (hereinafter called "the said land").

2. The Mumpton City Council (hereinafter called "the Council") are the Local Planning Authority (inter alia) for the purposes of the provisions of Section 87 of the Town and County Planning Act 1971 as amended (hereinafter called "the Act of 1971").

3. On the 20th January, 1988, the Council upon application in that behalf made in accordance with Part III of the Act of 1971, granted conditional planning permission for the change of use of the said land from printing and stationery shop to a restaurant.

4. The said permission was granted subject inter alia to the conditions:-

    (a) The development to which the permission relates must be begun not later than the expiration of five years beginning with the date on which this permission is granted.

    (b) The premises shall not at any time operate as a take-away food shop and all food to be consumed on the premises.

    (c) The premises shall cease to operate at 11.00 pm on any day and shall not open before 9.00 am on the day following.

5. It appears to the Council that within the period of four years before the date of service of this Notice there has been a breach of planning control in that the said condition (b) above subject to which the said permission was granted, has not been complied with in the following respects, namely:

"the premises have been used as a take-away food shop"

6. The Council consider it expedient having regard to the provisions of the Development Plan and to all other material considerations to serve this Notice.

7. NOW THEREFORE TAKE NOTICE that in exercise of the power contained in the said Section 87 of the Act of 1971 the Council HEREBY REQUIRE YOU within a period of seven days beginning with the date this Notice takes effect to take the following steps to secure the compliance with the said condition:-

"to cease using the premises as a take-away food shop and to ensure that all food sold is consumed on the premises"

THIS NOTICE SHALL TAKE EFFECT subject to the provisions of Section 88(10) of the Act of 1971, on 22nd December, 1989.

DATED this Tenth day of November, 1989.

CITY SOLICITOR
Town Hall, Mumpton

YOUR ATTENTION IS DIRECTED TO THE ACCOMPANYING NOTES WHICH EXPLAIN YOUR RIGHT OF APPEAL AGAINST THIS NOTICE. YOU SHOULD READ THEM CAREFULLY.

[*Note*: There are three possible defects here.

(1) It is unnecessary addressing the notice to named persons.
(2) The use of the four-year period in a change of use case.
(3) The compliance period is too short.

However, none of these nullify the notice.]

Table of cases

AG v. Bastow [1957] 1 QB 514 119
AG v. English [1982] 2 All ER 903 168
AG v. Howard United Reform Church Bedford [1976] 2 WLR 961 .. 147
AG v. Morris [1973] 227 EG99 .... 117, 119
AG v. Smith [1958] 2 QB 173 117
Avon CC v. Millard [1985] 50 P and CR 275 121

Backer v. Secretary of State [1983] JPL 167 47
Barnet BC v. Eastern Electricity Board [1973] 2 All ER 309 154
Barrie (James) v. Lanark DC [1979] Sc 74
Barvis v. Secretary of State (1971) 22 P & CR 710 12
Bath City Council v. Secretary of State [1984] 47 P & CR 663
  .... 52, 86, 132, 150, 151
Beaconsfield DC v. Gams (1974) 234 EG 749 121
Bedford CC v. CEGB [1985] JPL 43 .... 14, 117
Bell v. Canterbury DC [1986] 52 P & CR 428 158
Belmont Farms Ltd v. Minister of Housing and Local Government (1962) 13
P & CR 23
Bolivian Tin Trust Co. Ltd v. Secretary of State [1972] 1 WLR 1481 .. 49
Borough of Morecombe v. Warwick (1958) 19 P & CR 307 68
Bradford MBC v. Secretary of State [1986] JPL 598 121
Bristol City Council v. Secretary of State [1988] 56 P & CR 49 49
Britt v. Buckinghamshire CC [1964] 1 QB 77 8
Bromsgrove DC v. Secretary of State [1988] JPL 257 15
Brooks v. Gloucestershire County Council (1967) 19 P & CR 90 16
Brooks and Burton Ltd v. Secretary of State [1977] 1 WLR 1294 15
Bullock v. Secretary of State [1980] JPL 461 153
Burdle v. Secretary of State [1972] 1 WLR 1207 18
Bush v. Secretary of State [1988] 56 P & CR 58 156
Button v. Jenkins [1975] 3 All ER 585 88

Carpet Decor v. Secretary of State [1981] JPL 806 .... 43, 44, 56
Central Regional Council v. Clackmannan DC [1983] Sc 134
Cheshire CC v. Secretary of State [1988] JPL 30 7
Chiltern DC v. Hodgetts [1983] AC 120 .... 100, 101
City of Dundee DC v. Peddie [1983] Sc 134
City of London Corporation v. Secretary of State [1971] 23 P & CR 169
  .... 27, 44
Cleaver v. Secretary of State [1981] JPL 38 62
Coleshill Investments v. Minister of Housing [1969] 1 WLR 746 .... 12, 13, 14
Copeland DC v. Secretary of State (1976) 31 P & CR 403
  .... 44, 46, 56, 63, 64, 84, 85
Cord v. Secretary of State [1981] JPL 40 62

Table of cases

Cynon Valley DC v. Secretary of State [1986] 20, 31, 43

Davy v. Spelthorne DC [1984] AC 262 .... 8, 89, 92
de Mulder v. Secretary of State [1974] QB 792 .... 19–20, 58, 64–5
Denham v. Secretary of State [1984] 47 P & CR 598 47
Dudley BC v. Secretary of State [1986] JPL 689 61
Duffy v. Pilling [1977] 75 LGR 159 105
Duffy v. Secretary of State [1981] JPL 811 19

Earl Car Sales Ltd v. City of Edinburgh DC [1984] 134
East Barnett DC v. British Transport Commission [1962] 2 QB 484 ... 14
East Hampshire DC v. Secretary of State [1978] JPL 582 87
Eldon Garages v. Kingston-on-Hull BC [1974] 1 WLR 276 ..... 9, 56, 57
E.L.S. Wholesalers (Wolverhampton) Ltd v. Secretary of State
    [1987] Times May 19 38
Essex CC v. Secretary of State [1974] JPL 226 24
Ewen Developments v. Secretary of State [1980] JPL 404 47

Fairchild v. Secretary of State [1988] JPL 472 96
Fawcett Properties v. Bucks CC [1961] AC 636 33
Ferris v. Secretary of State [1989] 57 P & CR 127 ...... 9, 35, 53, 55, 58
Forkhurst Ltd v. Secretary of State [1982] JPL 448 87
Fraser v. Secretary of State [1988] JPL 344 7
Fuller v. Secretary of State [1988] EG 55 19

Garland v. Minister of Housing [1968] 20 P & CR 93 .... 44, 85
Gill v. Secretary of State [1985] JPL 710 23
Glamorgan CC v. Carter [1963] 1 WLR 1 49
Glover v. Secretary of State [1981] JPL 110 87
Gouriet v. Union of Post Office Workers [1978] AC 535 119
Groveside Homes Ltd v. Elmbridge DC [1978] 284 EG 940 155
Gwillim v. Secretary of State [1988] JPL 263 87

Hamilton DC v. Alexander Moffat & Son (Demolition) Ltd [1984] Sc 135
Hammersmith LBC v. Secretary of State [1975] 30 P & CR 19 86
Hartley v. Minister of Housing [1970] 1 QB 414 21
Hertmere BC v. Alan Dunn Building Contractors Ltd [1985]
    84 LGR 214 169
Hewitt v. Leicester Corporation [1969] 1 WLR 855 68
Hilliard v. Secretary of State [1978] JPL 840 28
Hounslow BC v. Secretary of State [1981] JPL 510 61
Howard v. Secretary of State [1975] QB 235 76
Hughes v. Secretary of State [1985] JPL 486 84

Iddenden v. Secretary of State [1972] 1 WLR 1433 64
Institute of Patent Agents v. Lockwood [1894] AC 347 134
Ivory v. Secretary of State [1985] JPL 796 61

James v. Brecon County Council (1963) 15 P & CR 20 12
Jeary v. Chailey RDC [1973] 26 P & CR 286 34–5
Jennings Motors Ltd v. Secretary of State [1982] 1 All ER 225 28
Johnstone v. Secretary of State [1974] P & CR 424 .... 18, 107
Jones v. Secretary of State [1974] 28 P & CR 362 17
Jones v. Stockport Borough Council [1984] JPL 274 23

Kent CC v. Batchelor (No. 7) [1979] 1 WLR 213 .... 120, 150
Kerrier DC v. Secretary of State [1981] JPL 193 57
Kingston-on-Thames DC v. Secretary of State [1973] 1 WLR 525 27
Kingswood DC v. Secretary of State [1988] JPL 249 .... 10, 87

Lamb v. Secretary of State [1983] JPL 303 24
Lenlyn Ltd v. Secretary of State [1985] JPL 82 88
Lewstar Ltd v. Secretary of State [1984] JPL 116 36
Lewis v. Secretary of State [1971] 23 P & CR 125 17
Lilo Blum v. Secretary of State [1987] JPL 278 36
Lipman v. Secretary of State [1976] 33 P & CR 95 60
London Corporation v. Cusack-Smith [1955] AC 337 67
London Dockland Development Corporation v. Rank Hovis Mcdougal
  Ltd [1986] 88 GLR 101 119
London Parachuting Club Ltd v. Secretary of State [1988] JPL 478 ... 86
London Residuary Body v. Secretary of State [1988] JPL 637 ..... 15, 97
L.T.S.S. Print and Supply Services Ltd v. Hackney BC [1976]
  1 QB 633 .... 31, 95

Macdonald v. Glasgow Corporation (1960) 11 P & CR 318 128–9
Maidstone BC v. Mortimer (1982) 43 P & CR 67 .... 101, 155
Manchester City Council v. Secretary of State [1987] 54 P & CR 212 .. 39
Mansi v. Elstree RDC [1964] 16 P & CR 26 .... 62, 81
Marine Associates v. City of Aberdeen DC [1978] Sc 132
McDaid v. Clydebank DC [1984] JPL 579 .... 129, 130
McNaughton v. Peter McIntyre (Clyde) Ltd [1978] Sc 132
Metallic Protectives Ltd v. Secretary of State [1976] JPL 166 61
Midlothian DC v. Steveman [1986] JPL 913 171
Miller-Mead v. Minister of Housing [1963]
  2 QB 196 .... 9, 44, 52, 56, 59, 73, 129, 163
Mills and Allen Ltd v. City of Glasgow Corporation [1980] JPL 409 168
Moody v. Godstone RDC [1966] 1 WLR 1085 68

Table of cases

Murfitt v. Secretary of State [1980] P & CR 254 47

Nash v . Secretary of State [1986] JPL 128 48
Nelsovil Ltd v. Minister of Housing [1962] 1 WLR 404 .... 35, 76
Newbury DC v. Secretary of State [1981] AC 578 .... 28, 46, 78
Newbury DC v. Secretary of State [1988] JPL 185 97
Norfolk CC v. Secretary of State [1973] 1 WLR 1400 33
Northavon DC v. Secretary of State [1980] 40 P & CR 32 ..... 21, 22, 25
North Warwickshire DC v. Secretary of State [1985] 50 P & CR 47 ... 23

O'Reilly v. Mackman [1983] 2 AC 237 .... 5, 90
Ormston v. Horsham RDC (1965) 17 P & CR 105 132

Panyani v. Secretary of State [1985] 50 P & CR 109 15
Peacock Homes v. Secretary of State [1984] JPL 229 .... 43, 48
Percy Trentham v. Gloucestershire CC [1966] 1 WLR 506 17
Perkins v. Secretary of State [1981] JPL 755 47
Philglow v. Secretary of State [1985] JPL 318 16
Pilkington v. Secretary of State (1973) 1 WLR 1527 .... 27, 85
Pioneer Aggregates v. Secretary of State [1985] AC 132 26
Pirie v. Bauld [1975] Sc 127, 131
Pittman v. Secretary of State [1988] JPL 391 61
Plymouth City Council v. Quietlynn [1987] 3 WLR 189 92
Porritt v. Secretary of State [1988] JPL 414 .... 70, 81
Porter v. Honey [1988] 2 All ER 449 169

R v. Basildon DC (1987) 53 P & CR 397 73–4
R v. Greenwich LBC *ex parte* Patel [1985] JPL 581 .... 69, 71, 103, 109, 131
R v. Jenner [1983] 1 WLR 873 92
R v. Inland Revenue Commissioners *ex parte* National Federation
of Self Employed and Small Businesses Ltd [1982] AC 617 90
R v. Keeys [1989] JPL 28 .... 94, 105
R v. Kuxhaus [1988] 2 WLR 1005 97
R v. Leminster DC [1988] JPL 554 150
R v. Polly Newland [1987] JPL 85 98
R v. Reading Crown Court [1988] 1 All ER 333
R v. Richmond BC *ex parte* Macarthy and Stones [1989] *Times* 7 Feb . 38
R v. Runnymede BC [1987] JPL 283 61
R v. Secretary of State *ex parte* Ahern [1989] *Times* 29 March 85
R v. Secretary of State *ex parte* Hillingdon BC [1986] 1 WLR 192 7
R v. Secretary of State *ex parte* Jackson [1987] JPL 740 75
R v. Secretary of State *ex parte* JBI Financial Consultants Ltd
  [1989] JPL 365 75

R v. Wells St. magistrates Court [1986] 3 All ER 4 101
R v. Westminster City Council *ex parte* Monahan (1989) JPL 107 ... 120
R v. West Oxfordshire DC *ex parte* Pearce Homes Ltd [1986] JPL 523 33
R (Bryson) v. Ministry of Defence (1967) (NI) 144
R (Thatton) v. DoE (1982) (NI) 144
Ragsdale v. Creswick [1984] JPL 883 107
Rawlins v. Secretary of State [1989] JPL 439 .... 18, 64
Re Hughes Application [1986] (NI) 144
Rhymney Valley DC v. Secretary of State [1985] JPL 27 88
Richmond BC v. Secretary of State [1988] JPL 396 55
Rignal Developments v. Halil [1987] 3 WLR 394 101
Ringwood Investments v. Secretary of State [1979] JPL 772 86
Robbins v. Secretary of State [1989] *Times* 21 May 152
Robert Barnes & Co. Ltd v. Malvern Hills DC (1985) 1 EGLR 189 .. 114
Rochdale MBC v. Simmonds (1980) 40 P & CR 432 .... 44, 58
Rolf v. North Shropshire DC (1988) 55 P & CR 242 152
Royal Borough of Kensington & Chelsea v. Secretary of State
  [1981] JPL 50 15
Runnymede BC v. Ball [1986] 1 WLR 353 116
Runnymede BC v. Singh [1987] JPL 283 62
Runnymede BC v. Smith [1986] JPL 592 112

J. Sample (Warkworth) Ltd v. Alnwick DC [1984] JP 670 114
Scarborough BC v. Adams and Adams [1983] JPL 673 ... 67, 71, 89, 107
Scott v. Secretary of State [1983] JPL 108 57
Scott Markets Ltd v. Waltham Forest DC [1979] JPL 392 111
Shanley v. Secretary of State [1982] JPL 380 33
Somak Travel v. Secretary of State [1987] JPL 632 62
South Cambridgeshire DC v. Stokes [1981] JPL 594 100
South Staffordshire DC v. Secretary of State [1987] JPL 635 .. 28, 48, 63
Spook Erection v. Secretary of State [1988] 3 WLR 291 123
Square Meals Frozen Foods Ltd v. Dunstable Corporation [1974]
  1 WLR 59
Stevens v. Bromley BC [1972] Ch 400 67
Stoke-on-Trent City Council v. B & Q (Retail) Ltd [1984] AC 754 ... 118
Strandmill Ltd v. Secretary of State [1988] JPL 491 28
Swinbank v. Secretary of State [1987] JPL 781 .... 17, 18, 62–3
Sykes v. Secretary of State [1981] 1 WLR 1092 .... 23, 61

Tamlin v. Hannaford [1950] KB 18 123
Thomas (David) v. Penybont RDC [1972] 1 WLR 1526 44
Thrasyvoulou v. Secretary of State [1988] 3 WLR 1 .... 10, 79, 80
Trevors Warehouses v. Secretary of State [1972] 23 P & CR 215 .. 58, 60

Table of cases

Trustees of the Castell-y-Mynach Estate v. Secretary of State (1985) JPL 40 ... 21
Trusthouse Forte Hotels v. Secretary of State [1986] JPL 834 ... 37

Vale of Glamorgan DC v. Palmer [1984] ... 155
Vaughan v. Secretary of State [1986] JPL 840 ... 49, 51

Wadham Stringer Ltd v. Fareham DC [1987] JPL 715 ... 169
Wakelin v. Secretary of State [1978] JPL 769 ... 25
Wandsworth BC v. Winder [1985] AC 461 ... 92
Warrington BC v. Garvey [1988] ... 53, 105
Waverley DC v. Secretary of State [1982] JPL 105 ... 45
Wealden DC v. Secretary of State [1988] JPL 268 ... 12, 116, 118
Webber v. Minister of Housing [1968] 1 WLR 29 ... 16
Wells v. Minister of Housing [1967] 1 WLR 1000 ... 46
West Bowers Farm Products v. Secretary of State [1985] JPL 857 ... 21
Western Fish Products v. Penwith DC [1981] 2 All ER 204 ... 8
West Glamorgan DC v. Rafferty [1987] 1 All ER 1005 ... 7
Westminster City Council v. British Waterways Board [1985] AC 676
Westminster City Council v. Jones [1981] JPL 750 ... 116
West Oxfordshire DC v. Secretary of State [1988] JPL 324 . 10, 56–7, 85
White v. Secretary of State [1989] *Times* 10 Feb ... 27
Williams v. Minister of Housing [1967] 18 P & CR 514 ... 14
Winton v. Secretary of State [1982] 46 P & CR 205 ... 19, 27–8
Wilson v. West Sussex DC [1963] 2 QB 764 ... 33
Wood v. Secretary of State [1973] 1 WLR 707 ... 19
Windsor and Maidenhead Royal Borough Council v. Brandrose Investments Ltd [1983] 1 WLR 509 ... 121

Young v. Secretary of State [1983] 2 AC 662 ... 95

Table of statutes

1925 Law of Property Act s.198 .... 100–101, 107
1960 Caravan Sites and Control of Development Act 86
1967 Forestry Act 154, 158, 159
1968 Transport Act 161
1971 Town & Country Planning Act
   s.1B 182
   s.22 .... 1, 11, *et seq.*
      22 (1) 11
      22 (2) 12, 22
      22 (3) 25
      22 (3A) 25
      22 (4) 25, 171
   s.23 .... 30–31, 95–6
   s.24 28
   s.24A – E 29
   s.33 26
   s.34 8
   s.40 29
   s.41 44
   s.42 26
   s.43 26
   s.44 26
   s.45 28
   s.46 28
   s.51 .... 11, 28
   s.51A 11
   s.52 120
   s.53 .... 45–6, 175, 177
   s.54 .... 145–6, 182
   s.55 .... 148, 149
   s.56 147
   s.56C 153
   s.58 147
   s.58AA 147
   s.58B 163, 165
   s.58J 164
   s.58K 164
   s.60 .... 153, 159, 162
      60 (1) 156
   s.61 154

s.61A	157, 158
s.62	156, 157
s.63	165
63 (2)	166
63 (3)	167
s.64	165, 166
s.65	161, 162
s.87	3, 52 *et seq.*, 183–4
87 (1)	34, 47
87 (2)	34
87 (3)	42, 45
87 (4)	46, 47, 48
87 (5)	66, 81
87 (6)	54
87 (7)	54, 63, 108
87 (8)	54
87 (9)	63
87 (10)	64, 97
87 (11)	54
87 (12)	54
87 (13)	54, 96
87 (14)	93
87 (16)	95
s.88	72 *et seq.*, 184–5
88 (1)	70, 74
88 (2)	69, 77 *et seq.*
88 (3)	74
88 (4)	76
88 (5)	76
88 (6)	77
88 (7)	75
88 (8)	77
88 (9)	77
88 (10)	97
s.88A	69, 70, 80, 92
s.88B	37, 78
s.89	93 *et seq.*
89 (1)	99, 102, 104, 105, 108, 124
89 (2)	102
89 (3)	102
89 (4)	99, 103
89 (5)	100, 104–5, 107, 124
s.90	111 *et seq.*

90 (5)	112
90 (9)	113
s.91	108–9, 157, 170, 171, 175
s.92A	42
s.93	
93 (1)	93
93 (2)	77, 92, 100, 108
93 (3)	93
93 (5)	100, 108
s.94	49, 50
s.96	149, 150
s.98	151
s.99	151
s.100	182
s.101	151
s.101A	151
s.101B	164
s.103	157
s.104	161, 162
s.105	162, 163
s.107	11, 161
s.109A	168
s.110 (1)	83
s.110 (2)	69–70, 81, 103
s.114	151, 152
s.115	152
s.116	152
s.117	152
s.126	153
s.174	158
s.177	114
s.243 (1)	69, 70, 72–4, 106, 109, 178
243 (2)	77, 106–7
243 (3)	163
s.245	87, 89, 163, 178
s.246	72, 86, 88, 144, 178
246 (1A)	157
s.276	181
276 (5A)	8
s.277A	149
s.280	40, 41, 108
s.281	40, 41
s.283	68

283 (3)	67
s.284	40, 41, 14
s.290 (1)	13, 23, 66, 80, 123, 163, 172
Schedule 9	75
Schedule 11	182
Schedule 14	48

1972 Local Government Act

s.101	7
s.111	38
s.222	114, 117, 119
s.233	69
Schedule 16	13, 181
Schedule 17	181, 182

1972 Northern Ireland (Temporary Provisions) Act	138
1972 Town and Country Planning (Scotland) Act	177
s.85 (1)	129, 136
85 (3)	133
85 (10)	129, 130, 131
85 (11)	132
s.86	127, 131, 132, 133
s.87 (1)	133, 134
s.87A	135
s.88	129
s.270	128

1973 Greater London (General Powers) Act

s.25	26
1973 Local Government (Scotland) Act	125, 126
1975 Local Land Charges Act	100
1976 Local Government (Miscellaneous Provisions) Act	108
1977 Rent Act	107

1978 Interpretation Act

s.7	68
1979 Ancient Monuments and Archaeological Sites Act	147
1980 Local Government Planning and Land Act	7, 29
1980 Magistrates Courts Act	99

1981 Acquisition of Land Act

s.23	152
1981 Town and Country Planning (Minerals) Act	13
1982 Local Government (Miscellaneous Provisions) Act	120
1984 Greater London (General Powers) Act	26
1984 Town and Country Planning Act	123
1986 Housing and Planning Act	29, 65
1988 Land Registration Act	41

Table of statutory instruments and regulations

1969 Town and Country Planning (Tree Preservation Order)
  Regulations (SI 1969 No.17) 153, 154, 155, 156, 159
1971 Town and Country Planning (Minerals) Regulations
  (SI 1971 No. 756) 48
1972 Planning (Northern Ireland) Order 137, 140–43
1973 Planning (Development Plans) Regulations (Northern Ireland) ... 134
  Planning (Use Classes) (Northern Ireland) Order 1973 139
  Planning (General Development) (Northern Ireland) Order 1973 ... 140
1975 Town and Country Planning (Tree Preservation Orders) Amendment
  Regulations SI 1975 No. 148 158
1976 Town and Country Planning General Regulations
  (SI 1976 No. 1419) 69, 109
1980 Town and Country Planning (Prescription of Country Matters)
  Regulations SI 1980 No. 2010 181
1981 Town and Country Planning (Enforcement Notices and
  Appeals Regulations) SI 1981 No. 1742 .... 5, 54, 64, 76
  Town and Country Planning (Enforcement) (Inquiries Procedure)
  Rules (SI 1981 No. 1743) 5, 77
1982 Notification of Installations Handling Hazardous Substances
  Regulations 1982 (SI 1982 No. 1357) 165
1983 Town and Country Planning (Fees for Applications and Deemed
  Application) Regulations (SI 1983 No. 1674) 82
1984 Town and Country Planning (Enforcement of Control) (Scotland)
  Regulations 135
  Town and Country Planning (Special Enforcement Notices) Regulations
  1984 (SI 1984 No. 1016) 125–6
1987 Town and Country Planning (Use Classes) Order
  (SI 1987 No. 764) 5, 23–5, 30, 44–5
1988 Town and Country Planning General Development Order
  (SI 1988 No. 1813) 6, 20, 21, 28, 42, 44
  Town and Country Planning (Tree Preservation Order) Amendment
  Regulations (SI 1988 No. 1963) 153
1989 Town and Country Planning (Control of Advertisement) Regulations
  (SI 1989 No. 670) .... 165, 166, 167–8, 169.

Index

abandonment of use, 20–21, 96
advertisements, 25, 165 et seq.
   conditions, 167
   criminal liability, 168–9
   deemed consent, 167
   development control and, 165–6, 170–73
   discontinuance order, 168–9
   enforcement, 168–9
   fly posting, 168
   exemptions, 167, 173
   guilty knowledge, 169
   meaning of, 172–3
   Northern Ireland, 143
   time limits, 170
agreements, 120–21
agriculture and forestry, 14, 22–3, 159
alternative sites, 37
appeals, 2, 3, 8, 10, 34–5, 69–71, 72, 74–88
   advertisements, 167
   amendment or variation of enforcement notice, 84–6
   amenity notices, 162
   application for planning permission as, 37
   burden of proof, 9–10, 52–3, 76
   costs, 39, 83
   court to, 3, 8 (*see* High Court)
   delays, 3, 4, 10, 76–7, 99
   exclusive remedy as, 63, 69–70, 72–3, 105–6, 109, 163
   fees, 4, 82
   grounds, 77–82
   hazardous substances, 164
   information about, 54
   listed buildings, 150
   Northern Ireland, 139
   planning permission, grant of, 37, 78
   powers of Secretary of State on, 3, 8, 76–7, 83–6
   suspension of enforcement notice, 3, 4, 97, 98
   time limits, 54, 74–5, 86
   trees, 154
   who can appeal, 70–71, 74, 86, 87
   written representations, 76
balloons, 166, 167, 170, 173

boundaries, 53, 64–5 (*see* planning unit)
breach of planning control, description of, 55–9, 60
building operations, 12

calling in powers, 8
caravan, 12, 56
committees, 7
compensation, 4
   listed buildings, 152
   stop notice, 114–19, 175
   tree preservation, 158, 160
conditions, 26–7, 33, 38–9, 43–5, 48, 56–7, 59, 78, 79
conservation area, 149, 157, 167
content of enforcement notice, 53 et seq.
copy of enforcement notice, 66
courts challenge in, *see* High Court, judicial review
criminal liability, 98 et seq.
   adjournment, 99
   causing or permitting, 104–5, 107
   conditions and, 104
   continuing offence, 101–2
   date of offence, 102
   defences, 101, 102, 103, 106–7
   'duplicitous informations', 99
   guilty knowledge (*mens rea*) 100–101, 127, 148–9, 154–5
   occupier and, 103
   owner and, 102–4
   penalties, 98
   repeated offences, 103, 104–5, 107–8
   Scotland, 126–8
   service of notice, 69, 71, 73, 77, 103, 105–6
   subsequent owners, 102
   summary and indictable offences, 98, 108
   trees, 154–5
   using land, 104–5
Crown, 5, 122 et seq.

date enforcement notice takes effect, 54, 86, 88, 96–7

delegation of powers, 7-8
derelict land, 161 et seq.
   appeals, 162
   development and, 162
   enforcement procedure, 161-2
   listed buildings, 161
   magistrates' powers, 162, 163
   penalties, 161
   unoccupied, 161
development, 1, 12-26, 43, *see also* operations, uses, abandonment of use, planning unit.
development orders, 28-9
development plan, 36
discontinuance orders, 11, *see also* advertisements
discretion, exercise of, 34, 65

enforcement notice
   excluding challenge, 63, 72-4
   formalities, 52-3
   suspension of, *see* appeals
   taking effect of, 3, 59, 74, 93 et seq.
   withdrawal of, 93
   see also errors, omissions in enforcement notices, nullity of enforcement notice, uncertainty
enforcement officers, 2, 174
engineering operations, 13-14
enterprise zones, 29
entry to land, 40, 72, 93, 108-9, 175
errors in notices, 56, 80, 83-4
established use certificates, 6, 49-50
excessive enforcement, 62-3, 81
existing uses, 20-21, 30, 36-7, 95, 142

fact, questions of, 10, 86-7
farm shop, 23

Government polices, 37-9

hazardous substances, 163 et seq.
   authorities, 163-4
   consents, 163-4
   defences, 164
   enforcement notices, 164
   immunities, 165
   liability, 164
   notifications, 165
   statutory undertakers and, 163
High Court, 3, 72, 86-9 (*see also* judicial review)

hostels, 15, 25
houses, 23, 36

identification of land subject to enforcement, 64-5
information notice, 40-41, 114
information obtaining, 2, 39-42
injunctions, 4, 115 et seq.
inspectors, 4, 75, 82
intensification, *see* uses

judicial review, 72-3, 87-8, 89-91, 97-8, 109, 117
   Northern Ireland, 144
   Scotland, 134-5

landowner, knowledge of, 52, 60, 100-101, 132-3
land registry, 41
limitations, 43-4, 48
listed buildings, 145 et seq.
   building preservation notice, 146
   compulsory purchase, 148, 151-3
   damage, 147
   demolition, 146, 147
   exemptions, 147, 149
   guilty knowledge, 148
   listed building enforcement notice, 149-51
   Northern Ireland, 142-3
   repair and maintenance, 151, 152
   time limits, 151
local inquiries, 4, 75-7
local land charge, 42, 100-101
local planning authorities, 6-8, 180-81
   Northern Ireland, 138
   Scotland, 125-6

material change of use (*see* uses)
mining operations, 13
multiple occupation, 2, 60

National parks, 7, 181
negotiations, 7-8, 38
Northern Ireland, 136 et seq.
notice, doctrine of, 100-101
nullity of enforcement notice, 52, 56, 59, 69, 70, 72-3, 84-5, 89, 93, 103, 109, 131

occupiers, 15, 67, 70
offices, 15, 24
offices, liability of, 7–8
omissions in enforcement notices, 52, 74, 84
operations, 1, 12–14, 21–2, 43, 57 (*see also* time limit)
owner, 66–7, 102–3

planning gain, 120–21
planning permission, 1, 3, 4, 26–33, 78–9, 94–5
　interpretation, 31–2
　loss of, 26–8
　need for, 29–31
planning unit, 18–20, 55, 64–5, 119
prosecutions, 98–9
public inquiry (*see* local inquiries)

reasons for enforcement, 37, 54, 65
register of enforcement notices, 42, 100, 135
　Scotland, 135
register of planning applications and permissions, 42, 45–6
restoration of land, 52

Scotland, 124 et seq.
Secretary of State, calling in powers, 51
service of enforcement notice, 66 et seq.
　criminal proceedings and, *see* criminal liability
　failure to serve, 69–70, 81, 97, 104, 105–6, 130–31
simplified planning zones, 29
small businesses, 38
smallholding, 14
special enforcement notice, 122–3
standing to challenge, 86, 87, 90
steps required by enforcement notice, 59, 62–4
stop notice, 4, 111–15, 177–8
　Northern Ireland, 141
　Scotland, 133–4
　subdivision of land, 19, 25, 27

suspension of enforcement notice, 97–8

time limit for appeal, 74–5, 98
time limit for enforcement notice, 3, 46–9, 57–8, 80, 136, 175 (*see also* established use certificates)
　Northern Ireland, 140
tipping, 21, 25
tree preservation, 153 et seq.
　appeals, 154, 157
　compensation, 158, 159
　consents, 153
　conservation areas, 157–8
　exemptions, 159–60
　Forestry Commission, 158–9
　guilty knowledge, 154–5
　Northern Ireland, 143
　penalties, 154
　publicity, 155
　replanting, 155–7
　Tree Preservation Orders, 153–4
trespass, action for, 72, 109

uncertainty, 33, 59–62, 132–4
underenforcement, 63–4
unoccupied land, 67, 161
Urban Development Corporations, 7, 41, 115
uses, 1–2, 14 et seq, 43 (*see also* existing uses, planning unit)
　agricultural, 23
　ancillary, 17–18, 63
　composite, 16
　description of, in enforcement notice, 57, 58, 59
　intensification, 15, 39, 57–8, 60, 62
　material meaning of, 14–16
　multiple, 16–18
　seasonal, 16
　use classes, 5, 23–5

variation of enforcement notice, 83, 85

written representation appeals, 4, 75, 76